Teaching the New English
Series editor: **Ben Knights**

Teaching the New English is an innovative
the English degree in universities in the
new and developing areas of the curric
that are reforming in new contexts. Al
lectual and theoretical concepts of the
practicalities of classroom teaching. The volumes will be invaluable
and more experienced teachers alike.

Titles include:

Gail Ashton and Louise Sylvester (*editors*)
TEACHING CHAUCER

Heather Beck (*editors*)
TEACHING CREATIVE WRITING

Richard Bradford (*editors*)
TEACHING THEORY

Charles Butler (*editors*)
TEACHING CHILDREN'S FICTION

Deborah Cartmell and Imelda Whelehan (*editors*)
TEACHING ADAPTATIONS

Ailsa Cox (*editors*)
TEACHING THE SHORT STORY

Robert Eaglestone and Barry Langford (*editors*)
TEACHING HOLOCAUST LITERATURE AND FILM

Michael Hanrahan and Deborah L. Madsen (*editors*)
TEACHING, TECHNOLOGY, TEXTUALITY
Approaches to New Media and the New English

David Higgins and Sharon Ruston (*editors*)
TEACHING ROMANTICISM

Andrew Hiscock and Lisa Hopkins (*editors*)
TEACHING SHAKESPEARE AND EARLY MODERN DRAMATISTS

Lesley Jeffries and Dan McIntyre (*editors*)
TEACHING STYLISTICS

Andrew Maunder and Jennifer Phegley (*editors*)
TEACHING NINETEENTH-CENTURY FICTION

Peter Middleton and Nicky Marsh (*editors*)
TEACHING MODERNIST POETRY

Anna Powell and Andrew Smith (*editors*)
TEACHING THE GOTHIC

Andy Sawyer and Peter Wright (*editors*)
TEACHING SCIENCE FICTION

Fiona Tolan and Alice Ferrebe (*editors*)
TEACHING GENDER

Gina Wisker (*editors*)
TEACHING AFRICAN AMERICAN WOMEN'S WRITING

Teaching the New English
Series Standing Order ISBN 978–1–403–94441–2
Hardback 978–1–403–94442–9 Paperback
(*outside North America only*)

You can receive future titles in this series as they are published by placing a standing order. Please contact your bookseller or, in case of difficulty, write to us at the address below with your name and address, the title of the series and the ISBN quoted above.

Customer Services Department, Macmillan Distribution Ltd, Houndmills, Basingstoke, Hampshire RG21 6XS, England

Teaching Adaptations

Edited by

Deborah Cartmell
Professor of English, De Montfort University, UK

and

Imelda Whelehan
Professor of English, University of Tasmania, Australia

First published 2014 by
PALGRAVE MACMILLAN

Palgrave Macmillan in the UK is an imprint of Macmillan Publishers Limited,
registered in England, company number 785998, of Houndmills, Basingstoke,
Hampshire RG21 6XS.

Palgrave Macmillan in the US is a division of St Martin's Press LLC,
175 Fifth Avenue, New York, NY 10010.

Palgrave Macmillan is the global academic imprint of the above companies
and has companies and representatives throughout the world.

Palgrave® and Macmillan® are registered trademarks in the United States,
the United Kingdom, Europe and other countries.

ISBN 978–1–137–31112–2   hardback
ISBN 978–1–137–31115–3   paperback

This book is printed on paper suitable for recycling and made from fully
managed and sustained forest sources. Logging, pulping and manufacturing
processes are expected to conform to the environmental regulations of the
country of origin.

A catalogue record for this book is available from the British Library.

Library of Congress Cataloging-in-Publication Data
Teaching Adaptations / [edited by] Deborah Cartmell, Reader in English, De Montfort
University, UK; Imelda Whelehan, Professor of English, University of Tasmania, Australia.

p. cm. – (Teaching the New English)

Summary: "This volume looks at the ways in which adaptations can and have
been taught by leading academics in the field of Adaptation Studies from all
over the world. While aware that Shakespeare and canonical literature remain
the mainstay of adaptation study in English, Teaching Adaptations addresses
the challenges and appeal of teaching popular fiction and culture, video games
and new media content, which serve to enrich the curriculum, as well as exploit
the changing methods by which English students read and consume literary and
screen texts. The volume is structured to appeal to both those who are considering
teaching adaptations for the first time as well as those who are familiar with key
perspectives in adaptation criticism"– Provided by publisher.
Includes bibliographical references and index.

ISBN 978–1–137–31112–2   (hardback)

1. Literature—Adaptations—Study and teaching.   I. Cartmell, Deborah,
editor.   II. Whelehan, Imelda, 1960– editor.
PN171.A33T43 2014
809—dc23   2014026130

Typeset by MPS Limited, Chennai, India.

Contents

Series Editor's Preface

One of the many exciting achievements of the early years of the UK English Subject Centre was the agreement with Palgrave Macmillan to initiate the series 'Teaching the New English'. The intention of Philip Martin, the then Centre Director, was to create a series of short and accessible books which would focus on curriculum fields (or themes) and develop the connections between scholarly knowledge and the demands of teaching.

Since its inception as a university subject, 'English' has been committed to what is now known by the portmanteau phrase 'learning and teaching'. The subject grew up in a dialogue between scholars, critics, and their students inside and outside the university. Yet university teachers of English often struggle to make their own tacit pedagogic knowledge conscious, or to bring it up to a level where it might be shared, developed, or critiqued. In the experience of the English Subject Centre, colleagues found it relatively easy to talk about curriculum, but far harder to talk about the success or failure of seminars, how to vary modes of assessment, or to make imaginative use of virtual learning environments or web tools. Too often, this reticence meant falling back on received assumptions about how students learn, about how to teach or create assessment tasks. At the same time, we found, colleagues were generally suspicious of the insights and methods arising from generic educational research. The challenge for the extended group of English disciplines has been to articulate ways in which our own subject knowledge and forms of enquiry might themselves refresh debates about pedagogy. The need becomes all the more pressing in the era of rising fees, student loans, the NSS, and the characterization of the student as a demanding consumer of an educational product. The implicit invitation of the present series is to take fields of knowledge and survey them through a pedagogic lens.

'Teachers', people used to say, 'are born, not made'. There may be some tenuous truth in this. There may perhaps be generosities of spirit (or, alternatively, drives for didactic control) laid down in early childhood. But the implication that you cannot train or develop teachers is dubious. Why should we assume that even 'born' teachers should not need to learn or review the skills of their trade? Amateurishness about teaching has far more to do with the mystique of university status than with evidence about how people learn. This series of books is dedicated to the development of the craft of teaching within university English Studies.

Ben Knights
Emeritus Professor of English and Cultural Studies, Teesside University
Visiting Fellow, Institute of Education, University of London

Notes on Contributors

Rachel Carroll is Principal Lecturer in English at Teesside University and teaches courses on contemporary fiction, feminist theory, film and television adaptations, and African American writing. Her publications include *Rereading Heterosexuality: Feminism, Queer Theory and Contemporary Fiction* (2012) and an edited collection *Adaptation in Contemporary Culture: Textual Infidelities* (2009).

Deborah Cartmell is Professor of English at De Montfort University. She is co-editor of *Adaptation* and *Shakespeare*, and founder and former Chair of the Association of Adaptation Studies, and is currently editing the Bloomsbury History of Adaptation series.

Shelley Cobb is Lecturer in English and Film at the University of Southampton. Her research interests are film adaptation, women's cinema and literature, and women filmmakers.

Kamilla Elliott is a senior lecturer at Lancaster University. She is author of *Rethinking the Novel/Film Debate* (2003) and *Portraiture and British Gothic Fiction: The Rise of Picture Identification, 1764–1835* (2012).

Natalie Hayton has recently completed her PhD in English and adaptation studies at De Montfort University, Leicester. She is currently working on a project that explores the role of fairy tales in postfeminist retreatist fantasies.

Ariane Hudelet is Associate Professor in the English Department of Paris Diderot University, where she teaches literature and film, creative screenwriting, and TV series. She is the author of *Pride and Prejudice: Jane Austen and Joe Wright* (2006), and the co-author of *The Cinematic Jane Austen* (2009). She has also edited, with Shannon Wells Lassagne, three volumes on adaptation and is the co-editor of online journal *TV/Series*.

Alessandra Raengo is Associate Professor of Moving Image Studies at Georgia State University in Atlanta. Her scholarship explores the ontological implications of blackness in the field of vision. Her books include *On the Sleeve of the Visual: Race as Face Value* (2013) and, with Robert Stam, two co-edited anthologies: *Literature and Film* and *A Companion to Literature and Film* (2004 and 2005). She is currently investigating the aesthetics of 'liquid blackness' in contemporary art and film.

Laurence Raw is Professor of English in the Department of Education, Başkent University, Ankara, Turkey. His latest book is *Adaptation and Learning: New Frontiers* (with Tony Gurr, 2013).

David Sadler is Deputy Vice-chancellor at the University of Tasmania. Prior to joining UTAS he was Director of the Higher Education Academy (UK); Director of CSAP (Sociology, Anthropology and Politics Subject Centre). He previously also worked in the UK Foreign and Commonwealth Office. He specializes in International relations and is both a UK National Teaching Fellow and a Jean Monnet award recipient.

Jamie Sherry is Lecturer in Screenwriting at Bangor University and is Secretary of the Association of Adaptation Studies, as well as serving on the steering committee for the Screenwriting Research Network. He has published research on the process of adaptation through screenwriting and is currently completing the monograph *The Adapted Screenplay: Theory, Practice and Process* (2014).

Imelda Whelehan is a Research Professor at the University of Tasmania and Visiting Professor at De Montfort University. She is co-Chair of the Association of Adaptation Studies and co-editor of *Adaptation*. Her long collaboration with Deborah Cartmell has resulted in a number of collections, including *Adaptation: From Text to Screen, Screen to Text* (1999), *The Cambridge Companion to Literature on Screen* (2007), and the co-authored *Screen Adaptation: Impure Cinema* (2010).

1
A Short History of Adaptation Studies in the Classroom

Deborah Cartmell and Imelda Whelehan

Adaptation studies is a growth area in the Arts and Humanities and has brought numerous multidisciplinary perspectives to what used to be more commonly known as 'novel to film' or 'literature and film' studies. The impact of adaptation studies on English has been indisputably significant, and it could be argued that the study of adaptations has changed the way we teach the subject for good; at the very least it is now common to see English modules delivered with varying degrees of adaptation content across the globe, even if, as Thomas Leitch asserts, 'English studies has continued to treat film adaptation not so much with hostility as with benign neglect'.[1] While fictional texts and their feature film adaptations remain at the subject's core,[2] the study of adaptations has broadened to embrace 'literature' and the 'screen' in the broadest senses of each word. With a new theoretical richness and interdisciplinary confidence, adaptation studies has facilitated fresh approaches to issues of interpretation, rewriting, and refunctioning, enabling purposeful reflection on our contemporary obsession with reworking culture to suit our own needs.

In order to demonstrate how adaptation studies has changed, we take the case of the use of films based on Austen's fictions within literary studies. Like Shakespeare, Jane Austen is firmly embedded in the field of adaptation studies as an author who has repeatedly had the 'adaptation treatment', beginning with a chapter on Robert Z. Leonard's 1940 adaptation of *Pride and Prejudice* (starring Greer Garson and Laurence Olivier) in the first full-length study of literature and film, George Bluestone's *Novel into Film* (1957). By 2009, Austen and film had become a major critical preoccupation, as Pamela Church Gibson's summary of work on Austen and film demonstrates,[3] with a list that includes Sue Parrill's *Jane Austen on Film and Television: A Critical Study of the Adaptation* (2002), Linda Troost and Sayre Greenfield's *Jane Austen in Hollywood* (1998; 2nd edn 2001), Suzanne R. Pucci and James Thompson's *Jane Austen and Co.* (2003), Gina MacDonald and Andrew F. MacDonald's *Jane Austen on Screen* (2003), and David Monaghan, Ariane Hudelet and John Wiltshire's *The Cinematic Jane Austen: Essays on the Filmic Sensibility of the Novels* (2009). Claire Harmon's *Jane's Fame* (2009) and the online journal *Persuasions*, which frequently delivers articles on Austen films, demonstrate a modern tendency to move away from an absorption in the novels themselves to the fictions' afterlives. It now seems obligatory to include at least one chapter on 'Austen films' or 'Austen offshoots' in collected essays on her work, because studies of Austen are no longer complete until they show consideration of how her work provides inspiration for other trends in contemporary culture, from chick lit to dating manuals, to testing the ability of contemporary bestselling writers like Joanna Trollope and Val McDermid to 'reimagine Austen' all over again.[4]

Given the number of films of Austen's novels, it has been hard to ignore them in the classroom, and for many years much teaching has relied on them to explicate the text for a new cohort of students. Since the availability of videos in the 1970s, teaching often involved showing a short clip 'illustrating' a part of a novel or play as a means to open up discussion, but always as a path back to consideration of the book. While it is easy to appreciate the relevance of film clips within Shakespeare classes (given that the plays are performance pieces), showing novel adaptations was a practice harder to justify in the early days of video. Such a practice was, more often than not, scorned rather than applauded, a legacy of the chequered history of literature and film, when critics, in the first half of the twentieth century, blushed when suggesting that an author's work might be influenced by cinema.[5] Showing film clips, however, could be defended as a means of inspiring discussion that would often take the form of reflecting on what was wrong with the film adaptation, how it misunderstood the literary text, thereby empowering the students (as 'ENGLISH students') to feel a sense of superiority over those involved in the making of such films. In the not-so-distant past (certainly in our memories), the showing of films in literature classes was often stigmatized by academics and teachers, who believed such practice as lazy and, even more unforgivably, a devaluing of literature that unwittingly encouraged pupils to watch movies rather than read books. As Timothy Corrigan has noted, for most of the twentieth century, adaptation studies failed to capture the interest of film scholars (as the approach taken by their literary colleagues so frequently devalued the film text) and English academics (who regarded the use of film as either offering a cheap substitute for literature or as an excuse to bask in the superiority of literature over cinema).[6] Still within the field of Austen studies today, it is remarkable how little reflection there is on the implications of showing a clip from a film to 'illustrate' a novel, how little the film itself is valued as a product of many, rather than belonging to an individual, and how the concepts of popularization and commercial value are dismissed as either irrelevant or demeaning. Adaptation teachers have a steep hill to climb.

There is no doubt, however, that the field developed in English Studies through the inclusion of screen adaptations of canonical authors in the everyday practice of teaching and that authors and authorship still shape what is taught today. Following Shakespeare, Austen made a breakthrough, thanks partially to the numerous film adaptations since 1940 and thanks, too, to the fact that she is a major player in the English literature syllabus. Indeed these two facts are interrelated; today canonical status is not only assigned to a work by a single literary critical guru, such as F.R. Leavis, or by the number of citations it receives long after the death of the author, but is often bestowed in recognition of the number of films it has generated. We still have some way to go in breaking Austen adaptations away from exclusively author-centred approaches, as is the case with other canonical writers whose screen treatment is growing to industrial proportions. As several of the contributors to this volume suggest, following on from Robert Stam's introduction to *Literature and Film: A Guide to the Theory and Practice of Film Adaptation* (2003),[7] one way of approaching the afterlife of, say, Austen's fiction is to adapt Gérard Genette's concept of transtextuality to Austen adaptations, to think of her novels, not as sources but as 'hypotexts' and consider adaptations as texts in their own right, through an analysis of intertextuality (quotations or allusions to other texts), paratextuality (the materials surrounding the text, such as posters, reviews, trailers), metatextuality (the commentary on the text within the text), and architextuality (the title chosen, the structure adopted).

Scholarship on Austen and film is not the only critical turning point in adaptation studies. Since the mid-1990s adaptations themselves have had a significant part to play in popularizing an interest in the process itself, and in the people who contribute to it. Andrew Davies' role in scripting the 1995 BBC TV version of *Pride and Prejudice* was foregrounded in critical appraisals of the work, particularly in his 'unfaithful' development of a profound sexual tension between the two chief protagonists which lasted for most of the miniseries' five and half hours duration, and which is best remembered for a drenched and dishevelled Darcy encountering Elizabeth Bennet in the grounds of Pemberley. Colin Firth's performance as Darcy was also credited with focusing the attention of a new generation of female viewers, and the components of such a winning formula were discussed and dissected by the broadsheets and a 'making of' documentary and book. Davies by his own admission, 'sexed up' Austen and more or less got away with it; Patricia Rozema's feature film adaptation of *Mansfield Park* (1999) used sex *and* postcolonial critique to encourage a newly interactive Austen audience to read her against the grain. The initial furore around such versions was essential raw material in the seminar room, and while we look back at the 1990s as a time when we were stuck in the canon, these adaptation case studies redirected students' attention to how the canon was constantly reforming itself and could work in reverse thrust too, as is the case when costumes from Austen adaptations end up doing the rounds of stately homes as *ersatz* heritage artefacts.

Adaptation studies can open our minds to considerations often swept beneath the carpet in literary studies, regarding the popularization of a text through marketing, standardization (or genre), intertextuality, or plagiarism, and the targeting of specific audiences. What this offers students is an opportunity to go in countless directions; rather than each writing the same essay on, say, the representation of Pemberley in Austen's *Pride and Prejudice* and Joe Wright's 2005 *Pride and Prejudice* (with the inevitable conclusion, much to the chagrin of the adaptation teacher, that the book is better and more complexly articulated). Removed from the need to foreground the novel as ur-text, students explore aspects previously uncharted, such as soundtracks, costumes, *mise en scène*, trailers, posters, games, music, tie-ins, book covers using film illustrations, casting, genre, intertextual references to earlier films, and popular forms; the list seems endless. An example of this approach is a student essay that demonstrated how Joe Wright's *Pride and Prejudice* adapts 'Cinderella' (as much as Austen's novel) in the Pemberley sequence, with Elizabeth running away from her embarrassment at being found out, hotly pursued by Darcy (now Prince Charming). This analysis was a springboard for a consideration of the unacknowledged use of fairy tale narrative and iconography throughout the film, pushing aside the significance of Austen's narrative. Adaptation studies today, as is evident in the variety of articles in our journal *Adaptation* (OUP, 2008–) and in numerous volumes commenting on the state of the discipline, is far from fixed on seeing adaptation as a one-way, essentially dead-end journey from literary text to film, and is by no means restricted to canonical literature.

We began, at De Montfort University in 1992, teaching a third year course in Shakespeare on film which developed into a course on adaptations (initially, largely adaptations of canonical texts to placate our literary colleagues), which gradually introduced popular adaptations of children's fiction and graphic novels. The course expanded to three courses for years one, two, and three and then, as students progressed and demanded more, a taught Masters. We were able to show that, contrary to the fears expressed by some colleagues, learning adaptations made our students better 'readers' of both film and literary texts, and much more adept textual critics.

The MA was taught jointly with Film Studies colleagues, itself representing a sea change in the disciplinary organization of such courses, and included modules on Gothic, Popular Forms, Classic Adaptations, and Shakespeare. Work on genre and popular fiction, much as lecturers who have taught it know, stretches the students and encourages them to produce their most sophisticated work on the seemingly less sophisticated subjects, topics which challenged their literary and film studies training. We found adaptation an area also attractive to PhD students, possibly for the same reasons that it flourished at undergraduate level, in that it offered so much uncharted territory to explore and it so easily lent itself to fierce opinions and debate through shared experiences, but also because of its interdisciplinarity and the availability of original and challenging projects.

Teaching adaptations to all levels of students made us completely unembarrassed about the use of film clips. There is something to be said about the benefits of film clips offering a welcome break from the pressures of teaching, and postgraduates, like English teachers, find film a useful crutch in their first presentations of their research to their peers. The wheel, to an extent, has come full circle: showing films is sometimes still regarded as effortless and captivating, but it need not be a guilty pleasure, as it tended to be in English Studies in the last half of the twentieth century. As part of a doctoral training programme at De Montfort University's Centre for Adaptations, research students each present a film clip to their peers to view and then discuss in relation to their research project. At first the presenting student remains quiet, absorbing the comments of their colleagues, but as the discussion develops, the student takes an increasingly leading role in the seminar as their superior knowledge becomes evident, both to themselves and to their colleagues. These sessions are entertaining and informative as well as confidence building, providing a gentle introduction to the art of seminar presentation and teaching, while at the same time stressing that there is nothing wrong with showing clips.

In many respects, adaptation studies should not be ashamed of its history, especially in its quest to both empower and entertain, which it was implicitly criticized for doing for most of the twentieth century. Empowering readers (and viewers) is an important feature of the teaching of adaptation, and in this respect it is not new, but has a history that pre-dates the Leavises – indeed cinema itself. Early modern manuscript culture can be seen as an early form of 'adaptation studies' in which readers, oblivious to the sanctity of an 'original', were encouraged to revise, strikeout, and offer alternatives or solutions to questions posed by a text in manuscript, which was seen as essentially and importantly incomplete in itself.[8] What Chris Stamatakis describes as 'the rhetoric of rewriting', as it applies to Thomas Wyatt, is a model for adaptation studies as a whole that, in its numerous failed attempts to find 'a theory of adaptation' (significantly the title of Linda Hutcheon's seminal work in the field)[9] is, as this volume testifies, united in at least one thing: its view of both the adaptation and the adaptation critic as engaged in the process of 'rewriting'. Adaptation is essentially about a response to change.

This collection offers some suggestions, through accounts of the authors' teaching practices, of useful ways to respond to change at the heart of the teaching of English using adaptations. In 'Canons, Critical Approaches, and Contexts', Shelley Cobb identifies an emerging 'canon' of adaptation studies across the US, UK, and Australia, an ironic consequence of the institutional effects of curriculum development, even in area that attempts to destabilize literary and film studies canons. She notes that the term 'adaptation' is often suppressed in course outlines, once more drawing attention to the uneasy placing of adaptation studies in either the study of film or literature. She finds 'Shakespeare on Screen' the most common, followed by courses that include 'classic' novel adaptations, with Dickens, Austen, *Dracula*, *Frankenstein*, and *A Room with a View* the most frequently taught, although contemporary adaptations, including those of graphic narratives, recur on course outlines. Cobb argues that literary text- or genre-based approaches risk de-historicizing adaptations and she argues for an historical approach that reads adaptations made within the same period, so that questions relating to cultural, social, and industrial contexts are more rooted and therefore more graspable by students. Like the current state of English literary studies, adaptation teaching has taken a decidedly creative turn, both in the UK and abroad. Laurence Raw, writing about his experience of EFL teaching in Turkey, demonstrates how getting students to adapt texts and relate them to their own backgrounds enables them to deconstruct cultural values they previously took for granted. By getting them to assess their own adaptations, he encourages them to think about the commercial processes required to prepare an adaptation for audience consumption. This reflective and collaborative approach to learning produces students with increased language confidence and developed critical thinking skills.

In the next chapter, Ariane Hudelet considers the booming field of adaptation studies in France, which still clings to the model 'one book/one film' due to the present 'compare and contrast' mindset, as seen in the *concours* to become an English teacher (which introduced a compulsory text and adaptation in 1998) and whose selection of texts for examination tends to affirm the notion that the book is better. Hudelet proposes foregrounding theory, in particular, Stam's revision of Genette's transtextuality, to allow students to approach a film text from a variety of angles, helping to shift attention from linear hierarchies as articulated in the institutional *concours* and encouraging them to think of 'textual studies' as a blending of visual and theoretical literacy with the literary knowledge already assumed and privileged.

Imelda Whelehan and David Sadler's chapter focuses on teachers, offering an account of their experiences leading an Australian government-funded project to identify a 'community of practice' of adaptation scholars and provide a repository in which they can share and comment on each other's teaching materials. As they show, there are many obstacles to sharing in teaching, quite contrary to academic norms in research; this reality, coupled with the varied pressures to perform which beset the contemporary academic, make this project a somewhat utopian work in progress.

Echoing Laurence Raw in Chapter 3, Kamilla Elliott in Chapter 6 notes how adaptation studies struggles with traditional theorization because the adaptations themselves refuse to be fixed; Elliott reminds us that adaptation's very etymology means 'changing' and that its development has been arrested due to the continual urge to pin it down. Elliott recounts how, in exasperation, she tried to wrestle her students from the seemingly unshakeable belief that a book is better than a film by getting them to adapt: to learn in practice what they resisted in theory. For Elliott's students, *doing* adaptation blends aesthetic practices of creation with theory as reflection. Likewise, Jamie Sherry outlines how teaching screenwriting, a vital but undervalued part of the adaptation process, is a useful pedagogical tool for teaching the aesthetics and the industrial practicalities of adaptation. By focusing on the space between source and adaptation, other unexpected consequences arise which prompt a critique of the impact of English and Film Studies' pedagogical norms on practice-based assessment.

Alessandra Raengo considers how the black body 'appears as both the source and destination of the adaptation process', which because of its racialized otherness in film culture is the 'ultimate measure of fidelity'. Her chapter, using *The Jackie Robinson Story* (1950) and *Precious* (2009) as case studies, develops approaches to adaptation and embodiment by showing how, in Robinson's performance of his younger more athletic self, and Gabourey Sidibe's performance as Precious, the distinction between actor and role is collapsed. While Robinson's performance accords with Hollywood's assimilationist narratives, Sidibe's 'excessive corporeality' obstructs any kind of assimilation, visual or otherwise.

Looking at the transition between school and university, Natalie Hayton champions the study of adaptations for easing students into theoretical issues and debates through the study of children's literary adaptations and focuses on her experience in teaching one of our own courses, on adaptations of children's literature. As Hayton observes, such a course offers a surprisingly challenging and entertaining opportunity for students to move beyond their assumptions about texts and their adaptations, considering the imposition of other forgotten narratives – in this case fairy tales – within the adapted narratives. Fairy tale adaptations, so much a feature of most students' childhood viewing, offer a useful set of core knowledges which can be deployed in ways that decentre adaptation as one-to-one textual exchange.

Rachel Carroll also provides examples of how to better engage students, but rather than focusing on what are seemingly accessible and non-threatening adaptations, Carroll opts for contemporaneous adaptations with no critical apparatus to support them. Answering Cobb's call for an historical approach to the field, Carroll settles on the contemporary as a way of justifying the choice of texts and limiting the study to a specific period. She describes the materials gathered from her student project 'Adaptation Watch', tracing debates and issues, as they happen, in the examples of *Brideshead Revisited* (Julian Jarrold, 2007), *Wuthering Heights* (Andrea Arnold, 2011), and *Life of Pi* (Ang Lee, 2012). Her approach encourages focus on paratextual apparatuses as much as the adaptations, and invites students to scrutinize literary prize culture and pre-release marketing, and their roles in the construction of cultural value. Deborah Cartmell also adopts an historical approach by uncovering the origins of what has become known as adaptation studies in marketing materials of the early 1930s. With reference to F.R. Leavis and Denys Thompson's simultaneous repulsion and attraction to the language of advertising in *Culture and Environment* (published in 1933), this chapter argues for a return to teaching 'the pitch', in order to teach students (like Thompson and Leavis before us) to uncover what posters, trailers, and press books reveal about a film's audience. Cartmell shows that while Leavis, Thompson, and their peers' distaste for film adaptation motivated them to champion high literature through an analysis of the language of advertising and commerce, their critical achievement was to facilitate the opposite, and ironically anticipate the birth of media and cultural studies approaches some decades later.

This volume offers a variety of overviews, perspectives, and examples of teaching adaptation within English studies, as well as showing how the field is always straining at the boundaries of the subject and threatening to blur into film and cultural studies. As this collection testifies, it is an area much practised if not much discussed, and one that not only brings new material to the undergraduate and postgraduate curriculum, but also prompts innovative teaching and approaches to student learning. As many of the essays in this volume imply, adaptation studies capitalizes on students' informal knowledges to enhance their academic studies. While most undergraduates come to university as skilled readers of literary texts, they have rarely exploited their usually more innate skills of reading and intervening in popular and visual cultures. Adaptation studies blends the experience of consumption with that of academic criticism to produce graduates whose critical acuity even Leavis would be proud of. We share the wish, expressed by Ariane Hudelet in this volume, that our students succeed in transforming the discipline that still tends to hide adaptation studies in its outer reaches.

Notes

1. Thomas Leitch, 'How to Teach Film Adaptations, and Why', in D. Cutchin, L. Raw, and J. M. Welsh, eds, *The Pedagogy of Adaptation* (Lanham: Scarecrow Press, 2010), pp. 3–4.
2. See Shelley Cobb's discussion in Chapter 2.
3. Pamela Church Gibson, 'Jane Austen on Screen – Overlapping Dialogues, Different Takes', *Adaptation*, 2(2), 2009, pp. 180–190.
4. See http://theaustenproject.com (accessed 6.3.14).
5. Lara Feigel, *Literature, Cinema and Politics: 1930–1945* (Edinburgh: Edinburgh University Press, 2010); and Robin Wood, 'Leavis, Marxism and Film Culture', *Cineaction*, 87(8), p. 3.
6. Timothy Corrigan, 'Literature on screen, a history: in the gap', in D. Cartmell and I. Whelehan, eds, *The Cambridge Companion to Literature on Screen* (Cambridge: Cambridge University Press, 2007), pp. 29–45.
7. A seminal essay on adaptation and frequently cited, Robert Stam, 'Introduction: The Theory and Practice of Adaptation', in R. Stam and A. Raengo, eds, *Literature and Film: A Guide to the Theory and Practice of Film Adaptation* (Oxford and Malden: Blackwell, 2005), pp. 1–52.
8. See Chris Stamatakis, *Sir Thomas Wyatt and the Rhetoric of Rewriting: 'Turning the Word'* (Oxford: Oxford University Press, 2012).
9. Linda Hutcheon with Siobhan O'Flynn, 2006, *A Theory of Adaptation*, 2nd edn (Abingdon: Routledge, 2013).

2
Canons, Critical Approaches, and Contexts

Shelley Cobb

Although the teaching of adaptation in universities has been around for some time, the last 15 years have seen an explosion of scholarship and critical approaches that have influenced higher education syllabi in multifarious ways. However, even a brief look at course descriptions available online suggest that certain texts appear repeatedly on syllabi and that there are obvious similarities in the ways these courses are structured.[1] This chapter examines these tendencies by offering a brief survey of a range of modules on adaptation offered in a number of universities in the US, the UK, and Australia to show that there are some 'canonical' primary texts and critical texts that underpin the study of the field and to some extent define its terms. It will then explore the benefits and limits of these canons and conclude with a discussion of the value and limits of a mixed cultural studies approach used by the author.

The sample and context

Adaptation scholars might argue that our field does not have a canon, and that it is all the better for not having the rigidity constructed by the exclusionary practice of canon formation. There is no established textbook that has taken a hold of the discipline in the ways that David Bordwell and Kristen Thompson's *Film Art: an Introduction* or *Classical Hollywood Cinema* has in Film Studies or the various Norton Anthologies have in Literary Studies. The academic critiques of the literary canon's bias toward authors who are Western, white, and male, and the widespread notion that such a critique is an attack on tradition and a dumbing down of the study of English, continue to reinforce the idea that a literary canon exists. Moreover, though debates about the film canon do not exist to anywhere near that same degree in the public sphere, arguably due to its lesser cultural capital, they do exist in academia.[2] While this is not the place for an analysis of the relationship between the literary canon, the film canon, and a (possible) adaptation canon, I would argue that the latter is constructed, inevitably, in relation to the first two: not just as a subset of one or the other, but, in some instances, as a riposte to both. This chapter is not an attempt to argue for or against an adaptation canon nor to consider the ways that scholarship on adaptations is building a canon. Rather, following John Guillory, who argues that canon formation is a product of the institutional forms of the syllabus and curriculum, I have tried to map an emerging canon of primary texts (and critical approaches) in adaptation studies by selecting a sample of adaptation course descriptions, schedules, and syllabi.[3]

My approach to constructing a tentative canon has been to establish a baseline of 'typical course content' for the study of adaptations as a discipline. I sought course descriptions/syllabi/schedules from universities in the UK, the US, Europe, and Australia and found 31 with enough detail to establish content. All were written in English. Fifteen courses were from the UK, ten from the US, four from Australia, and one from Austria. The number of UK universities is highest because I am more aware of the various adaptation courses in the country from having met colleagues at conferences and at a Teaching Adaptation Study Day, sponsored by the Higher Education Academy (UK), that I co-organized with Rachel Carroll of Teesside University, UK, in 2011. In addition, my sourcing of syllabi was inevitably circumscribed by what has been made publicly available via university websites and academics' individual webpages. I did, however, restrict the courses I considered to those that clearly focused on adaptation between media; in other words, I left out general Literature and Film courses, even if they had a session or two on adaptation. This was, ultimately, a matter of judgement, but many of the course titles and short descriptions made their emphases clear. I did not restrict the sample based on discipline, but the vast majority of these courses were found in English departments. There were three based in Film departments, and two listed as general Arts and Humanities courses. There are no doubt more adaptation courses based in Film departments than those I have found, but I would suggest that the ratio between English and Film within my sample is a fairly accurate reflection of the makeup of the discipline, a consequence of the history of teaching film within English departments, and Film departments' tendency to make institutional alliances with other forms of media studies (such as Communication Studies in the States and Cultural Studies in the UK). I also confined my sample to undergraduate teaching, leaving out courses found in graduate schools, community colleges, and high schools, in keeping with the focus of this anthology.

In spite of all these restrictions, there is still a notable variety in the ways these courses are organized, as one might expect in the HE sector, which is free from the standardization of curricula by the state. And yet some patterns did emerge, and the deviations from those patterns offer insights into what appears to be a flexible but recognizable canon of texts and approaches. First, though I have put them aside for this sample, I would like to note the prevalence of Literature and Film courses in the US and the UK that are not structured around adaptation. They are, in many cases, courses in English departments that teach film *as* literature (which is also a common course title). Others are courses taught in Comparative Literature departments.[4] The latter usually centre on a national context and tradition, such as the courses 'Chinese Literature and Film' and 'Italian Literature and Film' that I came across. The former, though sometimes a general course on 'the relationship between film and literature', are more often structured in two ways: around topics such as 'The Feast in Literature and Film', 'Politics in Literature and Film', or 'The City in Literature and Film', all of which employ a study of representation; or around genres such as 'Fantasy Fiction and Film', 'Detective Fiction and Film', or 'Horror in Literature and Film'. Although any of these titles leave room for adaptations to be a part of the course, they also imply that they are by no means exclusively, or even mostly, about adaptation.

The widespread prevalence of these courses, I would argue, is a product of the intertwined histories of both disciplines at the university level and literary studies' habit of appropriating all forms of narrative into its purview. These courses' containment of adaptations to only a section of their syllabi signals that they are doing something more than *just* adaptations, that the study of adaptations *per se* is only a small part, if not a marginal element, of the relationship between literature and film. I would not argue against a view that there are many connections between literature and film to be studied that are removed from even the loosest definition of adaptation, but neither type of course mentioned above seems to go this far. My intention is not to criticize these courses: in my time as a student, I enjoyed and learned much from several Literature and Film courses. My point is that adaptation is suppressed in the title and description of these courses, even as it appears, in some, on the weekly schedule or hovers around the edges of the course in the study of narrative and genre. Part of this suppression, I suspect, is an opposition to the habit of using adaptations at high school level to teach difficult and 'old' texts such as the plays of Shakespeare, or to entice students who find literature difficult or boring. I would also argue that the suppression is a continuing attitude that views adaptation studies as a bastardization of each discipline's critical traditions and distinctions. Adaptation courses that declare their identity do so in the context of the English and Film disciplines' intertwined but individual historical development, the institutional relationship between these disciplines (which can range from separate departments to film majors/degrees within English departments or across various departments), the existence or not of combined degree/double majors, and the presence or not of other Literature and Film courses.

Typical course content

Of the adaptation courses in my sample, three are structured around a literary author: two are titled 'Shakespeare on Screen' and one 'Screening Jane Austen'. Both explicitly declare in their descriptions or through their schedules that adaptation (and the looser term, appropriation) is the structuring principle of the texts to be studied. The descriptions of the Shakespeare courses list film adaptations only, while the Austen course considers both television and film. The university where the Austen course is listed no longer offers it as an option. Though I included only two in my sample, due to the lack of schedule detail in others, I found other courses titled 'Shakespeare on Screen'. Shakespeare's plays have been adapted since the early days of film and in various parts of world cinema, and there is a large scholarly industry of studying and researching

Shakespeare's plays on film and television. Both these facts and the status of the playwright within the English literary tradition, as well as his permanent place on school curricula in both the US and UK, make these courses viable. Though these courses foreground a single author, general adaptation criticism and approaches are a central part of the schedules. I was slightly surprised not to find more modules on adaptations of Austen or Charles Dickens, as they seem to offer the chance to consider the ways that adaptations contribute to the ongoing recognition of these authors and their works as canonically and culturally valuable, as a course on Shakespeare adaptations must.[5] Three of my sample courses are structured around national contexts: 'British Literature on Screen', 'Italian Literary Adaptations', and 'Modern Chinese Literature and Film Adaptations'. All of these explicitly structure their schedules around the study of adaptations. In keeping with the national Literature and Film courses above, the Italian and Modern Chinese modules study film adaptations made in Italy and China, respectively. The 'British Literature on Screen' course includes film adaptations from both Britain and the US. By looking at novels that have been adapted to screen multiple times, such as *Frankenstein* and *A Christmas Carol*, this last module offers the opportunity to consider the ways in which adaptations have superseded their sources in our mediated cultural memory.

Other than the above examples, the vast majority of the adaptation courses in my sample, although different in the primary and secondary texts assigned (with some key texts repeatedly appearing), were all structured similarly.[6] The adaptations on the syllabi are regularly described as a 'diverse range of texts': a selection of film, and sometimes television, adaptations from various periods of film history, usually from the beginning of sound to the present (though one includes a silent film, as does one of the Shakespeare courses), and largely English-language screen texts, though two include transnational adaptations of Shakespeare plays in addition to those on the 'Shakespeare on Screen' courses. Within those parameters, certain 'types' of adaptations regularly appear on the syllabi.[7] All courses include either a classic novel adaptation – the most common are novels by Dickens and Austen, as well as *Dracula*, *Frankenstein* and *A Room With a View* – or a Shakespeare play adaptation – *Romeo and Juliet* is the play listed most often. Several include Classical Hollywood adaptations, such as *Rebecca*, *The Thirty-Nine Steps*, and *The Postman Always Rings Twice*. Each course is made up of at least 50 percent contemporary novel adaptations such as *Beloved, Trainspotting, The Virgin Suicides, No Country for Old Men, Atonement,* and *Let the Right One In.* Pleasantly surprising is the amount of graphic novel adaptations that appear on these syllabi, such as *From Hell, Watchmen,* and *Sin City.* Adaptations that appeared on two or more syllabi include: *A Room With a View* (4), *Henry IV, Pride and Prejudice, Let the Right One In, Romeo and Juliet* (4), *No Country for Old Men, Harry Potter* (which adaptation in the series is not specified), *Rebecca, The Shining* (3), *Adaptation, Watchmen* and *The Turn of the Screw.*

Only one course in my sample listed a textbook on adaptation to go with the primary texts. A third did not make the secondary critical readings available publicly. The rest listed secondary critical readings that included at least three of the following: Linda Hutcheon's *A Theory of Adaptation* (2006), Robert Stam and Alessandra Raengo' *Literature and Film: A Guide to the Theory and Practice of Film Adaptation* (2005), James Naremore's *Film Adaptation* (2000), Brian McFarlane's *Novel to Film: An Introduction to the Theory of Adaptation* (1996), Christine Geraghty's *Now a Major Motion Picture: Film Adaptations of Literature and Drama* (2008), Sarah Cardwell's *Adaptation Revisited: Television and the Classic Novel* (2002), Thomas Leitch's *Film Adaptation and Its Discontents: From Gone with the Wind to the Passion of the Christ* (2007), Deborah Cartmell's and Imelda Whelehan's *Adaptations: From Text to Screen, Screen to Text* (1999), or *The Cambridge Companion to Literature on Screen* (2007). It is, of course, not a surprise that the recent spate of scholarship published on adaptations since 2000 would be the go-to critical readings for adaptation modules. The books that appeared most often were those by Hutcheon, Stam and Raengo, and McFarlane; their dominance suggests that intertextuality and narratology are key approaches. All three books offer both critical approaches as central to analyzing adaptations, though for Hutcheon narratology is subordinate to intertextuality, while McFarlane uses intertextuality as a secondary element of his narratological approach. In the introduction to Stam and Raengo's book intertextuality is presented as the condition of adaptation, while 'comparative narratology' is offered as the best approach for analysis.

Based on the findings above, 'typical course content' for the undergraduate study of adaptations includes: a classic novel/Shakespeare adaptation that can be considered in relation to the heritage film/costume drama debates (this is most often where television adaptations appear); a classical Hollywood-era film adaptation that, based on the films listed above, offers consideration of auteurism and adaptation or of the Hays Code's effect on the adaptation process; and multiple contemporary novel adaptations, which can be productively analyzed in terms of intertextuality and narratology. The occasional graphic novel adaptation or inter-media (e.g. television to film and vice versa) adaptation is, I presume, included in response to the scholarship in adaptation studies which takes the debates beyond the novel to film adaptation that is the ur-text of the discipline. This structure of the 'typical' adaptation course matches the stated learning outcomes that I found in many module descriptions that variously worded the following: to recognize both the differences between and similarities of literature and film, and to develop the ability to analyze both forms; to learn and apply key approaches to adaptation; and to compare a wide range of adaptation texts. Although some courses in my sample indicate that socio-cultural-historical concerns are included (and no doubt other courses that do not state this also consider culture, history, and identity in the study of their chosen adaptations), the main components of the typical course content above suggest that formalist and aesthetic concerns circumscribe the study of adaptation.

Consequently, the typical course content sets aside two influential critical approaches to literature and film: cultural studies and historicism. In his 'Introduction: the theory and practice of adaptation', Robert Stam argues that

> ... the whole constellation of currents – multiculturalism, post-coloniality, normative race, queer theory, feminist standpoint theory – revolving around issues of identity and oppression, also have an impact on the theory of adaptation...[and]...the implications for adaptation studies are multifold.[8]

The implications for Stam include revisionist views of the literary canon and literary history, the inclusion of oral literature, attention to cultural and racial dimensions of texts, and revisionist adaptations that 'rewrite' the source text through a political lens. The list of primary texts above suggests that these 'currents' have not impacted the typical course content in a significant way. The most repeated texts are by canonical authors – Shakespeare, Austen, E.M. Forster – or popular literature adapted by film auteurs – Alfred Hitchcock, Stanley Kubrick, the Coen brothers. Children's literature, contemporary vampires, and graphic novels are all on the margins of any canon, but the ones found on syllabi in my sample do not disrupt too strongly the 'quietly assumed, unmarked normativities which place whiteness, Europeanness, maleness, and heterosexuality at the centre, while marginalizing all that is not normative'.[9] Furthermore, the typical adaptation course that includes one or two pre-1960s films and then various films from the 1980s to the present is ahistorical: it is organized neither by the historicity of the source texts nor the historicity of the film/screen texts. In addition, none of the courses in my sample organize the schedule in terms of a history of adaptation as a film genre, following Thomas Leitch's argument in his article 'Adaptation, the genre'.[10] By virtue of choosing a 'wide range of texts' to study, the typical adaptation course appears to sideline industrial, historical, and socio-historical contexts in the study of adaptations.

Film adaptation: culture and context

In his book, *Film Adaptation in the Hollywood Studio Era*, Guerric DeBona has argued for the analysis of adaptations in the industrial and historical contexts within which they were produced in order to consider the 'cultural politics of redeploying literary texts during one of Hollywood's most exciting and creative periods'.[11] By limiting the parameters of his chosen texts to adaptations made in a particular historical period and in a particular industrial context, DeBona shifts the mode of analysis to be in line with Film Studies' approach to film history and cultural studies. This shift does not automatically preclude literary analysis, but moves the questions away from concerns regarding what of the source is included (or not) or altered in the adaptation to the questions in which I am also interested: why this particular text adapted at this particular time? Why are similar source texts or texts by the same author adapted simultaneously? What effects do these adaptations have on each other in terms of reception? What is the cultural value of the source text to the authors/makers of the adaptation? What contemporary cultural/political/social issues does the adaptation engage with? And how does analyzing an adaptation in relation to the cultural politics of the period of the film's production and release affect our understanding of intertextuality and offer a new way to think about the 'what's in/what's out' question, generic conventions, authorship, and reception?

Although constructing a course that limits the adaptations to a certain period of cinema history might seem restrictive for the student experience, I would argue that it offers a coherence that makes students see adaptations as a 'product and process of creation and reception', which are in a dynamic relationship with history, industry, society, and culture, the politics of which are not limited to the adaptation's textual relationship to its source.[12] When students must analyze more than one adaptation in light of the key socio-historical concerns circumscribed by the course schedule, the cultural desire for fidelity that they bring with them to class diminishes because the source texts become just one varying element in the making of meaning. Furthermore, a course like this can teach various approaches to adaptation. I have taught two adaptation courses structured around the historical context of the film adaptations: 'The Golden Year: American Films of 1939 as Cultural History' and 'Gender, Culture and Contemporary Film Adaptation'.[13]

Although 'The Golden Year' does not say it in the title, adaptation was the focus of the course.[14] The title does make clear, though, that the historical boundaries of the course were within the year 1939, a year in Hollywood production that is often known as 'The Golden Year' due to the many films released that remain well known and are considered 'classics' to this day; many of those were also adaptations. The course schedule included *Stagecoach* (John Ford), *Gone with the Wind* (Victor Fleming), *The Wizard of Oz* (Victor Fleming), *Wuthering Heights* (William Wyler), and *Gunga Din* (George Stevens), but it also could have included *The Women* (George Cukor), *Goodbye Mr. Chips* (Sam Wood), *Dark Victory* (Edmund Goulding), *The Old Maid* (Edmund Goulding), and others. The historical context is obvious, of course. The late days of the Great Depression and the beginnings of World War II before US involvement create a potent mix for thinking about American national identity and history in the various texts, and the various adaptations raised discussion of 'manifest destiny', isolationism, the individual versus the community, and British–American relations, as well as race and gender. With the question 'why this particular source text at this particular time?' underpinning the course, class discussion considered the cyclical nature of economic boom and bust, the repeated history of colonization, the romanticization of the nineteenth century, and the mythologizing of America's origins, which played their part in the imagining of America and its place in the world: an imagining that these films participate in by re-imagining a source text from a different context.

'Gender, Culture and Contemporary Film Adaptation' is confined to the slightly longer than ten-year period of 1993–2006.[15] For this course, I have variously included *The Age of Innocence* (Martin Scorsese, 1993), *The Portrait of a Lady* (Jane Campion, 1995), *Mansfield Park* (Patricia Rozema, 1999), *Fight Club* (David Fincher, 1999), *Bridget Jones's Diary* (Sharon Maguire, 2001), *Brokeback Mountain* (Ang Lee, 2005), *A History of Violence* (David Cronenberg, 2005), *The Hours* (Stephen Daldry, 2002), *Great Expectations* (Alfonso Cuarón, 1998), *Hamlet* (Michael Almereyda, 2000), and *Casino Royale* (Martin Campbell, 2006). The emphasis in this course, as the title suggests, is on issues of gender and culture. The key critical approach for this course is intertextuality. As articulated by Robert Stam, intertextuality makes space in the study of adaptations for the recognition of multiple texts, including discourses of cultural politics:

> ... intertextual dialogism refers to the infinite and open-ended possibilities generated by all the discursive practices of a culture, the entire matrix of communicative utterances within which the artistic text is situated, which reach the text not only through recognizable influences, but also through a subtle process of dissemination.[16]

For me, intertextual dialogism means considering not only the textual, historical, and industrial contexts of adaptations, but in addition their relationship to the cultural and identity politics of their time, as well as the cultural politics of adaptation itself. Stam's explication of intertextual dialogism makes space for us to study adaptations in their socio-historical and industrial contexts, but it is Dudley Andrew who, 30 years ago, called for 'adaptation studies to take a sociological turn ... Although the volume of adaptation may be calculated as relatively constant in the history of cinema, its particular function at any moment is far from constant'.[17] What I am suggesting is that all adaptations should be analyzed within the 'matrix of communicative utterances' in which they are situated, and that we should be considering their 'particular function at [their particular] moment'. A course structured around a particular histori-cal period and focused on socio-political contexts helps students to see more clearly the complex layers of intertextual dialogism and to situate adaptations in their context. I have argued elsewhere that *Bridget Jones's Diary* exemplifies intertextual dialogism in its mix of appropriation and adaptation of source texts, generic conventions, and feminist and postfeminist discourses.[18] As such, it is the anchor of this course that is focused on the gender politics of adaptations in the 1990s and 2000s.

The wider film culture of this period is a part of a post-feminist popular culture that, according to Angela McRobbie,

> ... continues to define and redefine the boundaries of gender, showing how much is at stake in the marshalling of gender identi-ties in terms of rigid difference even as those very differences are also being undermined so that the field of popular culture now comprises a to and fro movement between the doing and undoing of gender.[19]

The doing and undoing of gender in the contemporary period has been the subject of a continually growing body of work on post-feminist cinema by scholars such as Diane Negra, Yvonne Tasker, Hilary Radner, and Rosalind Gill.[20] My goals with this course are to introduce students to this body of scholarship on gender, film, and popular culture at the turn of the century, as well as to contemporary approaches to adaptation, and then to have them consider what role adaptation plays in postfeminist film culture.

McRobbie's book, *The Aftermath of Feminism: Gender, Culture and Social Change*, is a cultural studies analysis of the current state of feminism in popular culture. In it she unwittingly gives a reason to consider classical adaptations as symptomatic of postfeminist film culture. First, she links postfeminist popular culture to the cultural paradox of the young woman who 'despite her freedom [is] called upon to be silent, to withhold critique [of sexism]'.[21] She then sug-gests that the young woman's repressed anger returns as 'a kind of secret life, a devouring of classic feminist novels, for example, a love for Jane Austen, a passion for Emma Bovary'.[22] Part of the implication of this statement is that engagement with classic literary texts can be a way for repressed anxieties about contemporary gender relations to return in popular culture, displaced through the adaptation of the text, its historical context, and its cultural value. I would argue, then, that Jane Austen adaptations of the 1990s (as well as more recent ones) are key texts in postfeminist film culture for the ways in which they give space for the representation of the tensions between independence and romance and the cultural pressure on contemporary women to manage both successfully. *Mansfield Park* deflects this common postfeminist narrative onto the conventions of the heritage film and through the conflation of Austen's authorship with Fanny's character. Consequently, the postfeminist desire to contain the threat of the successful woman through heterosexual coupling is reinforced through Fanny's happy ending in which she becomes both an author and a wife, while the apparent authentic representation of eighteenth-century England in the *mise-en-scène* makes her achievement of both seem more triumphant and progressive than might be the case in a contemporary romantic comedy. This cultural distinction between heritage films and romantic comedies is further reinforced by the cultural value of the Austen novel. Moreover, the distinction is heightened by the cultural value of *Bridget Jones's Diary*, which, as a romantic comedy adaptation of a chick-lit appropriation of *Pride and Prejudice*, exemplifies Diane Negra's argument that 'mainstream cinematic romances are customarily held in low cultural esteem and their review discourses often reflect the low expectations attached to them'.[23] Teaching *Bridget Jones's Diary* on the same course as *Mansfield Park* requires the students to consider these cultural distinctions and the generic crossover of the postfeminist sensibility of the period.

Conclusion

In a course with 'a wide variety of texts' from different periods of film history, it is not possible to be sure that students know enough about the historical context of the adaptations to interrogate its intertextual dialogism deeply. Though it is more possible, it is also unlikely that the course will structure the primary texts around a cultural issue. Moreover, I would argue that a course that looked at, say, masculinity across a 'wide variety of texts' would risk de-historicizing the study of gender for students, and my goal with these courses, which is a product of my own research training and interests in film, media, and cultural studies, is to view adaptations as cultural products of their historical moments. Adaptations complicate this, of course, when they adapt source texts from a previous period, and some might argue that my approach de-historicizes the source texts, as there is not enough time to make sure the students have knowledge of those contexts. I do teach the source text and the film on separate weeks in order to give as much attention to the source texts' contexts as possible. Also, I teach this module in an English department, where I know the students will be learning about nineteenth and early twentieth-century literary contexts in their other courses. Recently, Film degree students have been allowed to take my course, and their training in Film Studies means that they more readily think about how film authorship, genre, stylistics, and national contexts affect the adaptation process. Their presence has reminded me that the goal of my teaching is to get the students to think about how the adaptations use their source texts to speak to its own cultural-historical moment. It has reminded me that over-emphasizing the socio-historical context of the source text can lead students to fall back on fidelity discourses and debates about what the adaptation is getting 'right or wrong'. In the end, I hope what all the students learn is to 'use [adaptation] as we use all cultural practices, to understand the world from which it comes and the one toward which it points'.[24]

Notes

1. I use the word 'course' for what in the UK would be called a module or a unit. 'Course' is the common term in the US.
2. See Virginia Wright Wexman, 'Evaluating the text: canon formation and screen scholarship', *Cinema Journal* 2 Winter, 1985, 62–65, and Jonathon Rosenbaum, *Essential Cinema: On the Necessity of Film Canons* (Baltimore: John Hopkins University, 2004). For an article that attempts to take the argument for a film canon beyond academia, see Paul Schrader, 'Canon Fodder', *Film Comment* 42 (5), Sept/Oct 2006, 33–49.
3. John Guillory, *Cultural Capital: The Problem of Literary Canon Formation* (Chicago: University of Chicago Press, 1993).
4. In universities that use a modular credit system, many of these courses are coded so that they can be credited for both English degree and Film degree students, and in the US as electives for other degree majors.
5. I found but did not include the course 'Charles Dickens: Novels, Journalism, Adaptation', because the first half of the module focuses

on the novels and journalism of Dickens and his 'persona' in historical context before moving onto screen adaptations.

6. I do not name individual courses because it would not help to distinguish between them; many of them had similar variations on the following title: 'Film Adaptation'.

7. In this section I have left out the director and year for these adaptations because some of these titles have multiple adaptation versions and this was not always indicated in the information I found.

8. Robert Stam, 'Introduction: A Theory and Practice of Adaptation', in *Literature and Film: A Guide to the Theory and Practice of Film Adaptation*, ed. Robert Stam and Alessandro Raengo (Malden and Oxford: Blackwell, 2005), p. 11.

9. *Ibid.*

10. Thomas Leitch, 'Adaptation, the Genre', *Adaptation* 1 (2), 2008, 106–120.

11. Guerric DeBona, *Film Adaptation in the Hollywood Studio Era* (Chicago: University of Illiois, 2010), p. 6.

12. Linda Hutcheon, *A Theory of Adaptation* (London: Routledge, 2006), p. xiv.

13. I found a course with a similar title to 'The Golden Year' listed at another UK university, but I was not able to ascertain any details of its schedule.

14. The title of this course was conceived by Professor Sarah Churchwell of the University of East Anglia; however, I was given free rein to choose texts and organize the schedule as I saw fit when I was made convener.

15. I currently teach this course under the title 'Film Adaptation: Culture and Context'.

16. Robert Stam, 'The Dialogics of Adaptation', in *Film Adaptation*, ed. James Naremore (New Brunswick: Rutgers University Press, 2000), p. 64.

17. Dudley Andrew, 'Adaptation', in *Film Adaptation*, ed. James Naremore (New Brunswick: Rutgers University Press, 2000), p. 35.

18. Shelley Cobb, 'Adaptable Bridget: generic intertextuality and postfeminism in *Bridget Jones's Diary*' in *Authorship in Film Adaptation*, ed. Jack Boozer (Austin: University of Texas Press, 2008), pp. 281–304.

19. Angela McRobbie, *The Uses of Cultural Studies* (London: Sage Publications, 2005), p. 71.

20. Key publications include: Yvonne Tasker and Diane Negra, *Interrogating Postfeminism: Gender and the Politics of Popular Culture* (Durham: Duke University Press, 2007); Hilary Radner, *Neo-Feminist Cinema: Girly Films, Chick Flicks and Consumer Culture* (London: Routledge, 2009); Rosalind Gill, *Gender and the Media* (Cambridge: Polity Press, 2006); for postfeminist masculinity in cinema see Hannah Hamad, *Postfeminism and Paternity in Contemporary US Film: Framing Fatherhood* (London: Routledge, 2013) and section two of Joel Gwynne and Nadine Muller, *Postfeminism and Contemporary Hollywood Cinema* (Basingstoke: Palgrave Macmillan, 2013).

21. Angela McRobbie, *The Aftermath of Feminism: Gender, Culture and Social Change* London: Sage Publications, 2009), p. 18.

22. *Ibid.*, p. 119. I reference this quotation in my chapter 'What Would Jane Do? Postfeminist Media Uses of Austen and the Austen Reader' in *Uses of Austen: Jane's Afterlives*, ed. Gillian Dow and Clare Hanson (Basingstoke: Palgrave Macmillan, 2012), pp. 208–227.
23. Diane Negra, 'Structural Integrity, Historical Reversion, and the Post 9/11 Chick-Flick', *Feminist Media Studies*, 8 (1), 2008, 51–68.
24. Andrew, *Film Adaptation*, p. 37.

3
The Paragogy of Adaptation in an EFL Context

Laurence Raw

When I joined the Department of English Language Teaching at Başkent University, Ankara, in 2007, while teaching part-time in the Department of American Culture and Literature, I prepared courses specifically tailored for students with a strong adaptation element.[1] I encouraged them to rewrite canonical literary texts in their own words in an attempt to promote close reading, as well as increasing awareness of the sound and the sense of the words. Among the most popular adapted texts were Shakespeare's *Romeo and Juliet*, Lewis Carroll's nonsense poem 'Beautiful Soup', and Roger McGough's children's poem 'The Leader'. Through such activities students discovered how literary texts related to their own backgrounds: 'The Leader' proved exceptionally popular as a means of questioning the familiar gender stereotypes of the dominant male/submissive female, and thereby helped them cultivate the kind of 'active literacy' (to use Thomas Leitch's term) that promotes creative activity and cultural development.[2] In terms of process, the students' tasks were very similar to those adopted by professional screenwriters working with other creative personnel on a film (directors, actors, producers) to adapt a literary text. While acknowledging the importance of individual imagination, everyone had to accept those common meanings and directions that shaped their intended audiences' reactions. By such means the students discovered how adaptations evolve through individual control and ownership as well as through group and/or societal interactions.[3]

More recently I have used the experience of such classes to address basic paragogical – rather than pedagogical – issues of adaptation, paying particular attention to the experiences of EFL (English as a Foreign Language) students. Derived from the Greek term for 'production', paragogy addresses the phenomenon of effective learning by identifying principles of good practice. They include: meta-learning as a basis of knowledge; regular and constructive feedback; treating learning as distributed and nonlinear; and understanding how learning is a lifelong process extending beyond the educational institution.[4] Students and teachers alike should reflect on their experiences both inside and outside the classroom as a basis for inter- and cross-cultural comparison.[5] This chapter offers a case study of a paragogy devised for a drama course taught in the Department of American Culture and Literature in spring 2013 at Başkent University. My analysis will concentrate on three distinct points – curriculum planning, learning outcomes, and assessment. The syllabus was planned collaboratively, incorporating a substantial amount of adaptation studies work designed to reflect on the relationship between drama and adaptation as a psychological process of transformation. The main focus of attention centred on *process* rather than outcomes: through regular feedback and discussion students had the chance to reflect on *how* they had adapted to the texts included in the syllabus. With the idea of lifelong learning in mind, the course concentrated on the development of abilities (communication and negotiation, as well as developing fluency and confidence in speaking a foreign language) rather than the acquisition of knowledge; this had a significant bearing on the ways in which it was assessed. I conclude this chapter by suggesting that this paragogical framework for teaching adaptation has transnational possibilities; it can be employed equally effectively in native speaker as well as EFL contexts. All students can develop their capacity to adapt (understood in this sense as the ability to respond to new phenomena and new situations) while acquiring the confidence to reflect critically on their own learning.

The three drama courses in Başkent's American Culture and Literature curriculum function as part of an overall programme designed to promote the understanding of literature from a variety of perspectives and thereby deepen understanding of the US past and present. Yet students often find that they cannot cultivate their critical faculties due to linguistic obstacles; the texts they are given prove difficult to understand. In the Turkish context, they are expected to be members of 'the language élite' – a group of highly competent EFL speakers who are both bicultural and bilingual, whose exposure to literary texts will 'help them compete on the market as professional translators/interpreters', as well as enhancing their teaching careers in schools and/or universities.[6] The major problem arises from a lack of familiarity with the rhetorical and literary devices in texts, such as complex metaphors, which students find difficult to unravel. An additional issue is that more often than not literary language might be so markedly 'deviant' from everyday English that it breaks the norms of language use (as set down in EFL textbooks, for instance). Hence the learning of literature might inhibit rather than facilitate the learning of communicative skills, which are the main goals of EFL teaching and learning.[7]

Bearing this difficulty in mind, we began the American Drama course by rejecting the idea that texts should be studied for their rhetorical and literary devices, and concentrating instead on how the experience of reading dramatic texts differs from that of other texts, specifically novels and poems. One student – who teaches English Language in a private school part-time as well as pursuing an undergraduate course in American Literature – brought in a quotation from actor/teacher Matt Buchanan, defining drama thus:

> [it is] an important means of stimulating creativity in problem solving. It can challenge [...] perceptions about the world and about [oneself] [....] A student can, if only for a few minutes, become another, explore a new role, try out and experiment with various personal choices and solutions to very real problems – problems faced in life, or problems faced in literature or historical figures.[8]

This extract proved invaluable in determining how our syllabus should be constructed. Although the students wanted to look at cinematic adaptations of American plays, and how they differed from the source texts, they were equally interested in discovering the 'various personal choices and solutions to very real problems' that every actor faces while trying to create a role on stage and screen. I suggested that we should look at the work of the psychologist Jerome Bruner, which views 'adaptation' as a psychological process of coming to terms with new phenomena. In *Making Stories* (2002), he suggests that we are all involved in a process of story-making;

creating different roles for ourselves and those around us throughout our lives. This process is accomplished 'with the guidance of our memories of the past and our hopes and fears for the future. Telling oneself about oneself is like making up a story about who and what we are, what's happened, and why we're doing what we're doing'.[9] Like screenplay writers creating adaptations, we draw on our own experiences to create new stories out of familiar as well as unfamiliar materials. In a group situation, such as a classroom, these stories are continually reshaped, not only by our own experiences, but also by the comments made about us by others. As a result 'our self-directed self-making narratives [...] come to express what we think others expect us to be like'.[10] When other people express different opinions about ourselves and our self-created narratives, we alter them; this process is termed *adaptation*. Bruner concludes: 'the nature and shape of selfhood are indeed as much matters of cultural concern, *res publica*, as of individual concern [...] selfhood involves a commitment to others as well as being "true to oneself"'.[11] In our American Drama course, students wanted to use the experience of performing the stories told in the texts as a basis for meta-learning. They felt that what they were doing was useful in itself, as a way to help them adapt to new material and new experiences. One of the group members, with an extensive track record of writing and performing plays, summed up his reactions thus: 'When you gain understanding on something [through performing and rewriting it], the knowledge itself becomes more valuable because it is not the [textual] knowledge itself anymore. You add your own perspective [...] once you gain understanding'.

In determining the choice of texts for the syllabus, we came up with a fascinating combination: classics like *Death of a Salesman* (1949) were studied alongside less familiar work such as David Rabe's *Hurlyburly* (1984). A popular choice was Sidney Kingsley's 1949 play *Detective Story*, filmed two years later with Kirk Douglas in the central role as Detective McLeod. While its portrayal of life in a New York police squad might seem over-familiar, it nonetheless proved attractive to the students, many of whom were interested in deconstructing a familiar icon from the American as well as the Turkish media – the hard-boiled detective.[12] After having read the play individually, students decided they wanted to create role-plays with McLeod at the centre, to see how and why he behaves as he does. Although good at his job, he self-righteously regards himself as a sovereign judge of the rights and wrongs of others, paying little heed to the rights of the American justice system. His attitude changes, however, once he discovers that his wife has been involved in the crimes he tries to investigate. In his dying moments (having been fatally shot by a burglar) he admits that he has neglected to forgive others for their mistakes. Having essayed the role of McLeod in a student-generated version of the play (in Turkish), one male student wrote that true strength of character had little to do with being 'a big muscled guy. If you have intelligence and compassion, you can defeat every hardship in this life [....] [From our adaptation] I understood the importance of determination; if you want to solve a problem, you have to be intelligent as well as kind [....] I've learned the importance of forgiveness'. This is a fascinating insight from someone brought up in a context where masculinity is still equated with brute force.[13] There is no doubt that current events shaped his judgment; in the recent disturbances taking place in İstanbul over the proposed closure of Gezi Park, some of the protestors tried to commemorate the death of one of their number by lighting candles. Immediately after, they were attacked by a group of baton-wielding supporters of the government chanting nationalist lyrics. The scholar Jenny White saw this incident as a prime example of 'militant masculinity', in which oppositional voices were brutally silenced.[14] Inspired by Kingsley's text, the student contemplates the possibility of more compassionate constructions of masculinity, and thereby creates a new narrative to tell himself about himself, one that challenges dominant ways of thinking about masculinity.

The experience of working with *Detective Story* proved very different for a female student, who demonstrated a marked preference for Wyler's film version as opposed to the printed text. By looking at the action in its socio-historical context, she found inspiration to create costumes for herself as she essayed the role of McLeod. Instead of an old trench-coat and battered trilby, she preferred to dress in a fedora, in the belief that the detective was ostentatiously proud of his abilities as a cop and wanted to show off to everyone around him. This might have been an 'unfaithful' adaptation of the source text, but it provided a suitable means by which she could address her lack of self-confidence, especially when it came to speaking in public, either in English or Turkish. Her presence as both initiator and performer drew attention to the complexities of the adaptive act in which media (the printed text as well as the adapted performance) are in constant reciprocal interaction not only with each other, but also with those responsible for the remediation. The experience not only gave her an insight into McLeod's character but helped her to reconsider 'what the meaning is of being male and female' in a basically patriarchal culture. Her comments aptly express what Kyle Meikle describes as a disinterring of 'quasi-objects [and their transcultural significances] buried among page, screen, speaker, and stage'.[15]

Our course concentrated on the *process* rather than the outcomes of the adaptive act. In an attempt to engage in cross-cultural comparison, students looked at how source texts were transformed into the film versions, concentrating in particular on the changes introduced into the screenplays. In Williams' film version of *Streetcar* (1951), for instance, they considered how and why the source text had to be toned down somewhat due to the constraints of the Production Code.[16] Students subsequently compared the reviews by US-based critics on the film's premiere with more contemporary evaluations as posted on the Internet Movie Database. Finally, they contrasted their own responses with those expressed by the critics. Through this process students not only understood how critical responses to *Streetcar* have changed over time and space, but more importantly discovered the truth of Bruner's point about stories possessing a cultural as well as an individual significance. In the Hollywood of the early 1950s, *Streetcar* had to be sanitized to remove supposedly unsavoury or contentious elements. As they performed their own versions of Williams' text (in Turkish as well as in English), the students discovered similar tensions between individual and societal issues. One remarked on how Stanley Kowalski appeared 'emotionally weak', despite his physical strength, but felt duty-bound to sustain an aggressive façade in a patriarchal society. Watching Marlon Brando's performance in the Kazan film convinced him more than ever of the need to acknowledge his feelings to the rest of the group. This might not be considered 'masculine' (in Turkish terms, at least), but it provided a means to relieve personal and emotional frustration and thereby develop self-confidence.

Such role-plays formed part of a syllabus designed to create what Guy Claxton has termed a 'learning gymnasium', comprising a series of tasks that became gradually more sophisticated as the course unfolded.[17] Reading the texts was followed by role-plays, in which students had to produce adaptations of their own using whichever language they felt comfortable with.[18] Such tasks were designed to help them develop their practical and creative faculties, as well as understanding the significance of adaptation through process-focused activities. One female student was initially apprehensive, as she had never experienced this kind of course before. After having produced a mini-adaptation (English dialogue only, no staging) of David Mamet's *Glengarry Glen Ross* (1984) – based on the play as well as the 1992 film – she discovered for herself why individuals experience such difficulties trying to communicate with one another. In meritocratic cultures such as early 1980s America or the contemporary Turkish Republic, success is measured solely in terms of wealth, status, and performance; failure is simply not entertained. Everyone puts on a brave face, even if that means resorting to aggression. In the Turkish university system, this is why English-medium education is considered so significant; it is perceived as a passport to professional success.[19] The student admitted that she felt intimidated by this kind of culture: 'When I tried to talk I was afraid, as I thought they [her interlocutors] would insult me due to my ideas and lack of English'. Exposure to Mamet's play helped her understand how silence denotes strength of character: one needs to speak only when necessary. Her comments reveal how a curriculum co-created by teachers and students gives everyone a sense of personal investment as they use the experience of adapting texts to develop themselves and their relationship to those around them.

How can teachers create a paragogy that promotes a learning gymnasium? They need to understand that meta-learning is non-linear: students have different ways of making sense of past experiences as well as opening up new avenues of research for themselves. Most of the comments incorporated in this piece were written at different times of the day and night on Facebook, almost entirely outside the classroom context. This was the preferred method of communication by most students, based on the belief that the online environment rendered them less stressed or embarrassed while communicating in English.[20] Another strategy they favoured was that of the flipped classroom, based on extensive reflection and feedback, in which they read the texts they had previously chosen for the syllabus and posted their questions before the class on their Facebook discussion group. In class they answered them on their own, and subsequently reflected on why they had posed the questions in the first place. Were they interested solely in thematic concerns, or were they more interested in cross-cultural comparison? I acted as the 'personal trainer' by listening to discussions and offering further feedback where necessary. At the end of each class, the students discussed among themselves what they had learned, and used their findings as a basis for determining what would be studied in future weeks. If that meant departing from the syllabus as constructed at the beginning of the semester, then so be it.

One activity that emerged from these class discussions was a student-created and staged adaptation of Edgar Allan Poe's short stories 'The Fall of the House of Usher' and 'The Tell-Tale Heart', retitled 'The Fall of the Tell-Tale Heart'. Having studied both texts in previous courses in the department of American Literature and Culture, they wanted to re-evaluate their experiences through performance, rather than simply analyzing them in terms of metaphors, similes, or other literary devices. One student summed up her objectives thus: 'I wanted to make the texts my own if I could'. The results were fascinating: one student admitted that the tasks of writing, rehearsing, and performing an adaptation 'formed a whole different bond between me and my classmates because we actually handled each other pretty well in stressful situations, which we could never do before this project. I learnt how to forgive and forget just for the sake of the work being produced and we had to work together. I realized that this is actually what takes the stress away and what makes you happy'. Her comments illustrate how the experience of creating dramatic adaptations can help to negotiate difficulties experienced by EFL students with texts written in English. As the performance date drew nearer and nearer, members of the group not only resolved the linguistic problems presented by the Poe texts, but dealt with practical problems (such as blocking, or timing exits and entrances) through negotiation.[21]

In terms of student development, this activity not only helped them negotiate what they perceived as the linguistic difficulties presented by the texts, but it helped them understand how working on an adaptation in an academic context prompts reflection on their experiences past and present. One female student admitted that, when she had encountered non-Turks – whether native speakers or representatives of other nations – in the past, and had to speak English with them, she felt tongue-tied. The performance helped her to 'take a step into the path of the future' by giving her renewed faith in her communicative abilities. In a 2011 report on the future of the humanities, based on a UK-based Arts and Humanities Research Council Initiative, Rónán McDonald claims that any arts-based subject should help to promote the kind of 'critical thinking' that did much to enrich intellectual as well as personal lives by subjecting 'our values to academic and historical consideration'.[22] Our paragogy offered a much more specific construction of critical thinking, based on a shared willingness (among teacher and students alike) to use the experience of adapting literary texts to promote personal as well as linguistic development.

The question of how these developments might be assessed is a vexed one for two particular reasons in the Turkish context. At Başkent University, as with the majority of higher education institutions, EFL students are accustomed to taking at least two sit-down exams, plus writing term papers in each of their courses. They are assessed both on factual knowledge – based on what they have learned from lectures and/or class discussions – and on their abilities to present that knowledge in English in essay form, with an introduction and conclusion. While such modes of assessment have their advantages – as a means of testing what students have learned during a course – they often prove daunting for students. Once again the issue here is one of linguistic competence: students enter the department of American Culture and Literature with expectations of joining the 'language élite', and feel somehow inadequate when they produce the kind of essays that, in the teachers' opinions at least, are not suitable for members of that élite.[23] The prospect of evaluating student development solely in terms of abilities (e.g. their improved self-confidence) might seem attractive, but we are still faced with the issue of how teachers can ensure fairness in a course dedicated to process rather than outcomes. We discussed these issues at the beginning of the course and came up with the following solutions. Students were invited to reflect on what they considered a 'high-grade' performance: one male student believed that it depended on the acquisition of 'real life' abilities, both linguistic and social, that would prove useful once he had graduated. Another female student agreed; as a teacher as well as a student she wanted to use the experience of adapting American Drama to achieve her goals, both personal and professional. The students elected to write two evaluation papers – extensively quoted throughout this chapter – that focused specifically on how (and whether) the experience of critiquing the texts on the syllabus had inspired them to adapt themselves. Every paper was read by all members of the class, as well as by me, and subsequently discussed as a group; this formed the basis for further discussion as to how future classes should be structured. At the end of the semester students were asked to write down five examples of how they had developed their abilities, and to grade themselves using the familiar letter form (A, A–, B+ and so on). I did the same; when we had finished, we exchanged our findings and worked out a final grade through collective moderation. Students also wrote a term paper based on one or two of the texts incorporated on the syllabus; the choice was up to them, but they were asked to show evidence of the kind of 'critical thinking' outlined above (i.e. how exposure to American drama can enrich one's personal life). These papers were read by everyone and grades determined through negotiation.

The emphasis throughout was placed on modes of assessment that would challenge traditional top-down constructions (in which the teacher assumes sole responsibility) and work towards more collaborative methods. This kind of 'assessment-as-learning', rather than 'assessment-of-learning' relies heavily on individual self-assessment, in which teachers and students train themselves to observe, analyze, and judge their performances across a variety of tasks – both written and performative.[24] In retrospect, perhaps we should have devoted more time to creating a list of statements that individual students could use to measure their performances (for example 'I feel I can negotiate with others', 'I listen to other people's views, regardless if they differ from my own', or 'I feel I can now make my own decisions'), using a sliding scale from 1 to 10. This strategy would help to counter the possible criticism that our assessment modes lacked academic rigour; after all, how can students with a limited exposure to American literary texts decide whether one of their essays is a 'good' piece or not? On the other hand, in an EFL context – where students are developing their language as well as their critical thinking abilities – the term 'rigour' often inhibits rather than empowers them. A common linguistic mistake (for example, omitting the definite article in front of a noun, a common fault in Turkish students)[25] might result in their grades being reduced on the grounds of linguistic competence. Our course confronted this issue head-on by focusing less on language issues and more on student development through adaptation; through a series of tasks accompanied by extensive reflection, they developed the kind of abilities that should prove indispensable in their future careers.

In this chapter I have argued that by embracing a paragogy based on the notion that 'adaptation' constitutes a process of coming to terms with the world (as well as altering source-texts), students can understand how the experience of literature can contribute towards their lifelong learning. The important issue here is one of flexibility; if we accept that learning is non-linear, we must therefore understand how the aims and objectives of any given course might change as the semester progresses. This kind of randomness might seem intimidating for teachers and students alike (especially in my own university, where students are usually given a week-by-week breakdown of their course syllabuses and the activities they are expected to do at the beginning of each semester), but can be readily overcome through the creation of a mutually supportive environment, in which teachers and students alike reflect on their experiences of learning. There are other methods by which this approach to learning can be sustained: in Georgine Loacker's English Literature course at Alverno College, Wisconsin, students kept a weekly journal in which they recorded their impressions of each group activity, presentation, or academic paper. Their comments formed the basis for intensive discussion about how student performances could be evaluated at the end of the course. One student wrote: 'I've always considered reader response to be used as a reflection of past ideas in my life and how the work reminded me or made me reflect, but I'm learning that the reader-response framework can shape my further thinking and change my thoughts to develop more'.[26] Even in a classroom of predominantly native speakers that is not necessarily dedicated to adaptation, the idea of meta-learning is significant as a means for students to determine the ways in which they have adapted to the texts included on the syllabus. Once students have acquired the confidence to reflect on their own abilities, they can assume a significant role in planning future programmes of study designed to help them develop such abilities.

While it might be attractive to claim that the future of teaching 'adaptation studies' lies in viewing adaptation from this wider perspective as a means of coming to terms with the world around us, I am not sure that it would work in practical terms. I think that more needs to be done in terms of looking at paragogies in different academic as well as geographical contexts as a basis for establishing effective transnational frameworks for teaching adaptation. Nonetheless, I think that my experiences at Başkent reveal the significance of alternative conceptions of teaching and learning. Hitherto teachers in Turkey have been accustomed to playing the role of 'sage on the stage', as they prepare syllabuses, give lectures, and mark exams with very little input from their students. Such strategies, they believe, are the bedrock upon which their authority as scholars and/or 'experts' in their subjects can be sustained. In my American Drama course the approach was far more collaborative; just like the students, I was involved in a process of continual learning and adaptation – understood in this context as the process of coming to terms with ourselves and the narratives we construct to make sense of the world. Students can use this knowledge as a basis for creating their own learning opportunities.[27] In March 2013 an article in the *Guardian* claimed that many teachers were wary of this kind of approach to learning, in the belief that it casts aside 'tried and tested scholarly communications systems' in favour of more experimental techniques.[28] While 'tried and tested scholarly communications systems' – for example, private study, group discussions, student-generated questioning – are undoubtedly important, I believe that we should also embrace the experimental, so long as such experiments can encourage greater student involvement in the processes of learning (for example, by using online methods of delivery and communication such as Facebook and Twitter). Such concepts lie at the heart of innovative paragogies in adaptation studies that not only revaluate existing teaching methods, but assume that lifelong learning among our students is of primary significance.

Acknowledgements

Many thanks to Merve Tutka, Serkan Korkmaz, Tefvik Can Babacan, Ekin Görür, Aybüke Işık and Esra Akçay, who played a major contribution in making the American Drama course work so well.

Notes

1. In the Turkish context, I would use the term 'learners' to emphasize the importance of the lifelong learning process rather than 'students' (*öğrenciler*) – a term that covers those attending primary and high schools, as well as university. Some teachers address university students as 'children' (*cocuklar*), thereby emphasizing the institutional continuities between high school and university.
2. Thomas Leitch, 'How to Teach Film Adaptations, and Why' (Keynote Address, Boğaziçi University, İstanbul, 33rd American Studies of Turkey Conference, 8 October 2008).
3. Leitch has recently spoken of the need to approach adaptation from a communal perspective as something that depends on the survival of the species. I would argue that this still does not minimize the importance of individual voices in the adaptive act ('What Movies Want', *Adaptation Studies: New Challenges, New Directions*, eds. Jorgen Bruhn, Anne Gjelsvik and Eirik Frisvold Hanssen (London and New York: Bloomsbury Academic Publishing, 2013), p. 173.
4. See Joseph Corneli and Charles Jeffrey Danoff, *Paragogy* (Winnetka, IL: Pub Dom Ed Press, 2012), *passim*.
5. For the sake of clarity, I employ the term 'teachers' in this chapter. I use the term 'educator' in the Turkish context to emphasize the idea of lifelong learning, rather than employing the term 'teacher' (*öğretmen*), which specifically describes those who work in schools, universities, or other educational institutions.
6. Adelina Ivanova, 'Educating the 'Language Elite': Teaching Translation for Translator Training.' *Translation & Language Teaching: Language Teaching & Translation*, ed. Kristin Malmikjær (Manchester: St. Jerome Publishing, 1998), p. 92.
7. Jennifer Hill, *Using Literature in Language Teaching* (London: Macmillan Education, 1987), p. 10.
8. Matt Buchanan, 'Teaching through the Arts: Drama as a Teaching Tool,' 26 July 2011, http://teachingthroughthearts.blogspot.com/2011/07/drama-as-teaching-tool.html. Accessed 25 July 2013.
9. Jerome Bruner, *Making Stories: Law, Literature, Life* (Cambridge, MA: Harvard UP, 2002), p. 64.
10. *Making Stories*, p. 66.
11. *Ibid.*, p. 69.
12. The 2012–2013 season witnessed the conclusion of *Behzat Ç*, a cult police detective serial on a private Turkish television station – running since 2010 – about a hard-boiled police detective, which attracted praise and criticism in equal measures. Even if the students did not watch it on a regular basis, they were well aware of its presence in the mainstream schedules.
13. See 'Masculinity in Turkey', *Simge's Blog*, 26 November 2009, http://simgeguzelis.blogspot.com/2009/11/10masculinity-in-turkey.html.

Accessed 26 September 2013, which shows how popular television serials such as *Kurtlar Vadısı* (*Valley of the Wolves*) perpetuated this stereotype.

14. Jenny White, 'What Does Militant Masculinity and Intolerance Look Like?' *Kamil Pasha*, 12 July 2013, http://kamilpasha.com/?p=7286. Accessed 26 July 2013.

15. Kyle Meikle, 'Rematerializing Adaptation Theory', *Literature/Film Quarterly* 4 (3) 2013, p. 181.

16. For a fuller discussion of these changes, see R. Barton Palmer and William Robert Bray, *Hollywood's Tennessee: The Williams Films and Postwar America* (Austin: University of Texas Press, 2009), pp. 120–128.

17. Guy Claxton, *What's the Point of School?* (Bristol: Oneworld Publications, 2008), pp. 127–131.

18. This is a contentious point. In most of their English-medium classes, students are required to speak in the foreign language only. I offer the freedom to speak whatever language the students wish in an attempt to emphasize the importance of developing abilities and self-confidence.

19. 'Better English skills would make Turkey's workforce more adaptable to economic reform as well as their immediate neighbourhood. Innovation and the production of high technology, by their nature, require interaction with the world.' Selim Koru and Jesper Åkesson, 'Turkey's English Deficit', *TEPAV* (*Economic Policy Research Foundation of Turkey*), Policy Note (December 2011). http://www.tepav.org.tr/upload/files/1324458212-1. Turkey_s_English_Deficit.pdf. Accessed 17 November 2013.

20. See Zuchen Zhang and Richard F. Kenny, 'Learning in an Online Distance Education Course: Experiences of Three International Students', *International Review of Research in Open and Distance Learning* 1 (1) 2010, http://www.irrodl.org/index.php/irrodl/article/view/775/1481. Accessed 27 July 2013.

21. A video of the activity can be seen at http://www.academia.edu/3290825/ Adapting_Edgar_Allan_Poe_The_Fall_of_the_Tell-Tale_Heart_2013. Accessed 26 September 2013.

22. Rónán McDonald, 'The Value of Art and the Art of Evaluation,' in *The Public Value of the Humanities*, ed. Jonathan Bate (London and New York: Bloomsbury Academic, 2013), pp. 289–290.

23. I recently wrote a blog post on the ways in which fear can inhibit student performance in the ELT classroom 'LEARning to Cope with Exams,' *All Things Learning*, 24 July 2013, http://allthingslearning.wordpress. com/2013/07/24/learning-to-cope-with-exams-guest-post-from-laurence-raw/. Accessed 29 July 2013.

24. Georgine Loacker and Glen Rogers, *Assessment at Alverno College: Student, Program, Institutional* (Milwaukee: Alverno College Institute, 2005), pp. 4–7.

25. In the Turkish language, there are no definite or indefinite articles.

26. Georgine Loacker, 'Introduction' in *Self Assessment at Alverno College*, ed. Georgine Loacker, p. 12.

27. See Imogen Casebourne, 'What Type of Student Are You?' *EpicLearning Group.com*, 9 November 2012, http://epiclearninggroup.com/uk/what-type-of-student-are-you/. Accessed 30 July 2013.
28. Martin Eve, 'Open Access and the Humanities: Reimagining our Future', *The Guardian Higher Education Network*, 25 March 2013, http://www.theguardian.com/higher-education-network/blog/2013/mar/25/open-access-humanities-future. Accessed 30 July 2013.

4
Avoiding 'Compare and Contrast': Applied Theory as a Way to Circumvent the 'Fidelity Issue'

Ariane Hudelet

Studying adaptation in France has become quite common. High school teachers use it regularly in class, and most educators acknowledge that in the early twenty-first century, literature and culture in general need to be approached through various platforms and media if we want to communicate them to new generations of students who are constantly connected to each other and to the world through screens and virtual reality. This evolution, in universities as in secondary education, is illustrated by the inclusion of adaptation within the recruiting system for future teachers. Students who want to become teachers in France need to take a *concours* (a competitive exam which selects applicants for a restricted number of positions every year), and write several papers on set works and topics that change each year. Ever since 1998, the syllabus for the *concours* to become an English teacher has followed the example previously set by the Spanish and Latin exams, so as to include – in addition to the traditional plays, novels, and historical periods – a literary work *and* its film adaptation. Since future teachers are supposedly trained in adaptation studies when preparing their exam, they should in turn be more able to teach diverse forms of adaptation to students and teach literature through media convergence. However, the system is still flawed. First, the film that is chosen each year sometimes seems to be picked randomly, as if the committee selecting the works first chose a famous work of literature and then considered whether one of its adaptations might not be added to it. As a consequence, the works that have been selected over the years sometimes seem doomed to confirm the 'book is better' prejudice, as when Franco Zeffirelli's very bland film *Jane Eyre* was picked to 'accompany' Charlotte Brontë's novel. Although other choices have been more ambitious (such as Altman's *Short Cuts* together with Carver's collection of short stories, or Nabokov's and Kubrick's *Lolita*s), the choice of one book/one film also limits the range of approaches and seems to encourage the traditional 'compare and contrast' technique that often leads to a descriptive tendency and a return to traditional hierarchies between the source text and the adaptation copy. Finally, education in the field of film analysis is not yet sufficiently widespread in France to enable all university professors to carry out in-depth analyses of both text and film, with their own specific analytical tools, and some instructors simply lack the proper methodology to tackle the analysis of film and adaptation.

Beyond the mere contents of these syllabi, what matters when teaching adaptation to all kinds of student audiences is to provide strong analytical tools, without forgetting the importance of enriching the culture of the students and helping them situate their own, often fragmented, experience with literature within a historical context, and in a theoretical perspective. Teachers in France, as in other countries, I suppose, are constantly trying to keep up with the evolution of society, of techniques, and of the modes of cultural production and reception. They try to teach classes with substantial, demanding content (notably in terms of history and culture) through innovative ways in order to keep their audience interested – in spite of what Jasper Fforde ironically called the 'short Now' in his recent novel *First Among Sequels*, when referring to the shortening of the average attention span.[1] My colleagues who teach literature complain every year that the students do not read the assigned books, and link this to the increasing rapidity of exchanges and communications, and to the students' habit of doing several things at the same time (texting and checking their Facebook account, while only sporadically listening to their teacher). I will suggest that adaptation classes, if approached in a sufficiently open and complex manner, can help bridge the gap between the more classical culture of many teachers and the younger generation, for whom new technology has radically altered the relationship with knowledge, communication, and culture.

It is in this spirit that I have taught an adaptation class in the English department of my institution, Paris Diderot University. It is an MA class addressed to students who have been studying English language and culture academically for four years.[2] Some of these students want to become teachers in secondary schools, a few will continue with a PhD in English studies, and many of them will try to fight through a difficult job market to get a job more or less in line with their abilities, and, it is hoped, related to culture. The purpose of this class is to provide them with an understanding of the issues of adaptation in the English-speaking world and to train them in the practice of film analysis, with which they are often less familiar than literary analysis. The aim is also to help them navigate between the close analysis of text and film, and the more comprehensive approach to works within their contexts and within a broad inter-textual framework.

For the weekly two-hour sessions we have over one semester, I divide the course into two main parts. On the one hand, we work on two successive case studies. Austen's *Pride and Prejudice* and its many film adaptations[3] allow us to focus on the variety of different approaches and on the contextualization of each adaptation, while Coppola's *Apocalypse Now* and Conrad's *Heart of Darkness* lead us to focus on the political and metaphysical implications of both works, and on the inscription of Conrad within a multiplicity of intertexts that nourish Coppola's film. The idea is also to alternate macro and micro analyses: from transversal reflections on the whole works (around such notions as feminism when adapting Austen, or myth when dealing with *Apocalypse Now* and *Heart of Darkness*), to close analyses of specific text passages or film clips that allow them to deconstruct verbal or film language in order to understand how certain effects are produced.

On the other hand, in addition to this more traditional focus on case studies, students are also required to read a critical text that provides a synoptic view of the issues of adaptation – in this case, Robert Stam's introduction to Stam and Raengo's *A Companion to Film Adaptation*[4] – and apply what they have been reading to one example of their choice. This is what I will focus on now, because this assignment allows greater interaction among the students, and it helps the students to appropriate critical tools and to apply them to their own relationship with culture. Every class thus begins with a discussion of Stam's ideas, initiated by the oral presentations of two students. Each student shows a film clip (less than three minutes long) to the class and analyzes it in the light of the passage from Stam's introduction, which they have been assigned that day. After a brief presentation of the works they have chosen, they have to present a close analysis of the clip, clarifying and implementing the tools and notions raised in the critical text. Since Stam refers to many different theories or concepts, they have also had to check their Bakhtin, Genette, or Kristeva, and look up whatever they were not familiar with. It thus encourages them to appropriate critical tools and to apply them to something they were familiar with (the clip they picked), before applying them to material that they may be less comfortable with (Austen/Conrad adaptations). It also allows them to teach *me* about works that I do not always know, and I have found this very enriching as a teacher, as their tastes turned out to be quite eclectic.[5]

The appropriate selection of a clip itself implies that the notions evoked by Stam must have been clearly understood by the students. Since they can pick examples that they like or are familiar with, they are also more willing to do extensive research. By having to confront this familiar material with a type of text that they have not often been exposed to (critical theory), they are defamiliarized, and it often leads them to go beyond the descriptive level. Most of them become conscious of the constellation of intertextual relationships in which works of art are inscribed (many of the works chosen were adaptations of adaptations, such as *The Hours* or *A Thousand Acres*), and thus understand that the work of art is, to use Bakhtin's expression, 'a hybrid construction'.[6]

This type of assignment also makes the class livelier: students are forbidden to read from notes and must speak for a maximum of 10 minutes. The grades they obtained this past year reflected this greater involvement with the material – they were on average better than those they obtained during the two previous years, in which different types of assignments had been chosen. I would like now to focus on a few points that proved particularly fruitful in some of the presentations, which can also provide ideas for potential case studies in the classroom. I will quote from several papers (students were expected to hand in a written paper that developed their ideas more extensively after having made their presentation in class), sum up or paraphrase others, and sometimes add some material that we developed in the discussions that followed these presentations.[7]

From adaptation studies to studies of intertextuality

In his introduction, Stam first presents the long history of prejudice against adaptation, both on the part of literature specialists and on the part of film specialists. As most recent books on adaptations studies also do, he dismisses the criterion of 'fidelity', demonstrating its inadequacy and inefficiency as an analytical concept. This was one of the hardest things for the students, because the fidelity issue still tended to direct their spontaneous reactions when they discuss a film adapted from a work with which they are familiar.

Stam then shows how many concepts that were originally developed for the study of literature are still operative when applied to film adaptation. Genette's concepts of transtextuality and inter-textuality, for instance, help us distinguish the diverse types of dialogue that one text (or film) can entertain with another. As one of the students aptly wrote, such categories help us go beyond the one-to-one pairing underlying the fidelity approach:

> Intertextuality widens the kind of relationships that can unite two types of works of art, by overlooking the questions of fidel-ity, of original and copies, and by integrating the different forms of exchanges and dialogues between them [...] This perspective enables us to consider a whole range of relationships between two works of art, from the simple allusion, the quote or the reference, to the process of re-writing, but also of deconstruction, critique and re-creation of it.

One student chose to clarify Genette's analytical concepts by apply-ing them to Steven Daldry's adaptation of Michael Cunningham's novel *The Hours*, and to the relationship of both works with Virginia Woolf's *Mrs Dalloway*. Instead of merely mapping out the lineage between the three works, the use of Genette's notions allowed her to see how the three interconnected diegetic universes in *The Hours* (Virginia Woolf writing *Mrs Dalloway*, the reading of the book by a woman in the 1950s, and the story adapted and taking place at the beginning of the twenty-first century) manage to communicate both with each other and with the extradiegetic sources of inspiration. For her, the fact that the title of Cunningham's book and Daldry's film should have been another title picked by Virginia Woolf, before she decided to call the novel *Mrs Dalloway*, can be linked to the notion of 'architextuality' (generic taxonomies suggested or refused by the title or subtitle of a text): without directly pointing to the literary origin of the story (it is not entitled *Mrs Dalloway Returns* for instance), the title evokes (to the informed reader/viewer) the process of creation and revision that leads to a work of art, and implies that this should be seen as an ongoing process, one that is never completely finished. What we consider the final product (*Mrs Dalloway*, after a first draft called *The Hours*) has then become the starting point of another (*The Hours*, the novel, and then the film). The reference to the passing of time is then closely associated with the process of artistic creation and recreation, presented here as a sort of cycle.

In a second instance, she drew a parallel between the way *The Hours* gave us access to the creation of the novel and the notion of 'paratextuality' ('all the accessory messages and commentaries which come to surround the text and which at times become virtually indistinguishable from it').[8] Although *The Hours* is fiction, it is based on historical and literary research, and we do follow a character named Virginia Woolf, based on the real author, and thus learn about the context in which her work originated, as we would in a preface or academic article. 'Intertexuality' ('the effective co-presence of two texts in the form of quotations, plagiarism, and allusion')[9] is probably the most obvious feature, with the various references to the novel – notably through the repetition of many visual motives and quotations from *Mrs Dalloway* (such as the opening sentence of the novel, 'Clarissa said she would buy the flowers herself', or the water metaphor). Finally, the notion of 'metatextuality' ('the critical relationship between one text and another')[10] could be seen in the self-referential nature of a film and a text that are about the production and reception of a text and which integrate this feature into their very structure. The preference for editing and visual metaphors could also be seen as metatextual, or as an indirect criticism of a more 'straightforward' adaptation such as Ian Softley's 1997 *Mrs Dalloway*, which, more classically, used voiceover narration as an equivalent to Woolf's stream of consciousness technique. Another student, who also worked on Daldry's film, explained that, since Daldry chooses not to use voiceover to translate inner-speech, the film has to use other 'tracks' available to the film medium, notably action, behavior, colour patterns, or music. Focusing on the opening sequence of the film, he analyzed the *mise en scène* and editing and showed how a sense of imprisonment is expressed through repetitive close-ups of the three women, and by the fact that they are all shot lying in their bed while their partners are shot outside of the house. The student then went on to stress the importance of Philip Glass's music to connect the different pieces of the fragmented plot. The repetitive themes of the score and its melancholy tone indeed contribute to link these three women in spite of their different time periods, and to evoke the 'agony and the emotional barriers in their lives'.

This 'metatextual' or 'metafilmic' dimension was also understood by students as instances when the film adaptation provides a direct or indirect commentary on its own status as film, as opposed to the source that is adapted. One student thus analyzed the opening credit sequence of Zack Snyder's *Watchmen*, adapted from Alan Moore and Dave Gibbons's graphic novel. She argued that the sequence provides a reflection on the contrast between moving image and still images, and on the link between images and surveillance. She explains that the sequence is punctuated by photographs being taken, the viewer thus momentarily identifying with the anonymous photographer, while the filmic image imitates landmark images from American or world history. Retracing the gradual sidelining of vigilantes after the end of World War II, the sequence presents a montage inscribing the fictional characters into identifiable scenes that are part of collective memory thanks to painting (the retirement party of the Silk Spectre is thus presented in a parody of Da Vinci's 'Last Supper', with the pregnant woman instead of Jesus Christ), to photography (Alfred Eisenstaedt's famous 1945 photograph entitled 'The Tumultuous Celebration of V-J Day in Times Square' is re-enacted with a twist, since the kisser is now a beautiful woman and not a sailor), or archive footage (the Zapruder film of Kennedy's assassination is thus recycled, in an upgraded high-definition version, and extended to reveal the shooter at the end of the panning camera movement). As my student noticed, the treatment of filmic time points both to the comic book source (with fades to black between each scene evoking the space separating each panel, a deceleration of filmic time reaching quasi immobility to evoke graphic images) and to the filmic expansion (camera movements, zoom effects, variations of focus, and complex manipulations of filmic time). The sequence thus expands the complex reflection on time contained in Alan Moore's title, and in the symbolism of the comic book (the 'watch' motif, notably). When the sequence ends on the inscription 'Who watches the watchmen?' the indirect address to the audience who watch *Watchmen* is blatant and culminates in an explosion which concludes the sequence. The metafilmic dimension of the sequence thus addresses the viewer's memory and stresses the extent to which our memories today are informed and shaped by images – 'real' images such as photographs, paintings, and archive footage, but also fictional images such as graphic novels that have reached a cult status among aficionados, as *Watchmen* has. In the discussion that followed, we pointed out the different contexts in which the two works emerged. *Watchmen* was initially published in 1987 (during the Cold War), when issues of information and government control were crucial, whereas the film was released in 2009, when the manipulation of information through the expanded technologies of digital images had become commonplace and raised new concerns, both political and ideological.[11]

Not all students considered these categories useful; some criticized them, bringing up examples in which the different notions intersected or could hardly be differentiated. However, discussions showed that the use of notions defined by Genette and other theoreticians, such as Kristeva, Bakhtin, or Derrida, from post-structuralism to deconstructivism,[12] help shift our vision of adaptation away from linear hierarchies and towards a transtextual system in which notions of source and copy are interchangeable and reversible, so that adaptation can become a form of criticism. A good understanding of theoretical tools thus allows students to distinguish subtleties in the myriad of intertextual relationships between texts and films, and between cultural products in general. The distinction between parody, pastiche, and stylization, for instance, might not be easy to grasp for students at first, but by applying Bakhtin's concepts to adaptation, they seem to become much clearer. For instance, a scene from Brian De Palma's 1974 *The Phantom of the Paradise* provided very rich material for one of the presentations. In that film, which can be considered an adaptation of Gaston Leroux's 1909 novel *The Phantom of the Opera*, we see the 'phantom' of the film (a former composer whose music has been stolen by a producer against whom he seeks revenge) about to attack a singer chosen by the producer to interpret the composer's music against the will of the phantom.

Beef, the singer, is taking a shower and singing one of the Phantom's songs, in a situation that contributes to posit the scene as a parody of the famous shower scene in *Psycho*. The student analyzed how, beyond the single reference to Leroux's novel, the Hitchcock hypotext was also clearly recognizable through specific elements from the scene (the same white tiles on the walls, the same transparent shower curtain), in what is a parody more than a pastiche or stylization. She used Bakhtin's description of parody ('as in stylization, the author employs the speech of another, but, in contradiction to stylization, he introduces into that speech an intention which is directly opposed to the original one') to guide her study of the 'opposed intentions' of De Palma's scene with regard to *Psycho*. First, instead of the sober black and white look of Marion Crane's motel room, here the walls of Beef's room are a gaudy pink. Then, the look of the character (wearing a mobcap, taking drugs) also contributes to the change of genre, from thriller to comedy. Finally, the music starts from the beginning of the scene, and not, as in *Psycho,* at the moment when Marion is attacked in order to create surprise and fear. All these elements 'let the audience guess that nothing dramatic will happen', as my students concluded, and create a reversal since this time the viewer is supposed to be on the side of the attacker. She concludes on the Bakhtinian 'doubled-voice' discourse in De Palma's film, since 'the parody consists in the superposition of two visions shown in the hypertext', and very subtly remarked that this example fits the Bakhtinian notion of the author 'as the orchestrator of the pre-existing discourses':

> [H]ere the word 'orchestrator' is particularly well-adapted since it combines several references to different stories in the same movie, in order to create a comic process. The shower scene is not really critical of the original scene in *Psycho* but re-uses it as a symbol of the common culture to reverse the original meaning and thus to make the audience laugh.

Adaptation in context: reflections on the digital age

We saw in the previous examples how the necessity to apply theoretical notions to micro-analyses of a specific scene helped the students appropriate them as effective tools. By drawing their attention to the importance of the context of production of the different works, Stam's synoptic introduction also helped them historicize their experience of adaptation and connect issues that they would not have managed to combine without this theoretical background.

One part of Stam's introduction that sparked the most discussion was what he calls 'Adaptation in a Post-celluloid World',[13] which explains how film production and consumption, as well as adaptation theory, will be irrevocably changed by the digital revolution. Once the term 'celluloid' was explained to students (whose technical knowledge about film turned out to be minimal), the passage led to some enlightening studies of adaptations that rely heavily on recent technology, such as *Harry Potter and the Deathly Hallows* or the British miniseries *Sherlock*. One student chose to consider Spielberg's *Minority Report*, adapted from a novel by Philip K. Dick. She focused on the scene in which the main character, Anderton, a 'pre-crime' agent supposed to detect upcoming crimes and prevent them from happening, watches a projection of the next prediction, and realizes at the end that he is the perpetrator of the crime. The effectiveness of the scene is based on the equivalence between the abundance of high-quality CGI and the high technology devices used in the diegesis. In this scene, which seems to have become a blueprint for many others in science fiction and beyond,[14] the transparency of the devices seems to confirm the impossibility of any crime being committed, since society has developed an omniscient system to prevent it. As the screens are transparent, images can be seen from any angle, and the film gives the powerful impression that 'nothing can be hidden; everything is known to guarantee safety and protection'. Many shots thus use this transparency to allow the juxtaposition of two images within one: the image on the screen, and Anderton behind/through it, for instance. It is used at first to indicate Anderton's confidence, his apparent control of the events to come – as exemplified by one low-angle shot at the beginning of the sequence, depicting him through the screen, with his arms slightly raised like a conductor. The screens are also presented as interactive, since Anderton shifts from one image to the next and blows up a detail by direct manipulation of the screen. Eventually, the interplay between digital mediation and 'reality' is used in a reverse logic when Anderton's desperate expression at what he has discovered is enhanced by the final closeup on his face in the digital projection, superimposed on his real face thanks to the transparency effect. As the student concluded, Philip K. Dick's novel never mentions such an abundance of devices and technology, and the cinematic scene relies of course on the spectacular appeal of such technological display, but this adaptation also reflects on the notion of the inter-activity between media and people, and the immersive dimension of the moving-image experience that characterizes the visual evolution of the turn of the twenty-first century – it thus materializes the very different horizon of reception in which a text such as *Minority Report* is read, imagined, or represented by new generations.

The link between technology and adaptation also seemed to liberate the imagination of the students. One of them studied the use of a 'performance capture suit' in *Rise of the Planet of the Apes*, where the main character, Caesar, is played by actor Andy Serkis, who takes the form of a chimp, not by putting on makeup and a suit, but with a performance capture suit – a technology of markers and sensors that picks up facial expressions and movements, which are then stored by a computer, before using the data to turn the actor into a photorealis-tic ape.[15] After reflecting on the nature of such a filmic character, the student wondered whether this technique could not confirm some of Stam's speculations in 'Adaptation in a Post-Celluloid World', such as the possibility of bringing to life what no longer exists, resurrecting a deceased actor for instance, by having an actor perform 'under the features of a dead actor'. This was already partly done, as my student noted, in 1994, when a virtual actor, using CGI, replaced the face of leading actor Brandon Lee, who died during the shooting of *The Crow*. The modern technology of the performance capture suit, and its likely future improvements, could also lead us to imagine other applications, as my students went on to explain. It could for instance be imported outside the world of film production, with devices that could enable 'anybody to put on a suit and become somebody else in a TV series, or in a movie, in a video game fashion'. Returning to theory, she concluded:

> [T]he performance capture suit brings forward the revolution of the Hypertext and the writerly text of Barthes, where the specta-tor is no longer passive in a state of consumerism but becomes a producer of action, giving life or a new life to a narrative.[16] In the case of adaptation, spectators could become the main agent

of the adaptation that would be shaped by their choice and their knowledge and reception of a story.

We then debated the limits of such imaginary projections, and the place of scripts and screenwriters in adaptation: would 'the spectators/gamers' putting on a suit be actually adapting the story, or would they merely select a path within a limited set of adaptive options?

The student also raised the issue of copyright: do copyright laws protect the 'recycling' of a virtual actor? What degree of control does the actor have over his digital clone? This indeed raises difficult legal issues about copyright and ownership, and brings us back to another question, that of the author, be it single or collective, dead or alive – an issue which has been haunting adaptation studies for a long time as well.

These few examples taken from students' papers have contributed, I hope, to show the quality of the analyses made possible by the confrontation between a critical text and the students' choice of examples. As academics we all have various attitudes towards theory. Some of us relish its abstraction, whereas others remain suspicious of its pseudo-universality and the sometimes abstruse technicality of its vocabulary.[17] I hope this case study has shown how an adaptation class is a perfect place to help students understand the usefulness of theory, which is notably designed to help us take some distance from reality or representations, in order to return to them with new perspectives and interrogations. I also hope adaptation will find its way to the centre of the pedagogy of texts, following Thomas Leitch's lead when he asks for a new field 'that might well be called Textual Studies – a discipline incorporating adaptation study, cinema studies in general, and literary studies'.[18] Such a discipline, whatever we decide to call it, allows the students to develop a great variety of skills, as was demonstrated in the assignment used for this case study. Students need to combine close readings of texts and moving images, and research the contexts of each work and the critical theories that are mentioned by Stam. The format also forces them to select the most meaningful elements for study, and to convey them in a pedagogical and concise manner to their peers. Most of the time, this combination of skills led them to understand the limitations linked to the simple 'compare and contrast' exercise envisaged in the *concours*. I am confident that the new generation of students, so deeply immersed in an interconnected technological world, will also produce teachers who will promote this new discipline of 'Textual Studies', and will prove more creative than the tests that are now used to recruit them.

Acknowledgements

Many thanks to Anaïs Benoist, Aline Barbier-Pellet, Francesca Camporese, Maxime Montagne, Tiffany Nortier, and Nastasia Rivière, whose papers I quoted in this article, and to all other students from the class 'Studying Films, Studying Texts: Issues of Adaptation', Fall Semester 2012, Université Paris Diderot, for their active and stimulating participation. Direct quotations from the papers are within quotation marks. The rest is my reformulation of ideas expressed during in-class discussion.

Annex

List of works selected by students.

And Then There Were None/Identity (Agatha Christie, 1939/James Mangold, 2003).

Animal Farm (George Orwell, 1945/John Halas and Joy Batchelor, 1954).

La Dame aux Camélias/La Traviata (Alexandre Dumas fils, 1848/Willy Decker & Brian Large, 2005).

Dangerous Liaisons (Choderlos de Laclos, 1782/Stephen Frears, 1988).

Do Androids Dream of Electric Sheep/Blade Runner (Philip K. Dick, 1968/Ridley Scott, 1982).

Dracula/Horror of Dracula (Bram Stoker, 1897/Terence Fisher, 1958).

Great Expectations (Charles Dickens, 1861/Julian Jarrold, 1999).

Harry Potter and the Deathly Hallows (J.K. Rowling, 2007/David Yates, 2010–2011).

The Hours (Michael Cunningham, 1998/Stephen Daldry, 2002) (for four students).

The Lady from Shanghai/Manhattan Murder Mystery (Orson Welles, 1947/Woody Allen, 1993).

The Legend of Sleepy Hollow (Washington Irving, 1820/Tim Burton, 1999).

Little Red Riding Hood/Little Rural Riding Hood (fairy tale/Tex Avery cartoons, 1949).

Memento Mori/Memento (Jonathan Nolan, 2001/Christopher Nolan, 2000).

The Minority Report/Minority Report (Philip K. Dick, 1956/Steven Spielberg, 2002).

The Phantom of the Opera/The Phantom of the Paradise (Gaston Leroux, 1910/Brian de Palma, 1974).

The Pilgrim's Progress/Scott Pilgrim (Bunyan, 1678/Bryan Lee O'Malley, 2004–2010/Edgar Wright, 2010).

The Planet of the Apes/Rise of the Planet of the Apes (Pierre Boulle, 1963/Ruppert Wyatt, 2011).
Pylon/The Tarnished Angels (William Faulkner, 1935/Douglas Sirk, 1957).
The Red and the Black/Scarlet and Black (Stendhal, 1830/Ben Bolt, 1993).
Romeo and Juliet/Romeo + Juliet (William Shakespeare, 1595/Baz Luhrmann, 1996).
A Song of Ice and Fire/Game of Thrones (George R.R. Martin, 1991–2011/ Stephen Benioff & D.B. Weiss, 2011–present).
Speak (Laurie Halse Anderson, 1999/Jessica Sharzer, 2004).
Stardust (Neil Gaiman, 1999/Mathew Vaughan, 2007).
A Study in Scarlet/Sherlock, 'A Study in Pink' (Sir Arthur Conan Doyle, 1887/ Steven Moffat & Mark Gatiss, 2010).
The Third Man/The Good German (Carol Reed, 1949/Steven Soderbergh, 2006).
A Thousand Acres (Jane Smiley, 1991/Jocelyn Moorhouse, 1997).
To Kill a Mockingbird (Harper Lee, 1960/Robert Mulligan, 1962).
The Virgin Suicides (Jeffrey Eugenides, 1993/Sophia Coppola, 1999).
Watchmen (Alan Moore & Dave Gibbons, 1986–1987/Zack Snyder, 2009).
Water for Elephants (Sarah Gruen, 2006/Francis Lawrence, 2011).
Who's Afraid of Virginia Woolf? (Edward Albee, 1962/Mike Nichols, 1966).

Notes

1. Fforde's explanation about why the 'short Now' came to be is a little complex (a dangerous manipulation by the 'chrono guard' who regulate time-travelling). Its consequences, in the novel, are the expansion of reality TV and the decreasing taste for books: 'Short attention spans, a general malaise, no tolerance, no respect, no rules. Short-termism. No wonder we were seeing Outlander read-rates go into free-fall. The short now would hate books; too much thought required for not enough gratification.' J. Fforde, *First Among Sequels* (London: Hodder and Stoughton, 2007), p. 287.
2. One should take into account the fact that most of them have previously had seven years of English classes in junior high school and high school.
3. Robert Leonard's 1940 adaptation for MGM, the 1995 BBC miniseries, Gurinder Chadha's 2004 *Bride and Prejudice*, Joe Wright's 2005 *Pride & Prejudice*, and brief extracts from *Lost in Austen* (2008). I will try to include *The Lizzie Bennet Diaries* webseries in the future.
4. R. Stam, 'Introduction. The Theory and Practice of Adaptation', in R. Stam and A. Raengo, eds, *A Companion to Literature and Film* (Oxford: Blackwell, 2004), pp. 1–52. I could have as easily chosen other seminal introductions by Deborah Cartmell and Imelda Whelehan, James Naremore, or Thomas Leitch for instance – Stam's text was chosen because of its convenient division into brief subparts and because it offered a very broad synthesis of the issues raised by adaptation studies.
5. See the annex containing the list of works selected by students in the fall semester of 2012.

6. M.M. Bakhtin, *The Dialogic Imagination: Four Essays*, ed. Michael Holquist (Austin: University of Texas Press, 1981).
7. I have also corrected the English mistakes whenever necessary.
8. R. Stam, 'Introduction', p. 28.
9. Ibid., p. 27.
10. Ibid., p. 28.
11. I recommended that the student read books related to this visual turn and visual studies, such as W.J.T. Mitchell, *What Do Images Want* (Chicago: University of Chicago Press, 2005).
12. R. Stam calls it 'The Influence of the Posts'. R. Stam, 'Introduction', pp. 8–9.
13. R. Stam, 'Introduction', p. 11–14.
14. Many scenes in science fiction today use a similar aesthetic based on a rather low-lit space, dominated by grey and blue tints and transparent screens – in class we evoked the recent *Star Trek* films directed by J.J. Abrams, or some television series such as *24*, or even scenes from the British miniseries *Sherlock* (in S02 E02, when Sherlock goes to his 'mind palace', the air seems to become a transparent, interactive screen.)
15. Serkis is familiar with the technique since he also played Gollum and King Kong.
16. See R. Stam, 'Introduction', p. 13.
17. For detailed reflections on the status of theory within adaptation studies, see T. Leitch, 'Twelve Fallacies in Contemporary Adaptation Theory', *Criticism*, 45(2), 2003; and B. Westbrook, 'Being Adaptation: The Resistance to Theory', in C. Albrecht-Crane and D. Cutchins, eds, *Adaptation Studies. New Approaches* (Madinson: Fairleigh Dickinson University Press, 2010), pp. 25–45.
18. T. Leitch, 'Twelve Fallacies', p. 168.

5
Learning to Share: Adaptation Studies and Open Educational Resources

Imelda Whelehan and David Sadler

This chapter does not discuss a particular approach to teaching adaptation studies. It is about finding more ways to share information about what we do in the classroom, getting feedback on our own teaching innovations and practices, and adding to our own resources though properly cited access to other people's ideas and practices. It is a utopian ambition in many ways, an idea beset with so many problems that reflects the realities of most academics' daily lives. In an area such as adaptation studies, opportunities for sharing within institutions may be minimal, with modules/units sometimes scattered across a number of disciplines, produced by individuals who may be isolated in their own departments or schools. Sharing resources is not about cutting corners or abdicating responsibility, autonomy, or curbing creativity; it may allow for faster innovation and change or diversity in the curriculum. In this way students profit from a cross-fertilization of ideas, and lecturers can browse materials produced by others as a way of refreshing as well as reflecting upon their own teaching. Different approaches to teaching may enable another person to pilot a new approach in their own department and perhaps gain professional recognition in the area of learning and teaching, a feature of academic life too often unrewarded.

During the course of this chapter, we explore the challenges and opportunities presented by sharing learning resources in adaptation studies by analyzing our own experiences of leading a funded project which enables a community of academics who might experience difficulties finding each other by traditional means. The project – entitled 'Bridging the Gap: Teaching adaptations across the disciplines and sharing content for curriculum renewal' – and led by Whelehan and Sadler – was funded by the Australian government's Office for Learning and Teaching (OLT) for one calendar year in 2012. The OLT, like the UK's Higher Education Academy (HEA) fosters good practice and innovation in learning and teaching by funding projects and rewarding individual excellence. The core aims of the project were to develop a 'community of practice' of adaptation scholars in Australia, based around the sharing of resources in this interdisciplinary field, facilitated by an open access repository designed to house and provide access to donated artefacts. A further output from the project was the development of a Toolkit (Good Practice Guide) which provides guidance on using and uploading resources to the repository, particularly in relation to guidance on copyright matters in an Australian context, which has application beyond this project and is available to share and reuse (with acknowledgement) in common with all other objects in the repository.[1]

The first challenge to the ambition of sharing teaching resources was presented by Australian intellectual property laws within academia, which attribute ownership of teaching materials to the institution rather than the individual; therefore all individuals seeking to upload their work to an open access repository require institutional permissions. In order to populate the repository at its pilot stage partners were sought in other institutions. Their primary role was, in their engagement in the broad area of adaptation studies, to provide samples of material used in the course of their own teaching. In addition to this, they formed the project team, attending quarterly meetings, reviewing papers related to the progress of the project, and discussing the opportunities Open Educational Resources (OERs) might present to their own professional experiences. The project team, led by the authors who are both based at the University of Tasmania, comprised colleagues from Monash University, the University of Queensland and the University of Western Australia.[2] In addition to the Core Team a reference group with specific expertise in areas such as OERs and copyright, and an expert in Creative Commons,[3] Professor Anne Fitzgerald of Queensland University of Technology, provided highly specialized advice on intellectual property law and the legal issues presented by the establishment of open access repositories.

OERs are still a relatively new concept in the academic domain, founded in 2001 with the Massachusetts Institute of Technology (MIT) release of 50 freely available courses through the OpenCourseWare initiative. The ambition and the creation of a space for storage of teaching materials provided an important case study in this domain, and the question of whether it is better to have a more generic open access repository for a much broader community remains a moot point. The two core aspects of the project – the Community of Practice and the repository – were useful in testing the customs and habits of university teachers in research-intensive universities in Australia, and the possible restrictions to sharing presented by the disinterested effects of the law.

The rest of the chapter reflects on the aims of the project and the issues we encountered along the way. It offers a working definition of the term 'community of practice' – a phrase more commonly used in education scholarship – and explains why we used this concept as a way of testing the potential of such a community to transcend traditional disciplinary boundaries and bridge both the epistemological and physical gaps created by ideological and physical spaces between disciplines.

Communities of practice

The project emerged from two intellectual bases: Whelehan's long-standing involvement in the sphere of adaptation studies as it has developed over the last two decades, and Sadler's engagement with the education theory concept of a 'Community of Practice', which is based on the premise that sharing our approaches to learning and teaching strengthens our own practice and yields high returns if the community in its shared purpose adds value far in excess of what we can give to our students though our individual efforts. This concept, developed by Etienne Wenger and Jean Lave, can apply to processes of learning and engagement in all kinds of organizations, but we focus on it as applied to a learning and teaching context as a means of exploring how much further learning can progress through sharing. This is a departure from a core belief, still embedded if not always articulated in this way, that learning is about an individual journey: 'to assess learning we use tests with which students struggle in one-on-one combat, where knowledge must be demonstrated out of context, and where collaborating is considered cheating ... and most of us come out of this treatment feeling that learning is boring and arduous, and that we are not really cut out for it'.[4] Theories of communities of practice assume a social model of learning, one that is about participation and engagement rather than models of learning which are either classically transmissive (tutor–student) or based solely on individual dynamics and capacities for learning. In this sense, Wenger and Lave offer a model where learning within a community allows for new *and* experienced participants to learn, and for the community to define what its main common interests are and what it is seeking to do or produce. Communities of practice are, in this broad sense, ubiquitous, but in a higher education context are often described as communities of learning.

The first characteristic of a community of practice is that of mutual engagement. As Wenger explains, this kind of community does not have to represent proximity, but rather shared aims that are better achieved through a collective identity. At their best such communities foster collaboration; at their worst they can entrench approaches that achieve meaning through custom rather than more legitimate claims. We use this concept as a point of departure, while embracing the positive notion of 'community' in colloquial terms. The 'community' in academia connotes not just the student body, but also the collegiality of the academic ideal. These ideals may power many an academic aspiration, but greater administrative and other burdens placed upon the contemporary lecturer make realization of such ideals a challenge. By offering the possibilities of a virtual community through a repository that can be visited at the individual's convenience we make use of the idea of collegiality, exploiting the potential of digital life for higher education – that one's nearest colleague in terms of shared interests and teaching philosophy might be thousands of miles away and yet could be a source of hands-on support.

In selecting adaptation studies as a field for a pilot community of practice, we anticipated disagreement about the common features of such an area of study. Identifying a group that has irregular recognition in subject communities, specialist journals, and postgraduate programmes across the globe is a perverse choice in many ways; but to the authors (partly because of their own backgrounds) it was an obvious one. This is a community that thrives on virtual connectedness, which has grown through adapting discipline-based theoretical principles to cut through to the space in between. The title of the project 'Bridging the Gap' was inspired by Timothy Corrigan's observation that '[b]etween disciplinarity and adaptation, between literature and film, adaptation studies provide, I am convinced, especially ambiguous, risky, unstable, and enormously interesting opportunities today. ... It is in that gap that many of the most compelling ideas appear'.[5]

Ironically, the authors represent two communities often placed in conflict in the quotidian business of the modern university. Sadler, as an expert in Learning and Teaching, a UK National Teaching Fellow, and former director of the UK Higher Education Academy, and now Deputy Vice-Chancellor (Students and Education), represents teaching at the 'chalk face' and regimes of surveillance and monitoring; Whelehan, a research professor and specialist in this field, represents what is often portrayed as the other side of university life, the bit that scholars are always planning and earmarking time for as they sweat their way through another semester, the bit that can only be guaranteed through scarce external funding resources; and which can be denied by hostile peer review or impenetrable grading matrices which only reward the very few. What we knew before we wrote the project application, and we still know now, is that the perception of conflict between research and teaching is greater than the reality, and yet the increasing pressure to share publicly funded research makes it easier (if not always simpler) than it is to share teaching experiences.

Defining and managing the project

The Australia HE system, with some 40 universities in total, serving a domestic population of about 814,000 students in a population of around 23 million is a relatively small sector; but it is also one where huge distances divide many universities, and in which a number have a range of distant campuses that require a substantial investment in technologies related to online delivery. For the authors, at the time of applying for the project only four months into jobs in a new country, these were facts that only came into focus during the course of the project. Additionally, disciplinary boundaries take on certain cultural distinctions that make keyword searches applicable to the UK or US context much less reliable. As two individuals who had been thoroughly inculcated with the UK system of peer review through roles as Quality Assurance Agency (QAA) subject reviewers, through internal and external peer review of teaching materials and assessments, including external examining, and through peer observation of teaching, practices of peer review were assumed to be less problematic than they actually proved to be. In the Australian context such practices were either more institutionally specific, linked to particular alliances of institutions or, subsequently, a developing part of the national infrastructure for teaching.

Even if we did not encounter overt cultural barriers in consulting with potential partners, we soon realized that we were not always asking the right questions. Ironically, the research environment, with its cycles of peer review and appropriate citation of relevant research outputs, operates in a fairly recognizable global fashion. By contrast, learning and teaching do not operate in such global conformity, and agreements – for example on intended learning outcomes and associated curriculum design – are often nationally or culturally specific. In the UK, the experience with subject benchmarks is long-standing, but the challenges of codifying new areas or disciplines is well understood. In Europe, the 'Tuning'[6] process has addressed and encountered similar issues, whilst in Australia, the establishment of a discipline scholars' network has led to the voluntary and subject-led agreements on broad threshold statements of learning outcomes, but has not yet drilled down to the specificity of QAA-style subject benchmarks. This offers more flexibility for course-writing teams, but also discourages the development of a self-aware community of scholars. In many ways both the national setting and the selection of area of study made a more exciting test case because, while there have been some high-profile scholars writing about adaptation (for instance Brian McFarlane and Simone Murray), there are no associations or annual conferences of direct relevance to this area of study. In Europe and the US the conferences in particular – not to mention regular panels on SCMS (Society for Cinema and Media Studies) and other large subject gatherings – act as spaces for the exchange of ideas and contestation of disciplinary boundaries that necessarily migrate into teaching practices. Anecdotally, at least, it is noticeable to those of us who have participated in the increasing number of adaptation conferences since the late 1990s that published scholarship in the field has increased and agreed-upon core themes and approaches have undergone rapid changes. It seems safe to assume that teaching has been affected by such readily available and diverse approaches to adaptation, as access to secondary sources of such range and quality makes the development of modules and units more practical and attractive in terms of the provision of authoritative sources for students. While the range of published research outputs has the same potential impact on the field in Australia, one explanation for the relative lag in wider communication may be to do with the absence of conferences. For this reason an end-of-project symposium (held in February 2013) was factored into project planning.

While an open access resource is not restricted to one country, the primary aims behind this project were to prompt national debate and produce workable recommendations to the OLT to continuously improve teaching initiatives in the sector. The interdisciplinary character of adaptation studies as it grows and as people realize shared interests across traditional disciplines has the potential to be a different kind of community which tracks new pathways through the Humanities, the Arts, and even beyond. It was felt that individuals who can traverse the disciplines to create new pathways of knowledge may also be the teaching innovators who address their students' needs from different perspectives. But keeping ahead of new perspectives in adaptation studies requires an efficient scholarly network. Approaches to adaptation emerge across different disciplines in different ways and with different terminologies. This is potentially confusing for lecturer and student alike without some further guide to assist in navigation.

As noted above, the project encountered its first difficulties in trying to match the authors' experience of adaptations in the UK setting and establish how the scholars working on adaptation might or might not operate as a 'community'; additionally the aim of piloting an Open Educational Resource in a domain where intellectual property issues were different and where the practice of sharing in the teaching domain was even less usual, created a larger set of challenges. Moreover, it is well documented that the role of the academic is changing and becoming both more encompassing and more diverse. As Shelda Debowski notes, 'we have seen a growing rise in explicit performance expectations and changing role requirements, partly stemming from a formalization of university management and corporate governance'.[7] Lecturers today experience more pressures on their time and see initiatives such as Virtual Learning Environments as an initial added burden whose benefits do not always outweigh the huge initial investment of time. Teachers in universities are under increasing scrutiny and there is a thin line between providing an opportunity supported by a useful resource and providing one more piece of paperwork to add to the pile.

The interdisciplinary community

Our intuition was that there is a lot to share in adaptation studies and a great deal of common ground that links quite disparate practices, but that such units or courses were configured differently in Australia. In addition to the legacy of the novel/film courses, more apparent in the past, but still enduring (see Cobb, Chapter 2), it is possible to surmise that these interventions in adaptation studies wherever they occur are producing new knowledge within the existing 'old' disciplines and it may be that their creators feel they have little or no relation to adaptation studies. This is a crucial issue in a relatively small sector; crucial too will be cases when adaptation features in people's research interests and may only be formulated into teaching units after some time lag. Given the external funding of this project, we wanted to develop something that primarily had resonance for Australian users, but could then migrate out to global users and browsers, and in both aims we were possibly far too optimistic about the kinds of interest we could garner in a matter of months.

In 1983 cultural anthropologist Clifford Geertz, reflecting on hybridity in the social sciences, observed that 'there has been an enormous amount of genre mixing in intellectual life in recent years'.[8] In a sense, adaptation studies has taken 'genre mixing' to a new level, particularly in the Humanities disciplines, so that it stands as both an exponent of such blurring of boundaries and as a commentator on how such boundaries are transgressed in cultural productions. This problem of classification has deepened and enriched intellectual knowledge and problematized what we mean when we think of academic disciplines, to the point that such communities once expressed in this way seem unequal to the task of speaking for their putative members. The field of adaptation studies stands to gain from this kind of self-identity as a community. It emerges as an aspect of the curriculum across a number of disciplines, partly depending on academic cultural variations, and a great deal on the specialisms of individual academics. Historically, it has been most prevalent in English and Film studies pathways, but more recently elements of adaptation studies are identified within theatre studies, performance studies, modern language, history, cultural and media studies, and music. In the past, certainly, and even to some extent today, academics with such interests may find they have more in common with scholars outside their discipline and institution than within. Not only has the range of disciplines to which adaptation studies is of interest grown, but what is studied under that banner is very different. Adaptation students are less likely to simply study the word versus the image in looking for what does and does not translate in a screen adaptation of a literary work. We have moved gradually from asking how film can support our study of literature, to exploring aesthetic hierarchies that place the narrative forms in different artistic categories, to exploring adaptions of texts which have little aesthetic value, but much commercial potential, to broader questions of intertextuality, pastiche, and appropriation, refocusing attention on adaptation as a process rather than aesthetically valuing either 'origin' or 'adaptation'. Meanwhile, leading voices in the field have become increasingly vocal in their frustration with adaptation studies' critical shortcomings and theoretical absences, leading Kamilla Elliott to conclude that 'adaptation studies have not only failed theories; theories have also failed them'.[9] In such an era of debate, it seems only right that what students are taught can keep apace.

Conclusion: a project without an ending

By the project's end we had developed an Open Educational Resource that was freely available and to which people could sign in and upload their own teaching materials. This was formally launched at the end-of-project symposium and at that time we encouraged discussion about the perceived reluctance in the teaching domain for sharing, peer review and remodelling. The recommendations to the OLT at the close of the report included an exhortation to further encourage the exploration of how best to support and facilitate emergent areas of study as well as to see the greater availability of OERs as beneficial to the continuous development of learning and teaching as one means by which the scholarly community can be encouraged to reflect on their work, particularly by the peer review of the work of others. The legal issues behind Australian university's ownership of intellectual property of teaching materials and copyright laws around quotation and fair use set up formidable barriers against sharing, although the Good Practice Guide included substantial advice on copyright and intellectual property. All universities involved in the project had already agreed to the sharing of materials for this purpose. The use of third-party copyrighted material in teaching presents significant problems when it comes to sharing teaching materials online. Texts quoted or images reproduced and shown to students illustrate our arguments well in the classroom and are essential to teaching; but reproducing the same experience in the repository without contravening copyright laws requires judicious editing and sometimes further contextualization. One of the ways OERS cannot deliver all they promise is in this domain, and in relation to lectures and seminar material. Course outlines, assignments, quizzes, and further activities generated entirely by the academic make for more easily transferrable items.

We attempted to exploit social media to promote the repository more widely and it was advertised using Facebook, Twitter, and a blog located in the webpage portal of the OER. The site name 'Adapt' was chosen as a shortened form of 'adaptation' because this shortening evokes the verb form, helpfully underscoring the act of sharing of OERs through reuse and remodelling. It is not always easy to define the advantage to academics for using OERs, but some of the positives we came up with include potential time savings with trying to devise a new unit/module under pressure by adapting existing resources, enhancing one's reputation in the field by sharing high-quality resources, and the possibility of learning and refining through peer review. In order to encourage engagement with the project, Whelehan posted a blog defining adaptation studies, an extract from which follows:

> Adaptation studies is now less about which is the better, the original or the adaptation, and more about engaging with the process and understanding the motivations for an adaptation – whether it be explanation, homage, revision, critique, pure exploitation or something else. Adaptation studies facilitates an understanding of social change, narrative form, cultural difference, commercial imperatives, power relationships and so much more. ... A thorny question one might now ask is "when is an adaptation not an adaptation?" Luckily no one agrees on the answer.[10]

This was intended to provoke debate and discussion to encourage fellow scholars to embrace an inclusive rather than exclusive definition of the field. Later Sadler blogged about his own acquaintance with OERs and learning, acknowledging that 'it is really important to understand the barriers to placing your own resources into open and uncontrolled space. Teaching materials are usually the secret garden of academic life which are shared between the lecturer and their students, not usually open for peer review'.[11] As a project team we discussed what resources might be uploaded by project members to kickstart the site and encountered some healthy differences of opinion, if not a certain amount of reluctance to share the treasures of diverse secret gardens. It later turned out that this was equally a scepticism about what might be of use to others. Some participants preferred to write documents that described their teaching at a 'meta-level', or only include documents that described a particular approach rather than offered a reading of a single text or collection of texts. We soon found out that we had no idea what each of us meant when we were talking about teaching materials and that we all had different ideas about what might be of use to others. Our external evaluator, Alison Dickens, who had had intensive involvement with the setting up of HumBox[12] was very much of the view that anything used in the classroom or for preparation might be of interest and utility to others, and this was the working philosophy embraced by the authors. But the perceived inertia we witnessed in the sector in Australia is in part due to lack of time and/or willingness to jump all the hurdles required to enter and upload materials on the site, in addition to fairly large-scale ignorance about other OER initiatives, something certainly not restricted to an Australian context.

We finished the project still believing that embedding OERs in the working practices of academics would enhance teaching in the HE sector and encourage further and wider collaborations and increased reflective practice. As has been noted in the case of adaptation studies, while it has gone from strength to strength as a research area (witnessed by the growth in journals) its status as a pedagogical approach which traverses a number of disciplines has yet to be fully explored. If we are to claim that university teachers of adaptation studies could usefully form a nascent community of practice we have also to accept that the community would be diverse, international, and disparate in terms of core knowledges. When we devised the project, it was with the aim of testing the viability of such a community in Australia, and of helping establish a sense of community by developing an institutional repository through which people can upload materials related to their teaching practices with the aim of encouraging peer review and support continuous improvement for those individuals who submit materials, but also for those who take the opportunity to learn from others' work by remodelling and adapting (with attribution) to suit their own purposes. The aim was to share resources that might have a multitude of applications in learning; the challenge was to foster sharing as a practice with mutual benefits for all participants. A further challenge arose in the nature of national intellectual property and copyright restrictions, and one part of the project's aim was to find a way through these.

The tools for teaching adaptation studies themselves form the biggest barrier to the repository. The screen (cinema/TV/computer) has become very much the hub of adaptation studies in the classroom, and access to DVDs, downloads, and view-again television technologies like iPlayer and iView make it easier to access a broad range of material. This presents quite thorny problems for a repository of Open Educational Resources where individuals who are willing to make their work available through Creative Commons may want to share materials with third-party content (such as film stills and other kinds of clips); additionally copyright guidelines around 'fair use' vary enormously across national legal frameworks. The project needed to ensure that potential contributors were informed about the copyright environment and therefore a toolkit was designed to sit alongside the repository and provide advice.

The technical aspects of uploading are going to be off-putting to someone who encounters the ADAPT website and is willing to browse the repository and upload their own work. This is true of any such portal (including the well-used Humanities UK hub, HumBox), and there is no simple way to overcome this. The key responsibility of the project team members was to undertake to upload items to the repository to test its usability and to encourage others to follow by example. The project's lead peer reviewer made comments on the look and usability of the site as well as reviewing the materials uploaded. The comments drew attention to some of the repository's shortcomings. At this stage it is worth pointing out that even though a year seemed ample time to prepare material for and make live a repository, we had also to deal with a new Learning Management System which was not at that time geared up to such usage. The amount of materials at the project's end was itemized as two audio files, two articles, two PowerPoint presentations, and 17 other word or pdf files of various pedagogic materials, and this number has not increased significantly.

The project was successful as a test case about the usefulness of such a resource for an area with common teaching interests. But without extensive take-up it is difficult to know how sustainable this is, and this remains a challenge for small to medium OERs. Further steps envisaged include encouraging wider participation by linking the web address through the public online profiles of the project leader. In an Australian context we recommended that the OLT encourage HE institutions to allow the sharing of learning and teaching by agreeing to waive their theoretical IP rights and thus remove one bureaucratic layer for individual academics.

Some of the initiatives in adaptation studies teaching, as attested to in this volume (see for example Elliott, Raw, and Sherry) may not be easily captured as an artefact for sharing as teaching practice – but also many, like some of our project members, will feel more comfortable submitting meta-level reflective reports about why they do what they do in class rather than what they actually did. Some have mixed feelings about uploading lecture recordings which faithfully record all the stumblings and mumblings that accompany lectures delivered without a verbatim script, but for others this might inspire on a number of levels – not least understanding that we all teach under pressure and in imperfect settings; but such recordings capture a moment of engagement.

An unintended consequence of the project was the forceful recognition of the need to adapt in other senses; it shows how the copyright regime is out of step with learning needs and actual usage. This is something that is being endlessly debated in the research domain, and shows how the technology available for teachers is sometimes hampered by the content we can safely provide through it. Adaptation studies is one area where the use of film and other media presents real copyright issues, and the risk that material uploaded as one's own, deleting any screen grabs or clips that might have worked to contextualize the information in the classroom, becomes meaningless to those who might find it potentially useful. More positively as the external evaluator noted on the basis of her interviews with the core team, one participant observed that 'using the repository is like having a discussion with one's colleagues but that it offers the opportunity to connect to a greater number of colleagues'.[13] Whether a repository that addresses a subject community in this way can work is still open to debate, given that it requires stamina on the part of contributors, dedication and time on the part of the repository coordinator, and resources from the host institution which may not yield direct returns. In this way it is easy to see why repositories set up for institutions to share and promote internal innovations might be more immediately successful.[14]

What came to the fore most prominently by the time we presented the project at the symposium was why the lag between age-old habits and practices in research, particularly in relation to peer review and knowledge sharing, is so out of kilter with the secrecy and individuality that characterize most people's experience of teaching. This is particularly true of traditions of peer review, which is of course the regular path to scholarly publication, not to mention post-publication reviews, which help introduce research to the academic community. We argue that, at the very least, a greater adoption of the professional practices essential to our research careers might benefit individual teachers and subject communities, and improve the quality of student experiences in the range of resources available to them and their lecturers alike.

Notes

1. The authors would like to acknowledge the significant contribution of Project Officer Felix Wilson in this respect, in addition to his crucial coordination role across the whole project.
2. The project report can be located at this address: http://www.olt.gov.au/ project-bridging-gap-teaching-adaptations-across-disciplines-and-sharing-content-curriculum-renewal- We would like to extend our gratitude to Dr Lisa Fletcher, Dr Chris Worth, Assoc. Professor Frances Bonner, Assoc. Professor Jason Jacobs and Dr Hila Shachar, for their unerring support for the project, for their professionalism and for the many contributions they made to its outcomes.
3. Creative Commons are internationally recognized licences that allow reuse of resources without referring back to the copyright holder. This is used by government agencies to enable public use without permission.
4. Etienne Wenger, *Communities of Practice: Learning, Meaning and Identity* (Cambridge: Cambridge University Press, 1998), p. 3.

5. Timothy Corrigan, 'Literature on Screen, A History: In the Gap', *The Cambridge Companion to Literature on Screen* (Cambridge: Cambridge University Press, 2007), p. 42.
6. http://www.unideusto.org/tuningeu/teaching-learning-a-assessment. html. Accessed 4 February 2014.
7. Shelda Debowski, *The New Academic: A Strategic Handbook* (Maidenhead: Open University Press, 2012), p. 5.
8. Clifford Geertz, *Local Knowledge: Further Essays in Interpretive Anthropology* (New York: Basic Books, 1983), p. 19.
9. Kamilla Elliott, 'Theorizing Adaptations/Adapting Theories', in *Adaptation Studies: New Challenges, New Directions*, eds. Jorgen Bruhn, Anne Gjelsvik and Erik Frisvold Hanssen (London: Bloomsbury, 2013), pp. 31–32.
10. https://blogs.utas.edu.au/adapt/2012/04/18/what-is-adaptation-studies/. Accessed 7 February 2014.
11. https://blogs.utas.edu.au/adapt/2012/05/01/a-few-thoughts/. Accessed 7 February 2010.
12. http://humbox.ac.uk/. Accessed 10 March 2014.
13. http://www.olt.gov.au/project-bridging-gap-teaching-adaptations-across-disciplines-and-sharing-content-curriculum-renewal-, p. 53. Accessed 10 April 2014.
14. See http://www.nottingham.ac.uk/xpert/ a highly developed e-Learning base funded by JISC which encourages wider sharing of learning objects at the institutional level, but available to all. Accessed 10 March 2014.

6
Doing Adaptation: The Adaptation as Critic

Kamilla Elliott

In a recent talk, Thomas Leitch identified a central contrast between adaptation studies and translation studies: translation scholars tend to *do* translation; adaptation scholars tend not to do adaptation.[1] While I would not go so far as to back the saying, 'Those who can't do teach', this chapter addresses the pedagogical, critical, and theoretical value of *doing* adaptation. Doing adaptation opens insights, interpretations, and concepts inaccessible to conventional modes of theorizing, criticism, and expository writing about adaptations. It also offers new ways to engage the *aesthetics* of adaptations.

Disciplining adaptations

In their introduction to *The Pedagogy of Adaptation*, Dennis Cutchins, Laurence Raw, and James M. Welsh affirm that pedagogy typically begins by providing students with 'a particular approach ... or a heuristic that they could apply equally well in any situation'.[2] Approaches derive from theories, but theorizing adaptation studies is no simple affair. Adaptation scholars and studies are scattered across many disciplines – biology, psychology, technology, literature, film, theatre, art, music, media, communications, game studies, textual studies, intermedial studies, history, sociology, law, economics, politics, cultural studies (including gender studies, postcolonial studies, and other identity politics groups), and more. Each discipline theorizes adaptations differently according to its prevailing research questions, theories, and methodologies, often contesting these internally as well as with other disciplines. Adaptation studies, then, if not quite a theoretical Tower of Babel, is at least a field in which theories multiply and proliferate.[3]

Adaptations, which often engage more than one medium, have been particularly resistant to theorization by single-discipline theories. In spite of scholarly attempts to discourage adaptations and keep media in their separate spheres,[4] adaptations remain resolutely intermedial affairs that cannot live by one discipline's theories and methodologies alone. As critics began to recognize this and adaptation studies expanded beyond literature and film, scholars recommended an ever-expanding disciplinary and theoretical pluralism to explicate adaptations. In 2010, Brett Westbrook agreed with prior scholars advocating theoretical pluralism to offset the vast scope and range of adaptations: 'the vastness of the boundaries … can lead to a plurality of theories being pressed into the service of examining a particular point of the intersection between two texts, in all their glorious plurality', calling '[c]ritics [to] choose from a candy store of available approaches: semiotics, feminist criticism, Russian Formalism, media studies – the whole menu'.[5] Westbrook's recommended theories derive from various disciplines – linguistics, gender studies, literary studies, and media studies.

Yet often what we mean by 'theorization' is a form of disciplinary colonization: the application of principles, methodologies, values, and ideologies developed in one discipline to subject matter. The process is epitomized by these book titles: *The Language of Media*,[6] *Narrative across Media*,[7] *The Politics of Media*,[8] *The History of Media*, *The Philosophy of Media*,[9] *The Psychology of Media*,[10] *The Science of Media*,[11] and *The Economics of Media*.[12] These titles articulate processes of adapting media not to other media but to academic disciplines and their methodologies and theories. Each simultaneously illuminates and delimits the questions and issues addressed.

In 2012, Rainer Emig joined Westbrook in assessing that 'adaptation needs theory, but at the same time adaptation cannot and must not rely on one theory or even one clearly prescribed set of theories only … its multi- and interdisciplinary status also determines its multi-, inter- and transtheoretical attachments'.[13] Emig thus advanced theories gleaned from Foucault's New Historicism, Frederic Jameson's politics, Jean Baudrillard's cultural philosophy, Julia Kristeva's psychoanalysis, Jacques Derrida's semiotic philosophy, Judith Butler's gender theory, Homi Bhabba's postcolonial theory, and Jean-François Lyotard's sociology.

It seems to me that these arguments have not been taken far enough and that a fully pluralistic interdisciplinary theoretical approach to adaptations should go beyond the usual disciplinary suspects to include *every* discipline. Currently, only certain disciplines qualify as 'theorizing' ones in the humanities: typically philosophy, history, politics, sociology, economics, psychology, and linguistics. The markedly absent disciplines in these lists are the sciences (beyond the scope of this chapter, but addressed elsewhere)[14] and the nonverbal arts.

As well as being many other things, adaptations are art forms that cannot be fully explicated by or conformed to rational, logical, philosophical, or ideological constructs, theories, and methodologies. In *The Pedagogy of Adaptation*, Cutchins, Raw, and Welsh declare the impossibility of

teach[ing] students a particular approach to adaptations or a heuristic that they could apply equally well in any situation. ... [T]he more we study the issue, the more we find ourselves believing that the only legitimate response to art is more art.

Among other approaches to study, they suggest that students engage in the practice of adaptation, 'making the kinds of decisions and creating the sorts of interpretations filmmakers do when they approach a text to adapt it'.[15]

The idea that adaptations are art forms and should be treated as such is currently contested, although it held sway for most of the twentieth century. Under aesthetic formalism and New Criticism, adaptations were treated as aesthetic productions; the role of scholars was to assess their cultural value and disseminate it, or condemn and police adaptations if they were found aesthetically wanting. Following the principles laid out in Matthew Arnold's preface to *Culture and Anarchy: An Essay in Political and Social Criticism* (1869),[16] the role of art was to bring about individual and social perfection; the role of the critic was to locate the 'best' aesthetic productions and illuminate why they are best to students and the general public, contributing to social progress while curbing threats of anarchy and revolution from the uneducated underclasses.

In the last decades of the twentieth century, however, humanities academia underwent the revolution that Arnold feared, changing and challenging these views of aesthetics and the cultural role of scholars. The revolution included a challenge to humanist, formalist, aesthetic scholarship focused on high art, canonical works and their civilizing properties from Marxist, poststructuralist, and postmodern studies of all manner of cultural productions, studies that aimed to democratize culture by exposing the political underbelly of high art. Postmodern cultural studies entered adaptation studies in full force from 1996, when Deborah Cartmell, Imelda Whelehan, I. Q. Hunter, Heidi Kaye, and contributors to their essay collections read adaptations to destabilize 'the high/lowbrow divide' and to challenge 'cultural elitism'.[17] Adaptations were increasingly read not just as art forms, but as signs, narratives, cultural productions, ideologies, mental constructs, and commodities, assessed under theories besides aesthetics and studied in disciplines other than the arts. Aesthetic criticism was challenged on multiple grounds: its impressionism by structuralist and systematic theories;[18] its cultural values by left-wing dialectics and dialogics; its truth value by postmodern philosophy and poststructuralist intertextuality.[19]

And yet adaptations continue to be viewed primarily as aesthetic productions and judged according to Arnoldian cultural values by audiences, media reviewers, and the adaptation industry,[20] as well as by many academics. Rejecting aesthetic criticism altogether runs the risk of creating an inordinate gap between adaptations in culture and adaptations in academia. My pedagogical experience suggests that there is another way to study the aesthetics of adaptations: the way of *doing* adaptation, in which the aesthetic practice of producing adaptations functions as a form of criticism – even theorization.

The adaptation as critic

Oscar Wilde opens a historical and theoretical door into this possibility when he closes the gap between criticism and art in his essay, 'The Critic as Artist' (1891). Turning Arnoldian nineteenth-century critical conventions on end, he proposes that 'Criticism is itself an art. And just as artistic creation implies the working of the critical faculty, and, indeed, without it cannot be said to exist at all, so Criticism is really creative in the highest sense of the word'.[21] Inverting Wilde's inversion, I want to make an additional case for the Artist as Critic and, by extension, the Adaptation as Critic. I do not here advance the Adaptation as Critic in the same way that Neil Sinyard (1986) and others, myself included, have done in the past – a process of reading adaptations to analyzing how *other* artists have read and interpreted the works they adapt. In *Film Adaptation and Its Discontents*, Leitch advocates an approach to adaptations 'that subordinates the process of reading adaptations to the process of writing them'. By this he means engaging adaptations with 'a literacy whose goal is engagement, analysis, and reasoned debate' as opposed to 'the consumption of information from authoritative sources'.[22]

My pedagogical practice goes further than this and than Cutchins, Raw, and Welsh's practical tasks of 'making the kinds of decisions and creating the sorts of interpretations filmmakers do when they approach a text'[23] via treatments, storyboards, and scripts. It joins a growing movement of creative-critical scholarship, in which *scholars* engage in acts of creative production that engage with prior aesthetic works.[24] (See Appendix A.)

Traditional modes of humanities scholarship require students to produce convincing argumentation expressed in rational critical writing supported by evidence. Sometimes such writing draws on empirical epistemologies emulating the sciences; sometimes it engages the logical argumentation of philosophy; sometimes it pursues ideologies of cultural capacity rooted in aesthetic formalism or political cultural studies. Even essays written under theories sceptical of empiricism and rationality such as postmodernism, poststructuralism, and psychoanalysis nevertheless generally follow an expository structure in which a thesis is presented, an argument is pursued, supported by evidence, and a conclusion is reached. The creative-critical work I assign my students goes beyond the verbal and rational to nonverbal and nonrational adaptations of all kinds in all media, accompanied by a critical essay in which students interpret their own adaptations as criticism of the works they adapt.

Martin Mull coined a widely reiterated saying, 'Writing about music is like dancing about architecture'.[25] Echoed and extended by Elvis Costello in 1983 ('it's a really stupid thing to want to do'),[26] the expression dismisses rather than entertains the idea that nonverbal, nonrational disciplines can be 'about' each other. It implies the impossibility and ludicrousness of explicating a nonverbal art with a verbal art by analogy to a more impossible, more ludicrous interdisciplinary relation in which one nonverbal art becomes 'about' another one. But in a fully interdisciplinary, intermedial field of adaptation, every movement between forms and media is an act of criticism or theorization 'about' intermedial relations. This is not a vision; it has been my pedagogical experience since I began teaching literature and film in 1996. In keeping with Wilde's inversion of social norms and hierarchies, my argument, then, does not derive from scholarly research subsequently applied to teaching; I learned it from my students and have subsequently applied it to my research.

The notion of the adaptation itself as critic (even theorist) of what it adapts offers three central benefits: first, engaging in adaptation illuminates adaptation as a *process* in ways inaccessible to rational, empirical, philosophical, and ideological modes of criticism; second, engaging in acts of adaptation produces critical and theoretical insights that redress some of the impasses identified by scholars[27] between adaptation theory and adaptation practice; and third, it allows a wider array of disciplines to be applied to adaptations, offering new critical and theoretical insights into them. Beyond these advantages, doing adaptation challenges the vice-grip of abstraction, empiricism, didacticism, and moralizing in the humanities with aesthetic concretism and interdisciplinary play. Its ability to surprise supersedes the value of theory to predict.

The creative-critical project

When I began assigning a creative-critical project in addition to the usual essays, class tests, and exams in my literature and film course at the University of California, Berkeley in 1996, I did not have these goals in mind. Indeed, I was unaware of the theoretical and critical potential of creative work until student projects alerted me to it. My rationale was initially much simpler. I was astonished to discover how conservative 18–22-year-old students were about literary film adaptation. As lovers of literature taught largely by Arnoldian high school teachers, many lamented and protested against infidelities in adaptation. Even when I stressed how much films add to texts (music, costumes, sets, props, actors, camera work, etc., as well as new industry, cultural, and historical contexts), they perceived film adaptations solely in terms of literary loss, not filmic gain. They were moreover reluctant to engage film adaptations as criticisms of literature, preferring to see them as failed translations.

No matter what I said, no matter which scholars they read protesting against fidelity criticism, they continued to protest against infidelity in adaptation. In exasperation, I resorted to pragmatics: I assigned them a task of doing adaptation, hoping that they would learn in practice what they resisted in theory: how difficult – even impossible – it is to produce a faithful adaptation. The project did just this for some students. One student adapted her own poem to a short film. But since she could not find a male actor willing to be filmed running naked down a road, she ended up using a woman, also unwilling to streak, draped in a sheet. Her critical reflection on the film indicated how these exigencies produced a filmic interpretation with homoerotic connotations unintended by the 'original' author of the poem – herself. Her film subsequently won a student film festival.[28]

My students have gone beyond filmmaking to produce adaptations in other media: writing, dramatizing, storyboarding, filming, novelizing, graphic-novelizing, drawing, illustrating, painting, sculpting, set designing, costuming, staging, scoring, puppeteering, acting, dancing, singing, editing, directing, casting, choreographing, gaming, video gaming, and producing marketing materials, film posters, book covers, news articles, political pamphlets, magazine spreads, scrapbooks, and multimedial installations. Students have furthermore engaged new and digital media, adapting works to Facebook pages, Twitter feeds, YouTube videos, blogs, vlogs, ringtones, and iPad apps.

If no student has yet danced about architecture, they have drawn about music, played rugby matches about theatre, gamed about films, drawn about musical tracks, computer programmed about graphic novels, baked layer cakes about book chapters, produced chemical explosions about character metamorphoses, made tactile interactive projects about audience response, and composed music about critical theory. They have adapted media to sign language, Parkour, cocktails, perfumes, jewellery, makeup, embroidery, furniture, baby mobiles, dolls, toys, puzzle books, detective files and cork boards, travelogues, chemical experiments, graffiti, musical instruments, and all manners of textiles from patchwork quilts piecing together various narratives to a suitcase cleverly adapting Robert Louis Stevenson's *The Strange Case of Dr Jekyll and Mr Hyde* (1886).

Beyond my initial intent in assigning the project, other critical, theoretical, and metamedial insights emerge both in the projects themselves and the critical essays that accompany them. The essays explicate students' production processes and interpret their work critically, engaging with other criticism and theory about the works they adapt.

Some student projects have explored narrative across media. One adapted Margaret Mitchell's *Gone with the Wind* (1936) to a board game, with character pieces for slave owners Scarlett, Rhett, Melanie, Ashley, and slaves, Mammy, Prissy, and Pork. The student painstakingly made game cards based on every mention of every act undertaken by each of these characters in the novel. Scarlett's pile was huge; Pork's was miniscule; the others lay somewhere between. The rules of the game stated that for every socially ethical action, a character moves forward a space; for every socially unethical action, s/he moves back a space; for every neutral action, s/he remains in place. The game was unwinnable: Scarlett had numerous cards, but was unable to reach the finish line because her actions were mostly unethical. While Mammy and Melanie were more often ethical than otherwise, they had too few cards to reach the finish line; Pork had no chance at all. The critical essay reflected acutely on primary and secondary characters in literature and the contrasts between ethics, winning, and losing in literature and gaming; it illuminated aspects of narrative in the novel that would have been opaque or invisible to single-medium criticism.

Other student projects have examined how changes in media adapt and rework cultural conventions and audience desires. In response to a lecture I gave on adapting linguistic nonsense in Lewis Carroll's Alice books to audiovisual filmic representations,[29] one student baked a three-tier cake adapting three chapters of *Alice's Adventures in Wonderland* (1865). It was beautifully decorated with hand-made characters and scenery from the books and various film adaptations, and a rabbit hole tunnel ran down through the layers. An accomplished chef, the student made each layer to gourmet standards. However, each layer used conventional ingredients in unconventional combinations. The layer adapting Carroll's chapter, 'Advice from a Caterpillar', featured a feathery light, white, poppy seed cake containing caramelized mushrooms and gummy worms. While individually delicious, together, the ingredients gave pause to the would-be consumer. The essay accompanying the cake addressed the adaptation of linguistic nonsense to gustatory nonsense, asking, if diners enjoy caramelized mushrooms and poppy seed cake separately, why not in combination? It further pondered why linguistic nonsense produces laughter, audiovisual nonsense produces wonder (as in the 1951 Disney film), and edible nonsense produces an admixture of desire and revulsion.

Other projects have illuminated the identity politics of media. One student adapted *Romeo and Juliet* to a ballet involving only four female characters: Juliet, her mother, the Nurse, and the Nurse's dead daughter. Stripping these characters from their male-dominated cultural and verbal contexts and bringing the Nurse's daughter, narrated but unseen and unheard in the play, into the adaptation clarified dynamics and interactions hitherto unobserved even by the myriad of feminist critics who had already fruitfully studied this play. Another student's artwork rematerialized the exploitation of Africa that Joseph Conrad's *Heart of Darkness* (1899) dematerializes in a diction of inscrutability and inexpressibility. Its base, a repurposed copper tabletop, was scratched, beaten, and damaged – and yet made to look glorious in contrast with its dark foreground, a stained and stitched, piecemeal map of Africa. The essay allocated multiple meanings to the copper disc – a serving dish presenting a butchered Africa on a plate for viewers' delectation; an opulent shield behind which Europeans hide from their historic colonial guilt; a cymbal (or rather a symbol of a cymbal) used by Africans, now silenced and hung on the wall as colonial trophy; a mirror in which readers of the essay see their own reflections. These are only the insights on two of the 13 pages in the essay; it would require a whole book to do justice to this and other student essays.

Some projects have focused on formal rather than ideological aspects of adaptation. While no dances have yet been danced about architecture, students have made architectural adaptations of books, films, and other media. Joining the usual suspects – film, theatre, and television set designs, each aesthetically interpretive and critically illuminating of the works they adapt – there have also been symbolic architectural adaptations of media. One student made a full-sized door into an art object, 'The entrance to Wonderland'. One side was all text; the other, all pictures and conversation. The essay probed relations among these forms in Carroll's book and in adaptation theories; the door recalled and delightfully problematized Saussure's analogy of form and content to two sides of a piece of paper. Another student created a Gothic dollhouse representing the psychology of Jekyll and Hyde. Its seven rooms were filled with texts, objects, and colours representing the seven deadly sins; the rooms doubled as chambers of the brain, and the central staircase doubled as the top of the spine. The project and its essay explored an immensely complex interhistorical intermediality set in dialogue with psychoanalytic theories.

Joining inventive and densely interpretive film, theatre, and television costume designs for actors to wear, students have also designed clothing to represent character more symbolically, such as reversible clothing or an unwearable two-sided mask for Jekyll and Hyde. One particularly ingenious dress design for Alice presented initially as her trademark Disney blue dress and white apron. But in the pocket of the innocuous white apron lay a cupcake bearing the words, 'Eat me'. Inside the cupcake was a key that unlocked a padlock opening the skirt to reveal an extensively unfolding underskirt/underworld of texts, objects, and images presenting a surrealist reworking of the novel's ambivalent state between dreaming and waking. Another student designed an Alice corset and used it to reflect on Victorian constraints upon women highlighted in Tim Burton's film of *Alice in Wonderland* (2010), its essay setting the corset in dialogue with historical studies of costumes and the costumes of Burton's film.

Students have also explored makeup and hair both for performance and in abstract and symbolic ways. Beginning with the phrase, 'How do you judge a book?', one student made a short film exploring how makeup produces character *and audience* psychologies, the latter implicated in – indeed inextricable from – critical interpretations, since critics begin as audiences. Another student film placed metamorphosing layers of camouflage paint and blackface on a white actor's face as part of an exploration of racism in *Heart of Darkness*. Using makeup, hair styling, and accessories alone, another student turned a single face into a host of Burtonesque Wonderland characters to probe the idea that Alice 'is' all of the characters in her dream, as she is in Jan Švankmajer's film, *Alice* (1988).

One student even challenged a sacred academic cow by adapting literary *theory* to music, scoring Mikhail Bakhtin's theory of the carnivalesque[30] in three movements: a Baroque section indicating the normal social order; a section in which the norm of the Baroque is disrupted by atonal music representing the carnivalesque and the incursion of a musical grotesque body (represented by a tuba); and a final section in which the Baroque has integrated and internalized the atonal carnivalesque. This project came as close to dancing about architecture as any I have seen – the music, though non-semantic, offered as many compositional complexities as Bakhtin's essay, vying with and exceeding its polyvocalism.

Other musical adaptations have explored how different sound tracks produce different interpretations of the same film scene or character. For example, Jekyll and Hyde film scenes have been scored using musical styles ranging from classical to folk to heavy metal and rap, sometimes in intriguing dialectical combinations that split high and low culture musically, after the Jekyll and Hyde split itself, producing innovative expressions of their interplay beyond logic and polemics.

Similar stylistic explorations have been undertaken using the visual arts. Seizing on the lines from *Jekyll and Hyde*, 'I can't describe him. And it's not want of memory; for I declare I can see him this moment',[31] one student represented Hyde in three styles of painting: nineteenth-century realist, nineteenth-century impressionist, and early twentieth-century cubist. The essay astutely explored how each style constructs different concepts of evil and monstrosity. Even the brick wall against which Hyde stood differed across aesthetic styles.

Not all projects have been intermedial – some have been intramedial. One student probed tragedy and narrative closure by juxtaposing and intercutting the endings of William Shakespeare's *Othello* and *Romeo and Juliet* in a theatrical stage performance. Two beds were set side by side on a stage, one holding the comatose Juliet, the other a wakeful Desdemona. Drawing on techniques of intercutting in film, the student cut suspensefully and powerfully between the dialogue and actions of the two plays. At the moment Desdemona dies, Juliet awakens; at the moment Juliet takes her life, Othello takes his. These intercuttings allowed for new reflections not only on the endings of the plays, but also on issues of gender and agency in narrative closure. The final lines of the dramatization, 'Look on the tragic loading of these beds; / This is thy work',[32] resonated as they have never done before or since for me.

Other projects have emphasized intercultural dynamics and interchanges in adaptation. Students have adapted Anglo-American literature to their own cultures. One witty, buoyant, melodramatic Bollywood adaptation of the film, *Gone with the Wind* (1939), unfolded the affinities and dissonances between Hollywood and Bollywood more clearly than any textbook or criticism I have assigned or any lecture I have given.

Some students have produced interhistorical adaptations; one recently set Jane Austen's *Pride and Prejudice* (1813) in World War I. The project, comprised of extensive historical research, a treatment, sample scenes from a screenplay, storyboards for two film sequences, and costume designs for a dozen characters, went far beyond the assessment's requirements. Beginning with a cinematic big bang in which the picturesque landscape that viewers have come to expect in Austen productions is both foreign (French) and destroyed by a bomb blast, the narrow constraints of trenches displaced the constraints of the domestic interiors that Austen and her adapters usually present. Taking the idle soldiers of Netherfield into the trenches of France, it explored the effects of war on marriage proposals and sexual behaviour and developed the novel's local concern about the scarcity of men on an international scale. The essay included research on how men in the trenches treasured pocket-sized editions of Austen's works as simultaneously an escape from fighting and an impetus for fighting for 'England'; it continued with a discussion of how the project adapts the novel's challenges to gender and class politics to the war that produced the first wave of twentieth-century feminism and changed the social order forever.

Some projects have been autobiographical. One student financing his way through university as a bartender designed cocktails for characters in *Gone with the Wind*, reflecting with wit and acuity on continuities between cocktail ingredients and personality traits (and the effect of cocktails on personality). Another student's project bordered on the illegal when he adapted Cornell Woolrich's 'It Had to Be Murder' (1942) and Alfred Hitchcock's *Rear Window* (1954) to a photomontage of his own rear-view neighbours, naming and characterizing them on the basis of their appearance and actions, and attempting to construe their activities into narratives, as the story and film do. As the film probes paparazzi ethics and the problems of engaging criminal voyeurism as an agent of legality, the student's essay pondered the ethics of rear window photography in the service of academic assignments.

Parodies such as this bring humour and acerbic critique to the assessment. Other projects have parodied classic popular texts by adapting them to television shows. One student adapted *The Godfather* to a particularly messy *Veggie Tales* animated episode, in which smashed fruit and vegetables lie bleeding. The essay reflected on why such animated vegetarian violence is comical and on the cultural and ideological issues implicit in adapting violent literary 'classics' into animated films for children, when violence is so strongly censored in other media.

Students have produced double-edged parodies of both adapted and adapting works. *Pride and Prejudice* has been adapted to *Made in Chelsea* and *Take Me Out*, exploring links between privileged and idle lives and male scarcity in the romance genre across centuries, parodying both novel and television show in the process. *Alice's Adventures in Wonderland* has been adapted to *Come Dine with Me*, uniting the trademark eccentric characters obsessed with food in both forms in a mutual parody that probes the role of food in the battle for social and economic power. Francis Ford Coppola's *The Godfather* has been adapted to 'The Godfather Meets Jeremy Kyle', an episode in which Kay raises her suspicions about Michael's illegal activities to Kyle. The film ends chillingly with a shot echoing the ending of Coppola's film, in which Kyle shakes hands with a vindicated Michael and closes the studio door on Kay. The essay reflects astutely on continuities between the gender dynamics of both media.

These projects exist in excess both of my brief descriptions and their accompanying essays, not only because I do not have space to reproduce the projects and essays here, nor because the essay word limit prevents students from explicating their projects further, but also because each project contains aspects that emerge and remain but are not subject to verbal explication. Not only do projects remain in excess of words, they also remain in excess of rationality and logic, producing laughter, tears, horror, excitement, and a myriad of other emotional responses. The best produce responses that cannot be reduced to emotions – what I can only describe as aesthetic gasps of wonder at their artistry, ingenuity, beauty, and power. Assessment criteria therefore expand from the criteria used to mark written work to include aesthetic criteria (see Appendix B).

Aesthetics resurge in these projects in ways that elude the high/low art debates that have marginalized aesthetics in critical discourse. Having students create their own aesthetic processes and projects frees them from the weighty aesthetic cultural burdens of traditional pedagogy, which seeks to inculcate students with dominant ideologies and values through the aesthetic productions of others, whether they be the high-art humanist values of capitalist cultures or the radical politics that oppose them. The adaptation as critic allows students to produce their own aesthetics and represent their own values; the critical essay that accompanies the adaptation requires them to set these in dialogue with prior adaptations, criticism, and theory. Instead of teaching students to abstract aesthetic and cultural practices into words, theories, philosophies, and ideologies, the adaptation as critic materializes criticism, while the companion essay reflects abstractly on that materialization and, in the best essays, on the relations between the two, as well as among media, disciplines, and theories.

Notes

1. Thomas Leitch, 'Adaptation and Translation', presented at 'Film Adaptation: A Dialogue among Approaches', Alfried Krupp Wissenschaftskolleg, Greifswald, Germany, 18 April 2013.
2. Dennis Cutchins, Laurence Raw, and James M. Welsh, 'Introduction' in *The Pedagogy of Adaptation,* ed. Dennis Cutchins, Laurence Raw, and James M. Welsh (Lanham, MD: Scarecrow Press, 2010), p. xvi.
3. For a panoply of definitions and alternative terminologies, see Julie Sanders, *Adaptation and Appropriation* (London: Routledge, 2005) pp. 3–4; Robert Stam, 'Introduction: The Theory and Practice of Adaptation' in *Literature and Film: A Guide to the Theory and Practice of Film Adaptation,* ed. Robert Stam and Alessandra Raengo (London: Blackwell, 2004), p. 25; Eckart Voigts-Virchow, 'Anti-Essentialist Versions of Aggregate Alice: A Grin without a Cat', in *Translation and Adaptation Theories in Theatre and Film,* ed. Katja Krebs (London: Routledge, 2013), p. 64.
4. Irving Babbitt, *The New Laocoön: An Essay on the Confusion of the Arts* (Boston: Houghton Mifflin, 1910); George Bluestone, *Novels into Film* (Berkeley: University of California Press, 1957).
5. Brett Westbrook, 'Being Adaptation: The Resistance to Theory' in *Adaptation Studies: New Approaches,* ed. Christa Albrecht-Crane and Dennis R. Cutchins (Cranberry, NJ: Associated University Press, 2010), pp. 43–4.
6. Lev Manovich, *The Language of New Media* (Cambridge, MA: MIT Press, 2001).
7. *Narrative across Media: The Languages of Storytelling,* ed. Marie-Laure Ryan (Omaha: University of Nebraska Press, 2004).
8. John Whale, *The Politics of the Media* (Manchester: Manchester University Press, 1977).
9. Michael Schmid, *History and Philosophy of the Media* (Munich: Grin Verlag, 2004).

10. George Comstock and Erica Scharrer, *The Psychology of Media and Politics* (Burlington, MA: Elsevier Academic Press, 2005).
11. Jennifer Burg, *The Science of Digital Media* (New York: Prentice Hall, 2008).
12. Linda Low, *Economics of Information Technology and the Media* (Singapore: Singapore University Press, 2000).
13. Rainer Emig, 'Adaptation in Theory' in *Adaptation and Cultural Appropriation: Literature, Film, and the Arts*, ed. Pascal Nicklas and Oliver Linder (Berlin: de Gruyter, 2012), p. 14.
14. Kamilla Elliott, 'The Adaptation of Adaptation: A Dialogue between the Sciences and Humanities', in *Adaptation and Cultural Appropriation*, ed. Pascal Nicklas and Oliver Linder, pp. 145–61.
15. Cutchins, Raw, and Welsh, 'Introduction', pp. xiv, xvi.
16. Matthew Arnold, *Culture and Anarchy: An Essay in Political and Social Criticism* (London: Smith, Elder & Co., 1869), p. viii.
17. Deborah Cartmell and Imelda Whelehan, 'Introduction' in *Pulping Fictions: Consuming Culture across the Literature/Media Divide*, ed. Deborah Cartmell, I.Q. Hunter, Heidi Kaye and Imelda Whelehan (London: Pluto Press, 1996), p. 2.
18. See, for example, Brian McFarlane, *Novel to Film: An Introduction to the Theory of Adaptation* (Oxford: Clarendon Press, 1996).
19. See, for example, the essays in *Film Adaptation*, ed. James Naremore (New Brunswick, NJ: Rutgers University Press, 2000).
20. See Simone Murray, *The Adaptation Industry: The Cultural Economy of Contemporary Literary Adaptation* (London: Routledge, 2011).
21. Oscar Wilde, 'The Critic as Artist', *Intentions* (Fairfield, IA: Akasha Classics, 2009 [1891]), p. 79.
22. Thomas Leitch, *Film Adaptation and Its Discontents: From* Gone with the Wind *to* the Passion of the Christ (Baltimore: Johns Hopkins University Press, 2007), pp. 11–12.
23. Cutchins, Raw, and Welsh, *The Pedagogy of Adaptation*, p. xvi. Indeed, the authors contend that 'Actually filming and editing their adaptations … are not necessary to help students understand the process and problems associated with adaptation' (p. xvi).
24. Many UK universities now offer postgraduate degrees in creative-critical writing.
25. Gary Speranza, 'Review of *Sam & Dave*', *Time Barrier Express*, 1979, n. p.
26. Timothy White, 'A Man Out of Time Beats the Clock', *Musician* (1983): 60, 52.
27. Hutcheon, *A Theory of Adaptation*, p. xiv; Elliott, *Rethinking the Novel/Film Debate*, pp. 5–6; Kamilla Elliott, 'Theorizing Adaptations/Adapting Theories' in *Adaptation Studies: New Challenges, New Directions*, ed. J. Bruhn, A. Gjelsvik, and E. Frisvold (London: Bloomsbury, 2013), pp. 19–45.
28. Due to university rules concerning student confidentiality, I am unable to name students.

29. The lecture was based on Elliott, *Rethinking the Novel/Film Debate*, Chapter 6.
30. Mikhail Bakhtin, *Rabelais and His World*, trans. Hélène Iswolsky (Bloomington: Indiana University Press, 1984 [1965]).
31. Robert Louis Stevenson, *The Strange Case of Dr Jekyll and Mr Hyde* (London: Penguin, 2007 [1886]), p. 7.
32. William Shakespeare, *Othello* (London: Penguin, 2007), 5.2.364–5.

7
Teaching Adapting Screenwriters: Adaptation Theory through Creative Practice

Jamie Sherry

Whilst many of the most innovative and progressive texts on adaptation theory still emerge from Literary and Film Studies, the attraction of the subject for a variety of scholars from divergent academic disciplines has seen the field expand to incorporate new methodologies and approaches. Despite this, the teaching of adaptation is still principally located in departments of English and Film, and its pedagogical function remains focused on illuminating students' understanding of literature, or to better understand cinema's inherent qualities via its relationship with other media. Furthermore, examinations of adapted films focus primarily on the relationship between the literary source text and resultant film text, failing to adequately interrogate the complex industrial and creative processes that take place *during* adaptation. The lack of attention to the teaching of *processes* of adapting can be seen as a more general tendency to overlook the many useful theoretical and creative functions of adaptation studies methodologies beyond comparative case-study analysis. As Dennis Cutchins, Laurence Raw, and James M. Welsh argue in their introduction to *The Pedagogy of Adaptation* (2010) 'we have not generally created useful theoretical models or participated in sufficient dialogue concerning how adaptations might be taught in different contexts'.[1] Whilst the call-to-action goes unresolved within the chapters of that book, the clear intention to broaden the scope of adaptation studies teaching is evidence of a shift towards alternative perceptions of remediations in film and television that foreground the spaces between source and adapted text. As the authors observe, the process of adaptation is vital to our understanding of the subject from theoretical and pedagogical perspectives:

> Our main contention is that the term 'adaptation' needs to be radically rethought. Arguably as a matter of academic conditioning, we have hitherto restricted our impressions of adaptations to the rather limiting framework of novels-into-film, rather than focusing on adaptation as process. Because our students and many of our best theorists are restricted by the novel-into-film paradigm, they also fail to understand how adaptation can be perceived as a creative process, much less how it might be used as a way of developing innovative techniques of classroom pedagogy.[2]

My own experiences of teaching adaptation over the previous decade include roles in English and Film departments, as well as my current position as a Lecturer in Screenwriting. These experiences have allowed me to view the pedagogical function of adaptation studies from three discrete vantage points. The outcome of this experience is a better understanding of how adaptation can benefit and enhance general learning in a classroom setting, and provide a fundamentally important role in the pedagogy of the arts and creative industries. However, the teaching of screenplay adaptation raises some essential pedagogical and sometimes philosophical questions, not always easy to answer, regarding the function of the subject outside traditional English and Film Studies departments. How does the assessed completion of an adapted screenplay augment students' understanding of adaptation theory? What function should adaptation theory have on a practice-based course that is designed to improve creative expression through screenwriting? What does the process of adaptation teach students about remediation from creative, theoretical, and industrial perspectives? What criterion should be adopted in the assessment of an adapted screenplay, and are students expected to reflect and comment on their work, or should it stand alone as a piece of practice-led inquiry?

This chapter will attempt to answer these questions by analyzing the aesthetic and creative function of the adapted screenplay in screenwriting provision, highlighting the lack of attention to screenwriting within adaptation studies and the scarcity of critical adaptation theories in screenplay writing. It will also outline my own attempts to deal with some of the pedagogical tensions outlined above by discussing the content of the course I run at Bangor University. The adapted screenplay is framed as an intertextual creative document, developed as a discrete, literary form with its own language, poetics, and structure whilst also being informed by source material. It is within this breach – in which remediation, differing textual forms, and intertextual referencing synthesize and vie for space – that adaptation can be understood as *process*.

Adaptation process and the interstitial screenplay

Whilst the screenplay is commonly regarded as a functional device used to facilitate and guide film, in the case of adaptations it also becomes the bridging, interstitial document linking the source material to the final adapted work. The adapted screenplay is a vehicle and a system of transference to enable the transforming of one media into another, as well as functioning as a uniquely fluid work oscillating between the source media and cinema. Jack Boozer's edited collection *Authorship in Film Adaptation* (2008) is the only critical text to actively engage with theories of adaptation applied to specific aspects of screenwriting and the adapted screenplay. Boozer debates many issues central to adaptation theory that, prior to his text, failed to be applied in a serious way to the screenplay. Boozer argues in favour of the crucial importance of the interstitial screenplay in the study of adaptation, positing that a 'revised contemporary sensitivity to adaptive film authorship would therefore also include the environments of all three texts – literary, script intertext, and film', concluding that each component of adaptation 'can be sites of personal and cultural struggle and perhaps revelation'.[3] Boozer correctly notes that the adapted screenplay has been traditionally 'viewed only as an interim step', whilst its marginal position in serious criticism is explained by its function as 'merely a skeletal blueprint for the adapted film and thus unworthy of serious consideration in its own right'.[4] Robert Stam notes that all cinematic works are forms of adaptation, observing 'that virtually all films, not only adaptations, remakes, and sequels, are mediated through intertextuality and writing', arguing that '[e]ven non-adaptation fiction films adapt a *script*'.[5] This stance is echoed in Thomas Leitch's view that 'several fundamental questions in adaptation theory remain unasked, let alone unanswered' before offering one of his own: 'Since virtually all feature films work from a pre-existing written text, the screenplay, how is a film's relation to its literary source different from its relation to its screenplay?'[6]

This notion of framing a film as adapted from a source screenplay is one that adaptation studies has not explored with any depth, despite the fact that audiences are increasingly familiar with a screenplay prior to seeing a film, in part thanks to the sharing of these documents online. Boozer argues that works of adaptation studies have 'generally overlooked the actual process through which a source text is transformed into a motion picture',[7] and in doing so limit the possibilities for further interesting contexts for research into the many processes and texts produced in the adaptation process. The probable cause of this may be found in the functional roots of adaptation studies within the academy, as a bolt-on subject with which to teach English and Film, therefore neglecting a 'more general theoretical account of what actually happens, or what ought to happen, when a group of filmmakers set out to adapt a literary text'.[8] Leitch observes that film adaptations of Shakespeare have been used in classes as 'the spoonful of sugar that helps the Bard's own text go down' an issue that prevents more rigorous inquiry into 'general considerations of what is at stake in adapting a text from one medium to another'[9] Jennifer M. Jeffers echoes these views of the shortcomings of awkwardly pragmatic adoptions of adaptation studies in the classroom, and similarly appeals for a more wide-ranging approach to adaptation that transcends comparative case study analysis:

> In an age when high school and even college teachers opt to show the film as a means to elucidate the literary text or even to *avoid reading* the literary text, we need to be especially vigilant in our critique, not of the film's fidelity to the literary text, but of the various decisions made *en route* from the language text to film text, and the important economic, political, historical, and cultural issues involved in the transformation.[10]

The analyses of the issues highlighted by Jeffers are central to the recent growth of screenwriting and screenplay theory, in which process and the spaces between texts are of paramount importance. The broadening of the types of texts that can and should be studied in academia, thanks in part to poststructuralist and postmodern critical theories, should have opened up the possibility for serious application to the screenplay. Yet, as Steven Price notes, despite 'the theoretical assault on the canon and established practices in criticism since the mid-1960s' there has been 'little effect on the status of the screenplay, which remains largely invisible'.[11] Steven Maras also observes that the unfortunate lack of academic focus on the screenplay and the process of screenwriting 'contribute to a situation where screenwriting is under analysed in film studies, and film theory underutilised in screenwriting'.[12] Price argues that one of the troublesome aspects of screenwriting is the *object* itself as both literary studies and film studies must account for 'the difficulty posed by the script as something troublingly both inside and outside the film'.[13] Furthermore, Maras notes that film studies 'does not always know what to do with screenwriting', whilst Freddie Gaffney argues that the marginalizing of the screenplay in academia 'may stem from the UK education system that is definitely unsure where to place screenwriting (too "Media" for English, too "English" for Media)'.[14] Kevin Alexander Boon argues that whilst 'Some mention of the screenplay occasionally makes its way into film scholarship', it is invariably 'overpowered by examinations of the film or a preceding work, such as a novel or a play that the screenplay has adapted for film'.[15]

This notion of the privileging of stable texts is an issue that becomes especially important in the study of screenwriting and the screenplay, and is especially significant in the study and teaching of adaptation. The assumed instability of the screenplay is exacerbated by the fact that the screenplay is usually multi-authored; sometimes writers of a screenplay are uncredited; there are often many versions of a screenplay in existence; for the majority of films there will be more than one functional 'screenplay' (the final draft screenplay, plus a shooting-script). For Price, this 'instability is compounded, particularly by film makers and theoreticians, in metaphors and rhetorical strategies that seek to eliminate the screenplay altogether' due to its 'troublesome ghostliness in relation to the film'.[16] The screenplay, Price concludes, is 'both absent and present, dead and alive, erased yet detectable'.[17] Yet the process of studying adapted screenplays, and furthermore the creative practice of writing an adapted screenplay, is a useful pedagogical tool for teaching the industries and aesthetics of adaptation, representing the complex relationships of texts that surround and exert various forces on remediations.

Prior to the recent surge in critical, academic texts on the role of screenwriting and the screenplay, the principal mode of publishing on screenwriting has been texts and 'self-help' manuals intended to 'teach' students and potential screenwriters how to perfect their craft. The perceived discrepancy regarding the teaching of screenwriting compared to more general creative writing, is evidenced in the general assumption that these manuals are utilized as primary reading for screenwriting courses. Price views screenwriting teaching 'almost exclusively as a vehicle of "creative writing"'[18] or at least skewed towards vocational and 'practical craft, rather than the subject of scholarly or historical analysis'.[19] Providing an example of perceived divergence between the teaching of literary fiction contrasted with screenwriting, Price observes:

> Consequently, a student researching the screenplay will almost undoubtedly be directed to one of the innumerable self-help manuals on the subject, whereas the same student studying fiction is far more likely to encounter (say) Wayne C. Booth's *The Rhetoric of Fiction* than *How to Write a Novel*.[20]

The reality is that very few of these 'how to' screenwriting manuals are used in the classroom beyond introductory courses on screenwriting. A handful of books dedicated to the subject of adaptation, offering guidelines for screenwriters, can be seen to regurgitate much that is found in some adaptation theory texts, albeit with less critical rigour. Surprisingly, given the screenwriter bias of these texts, what they significantly fail to do is to promote the notion of radical adaptation, or any overt experimental technique for retelling the source story. The commentaries in these texts are theoretically conservative, and anecdotal to a level that makes them critically worthless for screenwriting classes beyond allowing students to consider the dichotomy between empowering the screenwriter whilst simultaneously reinforcing the importance of fidelity to the source material. Whilst they all state that the faithful transposition of literature to screen is impossible, and instruct the screenwriter to make creative choices in re-telling their source material, they also promote the notion of finding and adhering to the 'spirit' of a text to achieve successful adaptation. This has the incongruous outcome of sanctioning 'infidelity', whilst bestowing authorial control on the source author, rather than the screenwriter it is attempting to instruct. Kenneth Portnoy's *Screen Adaptation – A Scriptwriting Handbook* (1998) is emblematic of this type of approach, utilizing short, accessible chapters which espouse his almost completely anecdotal views of how screenwriters should adapt source material. Portnoy is keen to make the point, as other manuals also do, that a slavish adherence to the source material is detrimental to the final film:

> Many become so enamoured of their novels or short stories that they forget the lessons about development of character and careful story construction ... Because of their obsession to remain faithful to the original writer, they forget that they are creating a new work, developing a new genre, and creating a new art form.[21]

Portnoy positions the process of adaptation as something mediated between the author of the original material and the screenwriter, rather than an autonomous, creative discourse with the source. He argues that 'because film is a totally different genre than the novel, some writers argue that an adaptation is basically like an original and should be created in a fashion that bears the stamp of its creator's personal vision' before concluding that 'the successful adapter must take a position somewhere between these two extremes'.[22] This type of vague and subjective observation on adaptation displays a lack of understanding of the screenwriting craft within an industrial context, often falling back on the platitude that the screenwriter 'should feel some obligation to preserve the integrity of the original material, if possible, but not at the expense of the new work'.[23] This position evokes screenwriting 'Guru' Robert McKee's embracing of the empowering, transformative process of adapting for the screenwriter, as his pupils are instructed directly that their 'task will not be one of adaptation but of reinvention. ... Be willing to reinvent'[24] before stating that screenwriters should convey story 'in filmic rhythms while keeping the spirit of the original'.[25] Problematically, the aim of the adaptation process is assumed to be the solving of problems and the overcoming of obstacles found in the discrepancy between literature and film. There is little sense in these manuals of the positive and productive relationship between texts in adaptation, nor a discourse on how these highlighted tensions can both create interesting art and lead to the empowering of student screenwriters at the interstitial point between two mediums.

Teaching adaptation screenwriting: industry, theory and practice

As noted earlier, I have taught the subject of adaptation in a number of institutions in a variety of departments, all of which placed differing levels of priority on the pedagogic outcomes of the course. Teaching adaptation studies in an English department is quite different from doing so in a Film Studies department, or as part of a Filmmaking degree programme. Consequently, teaching in a Creative Studies department at Bangor University, within the context of screenwriting provision, places different expectations on my provision, and the learning outcomes must be amended to fulfil these. My third-year undergraduate course 'Adapting for Film & Media' contributes to overall screenwriting provision in the school, whilst being open to students studying creative and professional writing, creative studies, film studies, and a variety of other programmes. However, because the course deals with the broad possibilities of adaptation in media, teaching involves a mixture of screenwriting theory, screenwriting practice, film studies, literary studies, cultural theory, and a range of creative media, including computer games, comics/graphic novels, music, visual media, and fine art. So, whilst one of the principal aims of the course is to engage with adaptation theory, the course primarily exists as part of a screenwriting pathway, and the responsibility to teach and support good writing practice, expression, and industrial contexts for the screenplay dominates these approaches and outcomes.

In order to deliver and manage these contexts, and to balance any inherent tensions, the course introduces students to key theories of adaptation studies, with workshops that deliver various discourses on the history and development of adaptation. The principal aim of the course is to improve screenwriting skills and creative expression, and to provide a vocational and 'real world' context for screenwriters remediating source material within the film and television industries. However, students are also expected to consume, deliberate upon, and express their understanding of theories of adaptation, remediation, and intertextuality, as well as their understanding of the craft, theory, and poetic aesthetics of screenwriting through the production of adapted screenplays and their accompanying paratextual material (one-page outlines, beat sheets, treatments, storyboards). These sessions also examine a range of concepts related to adaptation, including authorship, visual storytelling, narratology, and intertextuality. Whilst the weekly pattern follows a theme based around a specific case study or studies, these sessions function as lectures, seminars and creative workshops, anchored by the more general issues raised by carefully chosen adapted texts. As an example, whilst the opening session predictably screens and then critiques Spike Jonze and Charlie Kaufman's *Adaptation* (2002) and its published shooting script, students are also encouraged to debate concepts in Thomas Leitch's essay, 'Twelve Fallacies in Contemporary Adaptation Theory' (2003) in order to raise issues concerning fidelity and authorship from the very start of the course. Later weeks examine adapting specific literary devices in the films *We Need to Talk About Kevin* (2011), *A Cock & Bull Story* (2005), and *Naked Lunch* (1991), as well as amplifying children's literature, and the demands of experimental literature. Students are also encouraged to consider non-literary sources. Teaching sessions on adapting comics and graphic novels, video games, and short film to feature film remediation, allow the cohort to both utilize source material they are passionate about, and allow debates on cultural capital and the predominance of the novel in film and television adaptations.

As students produce drafts of work, sessions start to become more complex, including the study of 'unofficial adaptations' through intertextuality, allusion and parody, cultural appropriation, and discussion of palimpsestuous overwriting of source material by culturally dominant adaptations. These sessions analyze the many texts that surround adaptations of Joseph Conrad's novella *Heart of Darkness* (1899) in order to illuminate palimpsestuous relationships. During the session students interrogate the various screenplays developed in the production of Francis Ford Coppola's transformative remediation of Conrad's work in *Apocalypse Now* (1979). Rather than attempt to better understand Conrad's novella by examining its adaptations, the class aims to illuminate the usurping of source material through cinema's palimpsestuous overwriting, and to understand the extent to which successive adaptations can significantly infiltrate re-readings of their source. Furthermore, recent films such as Terry Gilliam's *The Brothers Grimm* (2005), Tim Burton's *Alice in Wonderland* (2010), and Spike Jonze's *Where the Wild Things Are* (2009) are examples of a tendency towards self-consciously remediating source material – in these cases fairy tales and children's books – in a postmodern way. Rather than using adaptation solely to illuminate literature, in keeping with its predominant use in Literary and English studies, or to understand cinematic remediation from a film or television perspective, the course attempts both, whilst also foregrounding the screenplay, the screenwriting process of adaptation, and the industrial function of adaptation, without privileging any of these forms. The screenplay is neither elevated nor demoted, but contextualized as both a *text* and a *work*, in keeping with its dual role as an autonomous, literary, and poetic form, and as a functioning document to inform and guide another form. Screenplays for the chosen case studies are primary reading week by week, something that becomes especially important in sessions that could easily drift into comparative analysis of source and film. A session on Lynne Ramsay's 2011 adaptation of Lionel Shriver's novel *We Need to Talk About Kevin* (2003) could simply include a comparative examination of the novel as it is remediated for film in the screenplay (co-written by Ramsay and Rory Stewart Kinnear), plus a study of the screenplay on film, and a comparison of the film and its source. Rather than solely focusing on the way that cinema uses devices in order to adapt the literary specificity of a first-person, epistolary novel (consisting of the main protagonist's letters to her dead husband), this session also examines how a screenwriter may employ screenwriting techniques to adapt this form. Furthermore, the screenplay is evaluated for its employment of language that infers the strong visual style of the resultant film through expressionistic, poetic screenwriting. The introduction of a third intermedial component opens up these debates beyond the perhaps more passive binary comparative case study analysis of source and adapted text. The screenplay interrupts these analyses, forcing a triangular discourse that, whilst prey to the banalities of some comparative analysis, also has the potential to highlight the variety of texts and paratexts that come to bear on adaptation projects. In *We Need to Talk About Kevin* students can consider some of the artistic flourishes that the writers use to convey their story, as well as more practical issues such as the visual conveyance of unreliable narration (a particular problem for screenwriters and filmmakers whose ambiguities are compromised by the literalism of cinema). These issues naturally foreground *specificity* and *equivalence* – factors vital to the pedagogic theories and practices of screenplay adaptation.

I have found that the Adapting for Film & Media course is characterized by a number of tensions, alluded to in the introduction to this chapter, concerning the pedagogical focus of adaptation screenwriting provision. Navigating these tensions ultimately becomes one of the main strengths of the course, as the academic and theoretical function of screenwriting vies for space within the purely creative demands and expectations of writing carried out by artist students, and the increasingly important preparation of students for the professional and industrial demands of the media industry. These three principal contexts for adaptation screenwriting have a symbiotic relationship in which each aspect of screenwriting pedagogy become mutually beneficial and co-dependent, as evidenced in the following diagram (Figure 7.1):

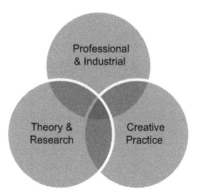

Figure 7.1 The three principal contexts for the teaching of adaptation screenwriting

From a creative practice perspective, adaptation screenwriting demands that students express themselves creatively, choosing source material that allows them to tell stories to communicate their personal, artistic vision, in accordance with more general creative writing pedagogy. Screenwriting is naturally on the periphery of formal creative writing provision in higher education, and is predictably viewed with a degree of academic snobbery, or as a 'craft' that merely facilitates other disciplines. Steve May observes that 'the provision of Creative Writing at undergraduate level is expanding in UK Higher Education Institutions' such that the subject has fractured to the point that 'to regard Creative Writing as a single, coherent subject is perhaps premature, given the diversity of its origins, forms and purposes across the Higher Education sector'.[26] Creative writing pedagogy transcends issues of vocation and publication by indicating that these courses are an aid to literacy, creativity, expression, and the notion that writing is a form of critical reading.

The contrast between creative writing and screenwriting can be found in the potential outcomes of both forms – whilst it is hoped that prose and poetry could potentially be published, the desired outcome for the screenplay is production (directed either by the writer or by another practitioner within the department). These possibilities for students' adapted screenplays foreground the issue of adaptation screenwriting as one part of an industrial process of pre-production that places emphasis on the realities of screenwriting in the modern media industries. Boozer notes these industrial complexities of the screenplay, and in particular the multiplicity of its creative and practical development into film:

> Unlike the solitary, imaginative origin of most fiction (however informed by a cultural milieu), the composition of an adapted screenplay takes place not only under the shadow of myriad narrative expectations but in a complex environment of business, industrial, and artistic considerations.[27]

The outcome of these industrial contexts for adaptation screenwriting is the placing of specific creative restrictions on the work being produced by students that forces them to consider commissioning strategies, the contemporary marketplace for adapted screenplays, financial aspects of optioning source material, and a strong focus on audiences. Students on this course are expected to carry out research in order to better understand the potential budget for their concept, and be able to indicate which set-pieces and scenes in their adapted screenplays could increase production costs. The portfolios of work that students submit for assessment consist of industry-standard documents of the type used by production companies in order to provide a 'real-world' context for pre-production strategies for adaptation projects, including a one-page outline, logline, beat sheet, treatment, commissioning proposals, and a shooting script. Students are also required to pitch their ideas to the cohort, as well as bringing drafts of treatments and screenplay extracts to workshop sessions in order to discuss them as both writers and script editors, and as commissioning producers.

Despite the creative and industrial demands of this screenwriting course, the replacement of critical and reflective essays with practice-based analysis of adaptation theory is one that opens up the possibilities for new methodologies for understanding remediation. In his analysis of cinematic adaptation teaching practices, Leitch discusses the tendency of his students to gravitate towards more established methodologies, and when 'given a free choice of approaches nearly always choose hermeneutical explication, evaluation, or critique according to whichever political or social bromides are currently fashionable'.[28] Cutchins, Raw, and Welsh echo the importance of practice as analysis in the teaching of adaptation, observing that 'Since students learn best by doing, they should be required to adapt texts from one medium to another'.[29]

Whilst practice-led, or practice-based, research is a subject usually discussed in terms of postgraduate study or in the context of postdoctoral research (partially as a response by UK-based creative practice academics to the demands of the 2008 RAE and 2014 REF), the principle of producing creative work as a form of active research also functions as a core philosophy for my own screenwriting teaching. In the context of writing adapted screenplays it is especially important as it raises questions regarding precisely what critical inquiry can be, in terms of symbiotically utilizing and then influencing theories of adaptation through practice-led research. Katy Macleod and Lin Holdridge argue that the act and outcomes of art process can be understood under the same terms as traditional Humanities-based criticism in a way that forces us to consider the very nature and function of 'theory'. They argue that 'art and the processes of art might be understood as academic research' in a way that evokes a 'complex of issues around theory: extant theory; theory within practice; the adaptation and renewal of theory through practice and the production of new theory'.[30] Drawing on Christopher Frayling's influential 'Research in Art and Design'[31] and in particular his use of the term 'research as art', Macleod and Holdridge argue for method, process, and art as research inquiry in which 'the thinking is ... embodied in the artefact, where the goal is not communicable knowledge in the sense of verbal communication, but in the sense of iconic or imagistic communication'.[32] Patricia Leavy notes that 'an artistic method ... can serve as an entire methodology in a given study' which 'allow research questions to be posed in new ways, entirely new questions to be asked, and new non-academic audiences to be reached'.[33] For Leavy, arts research can lead to a mutually beneficial relationship between production and theory which 'allow for "synergistic practices" that foster a holistic view of the research project'.[34] A similar ethos is employed by Hazel Smith and Roger T. Dean, who posit the idea that 'practice-led research and research-led practice ... are not separate processes, but as interwoven in an itera-tive cyclic web'.[35] This notion of creative practice *as* research, leading to credible findings and new insights is one that naturally struggles against prevailing methodologies formalized by the Humanities. Smith and Dean note these issues, whilst also pointing towards a seismic shift in our understanding of practice research both inside and outside universities:

> In the humanities, theory, criticism and historical investigation have been heavily prioritised over arts practice ... However, in the last two to three decades, the idea that arts practice might be a form of research has been developing ascendency .... Terms such as practice-led research have been developed by creative practitioners ... to argue – as forcefully as possible in an often unreceptive environment – that they are as important to the generation of knowledge as more theoretically, critically or empir-ically based research methods.[36]

For the purposes of teaching screenwriting and adaptation, these the-ories regarding practice as research, and the validity of the creative artefact as the outcome of those endeavours, become a fundamental tension in the pedagogy of screenwriting and adaptation. Helen Yeates has observed a 'subtly distinguishing category which has emerged from this survey of practice-led works' described as 'a kind of artisan-centred, theory-recrafting category' that can be applied to the practice of screenwriting in academia. Importantly, Yeates notes that the outcome of screenwriting research practice is inherently progressive and that some transgressive works utilize theory whilst also contrasting and confronting some of the more conservative, conformist structural tips provided by screenwriting manuals:

> One straightforward example is the constructing, demonstrating and application of a nuanced, character-centred model of feature film screenwriting, arguing through its very practice against the current popular 'gurus' with their more simplistic, plot-driven, how-to-dos screenwriting guides .... Rather, their projects embody reworkings and re-producings of the precise 'modus operandi' of their creative practice; such practice-led researchers examine and push the boundaries of the very practices themselves from within their own texts-in-the-making.[37]

Despite the fact that texts dedicated to the intersections of adaptation and screenwriting practice by screenwriter academics are naturally scarce, two offer insights into the possibilities for adaptation screenwriting teaching through practice-based research. Marilyn Hoder-Salmon's *Kate Chopin's 'The Awakening': Screenplay as Interpretation* (1992) is an account of the author's screenplay adaptation of Chopin's 1899 feminist novel that usefully attempts to understand the process of adaptation from a theoretical and practice-led perspective. Hoder-Salmon introduces her book as a critical study *in the form* of a screenplay, observing that 'Screenplay writing is the methodology'.[38] The adapted screenplay (which Hoder-Salmon includes in the book) exists 'as a form of criticism of the novel'[39] in order to highlight issues concerning the tendency to adapt male-authored literature. Hoder-Salmon wishes to access the source material through methods that transcend mere interpretation or the application of the Humanities' preferred critical ideologies, concluding that, 'It is perhaps the ultimate step in following current critical injunctions to "enter the text" in order to unmask its mysteries.'[40]

Mary H. Snyder's *Analyzing Literature-to-Film Adaptations: A Novelist's Exploration and Guide* (2011), offers a very different and highly personal account of the adaptation of literature to film, from the perspective of both a fiction writer and teacher of adaptation practice and theory. In this ambitious book, Snyder attempts to critique the processes, practices, and theories of adaptation from the viewpoint of the literary source material's originator. This leads Snyder to reflect on the strong poststructuralist bias of much contemporary studies, not as an academic or teacher, but as the author and originator of adaptable fiction, as she counters that her 'narrative didn't channel itself through me unconsciously, leaving me the conduit and nothing more'.[41] For Snyder asking her students to adapt source material into a screenplay in order to teach adaptation theories 'is more challenging and also more motivating than an analysis of additional excerpts'.[42]

Conclusion

Foregrounding the screenplay, and its many drafts and forms, in this process of adaptation is problematic due the ephemeral nature of the screenplay *function* – that of a bridging tool, or a temporary device that catalyzes source material into film. Not only is the screenplay a text that facilitates another text, and therefore 'by definition transitional and transformational',[43] it is also interpretively weighted towards its destination media. The textual analysis of the screenplay sees it framed within a discourse of its function compared to its 'intended' media, rather than as a discrete form with its own literary and poetic properties. The screenplay appears to exist in relation to the bridging of two formal texts (source novel and adapted film), and is regarded as merely aiding in this process of transformation, rather than functioning as a highly complex form of intertextual literature both inside and outside of the adaptation process. However, this chapter argues that the teaching of the adapted screenplay as a mediated, liminal, and interstitial form can enable students to identify adapting as a process, extricated but intangibly linked to the source material and adapted text. Furthermore, the writing of an adapted screenplay by students can transcend the pedagogical function of conveying creative and industrial screenwriting practices, or the illumination of literature and/or film. As well as allowing students to better understand decisions made in the adaptation process, the deployment of a practice-based methodology can potentially create new, radical ideas about adaptation theory that usurp the limitations of formal critical analysis. Nathaniel Kohn observes how the myriad, unpredictable forms, and aesthetics of screenwriting have this potential to function as both creative and theoretical:

> But screenplays are other (and more) than that; they are unique and uniquely (post)modern works, in part because authorship is neither privileged nor commonly shared and is often uncredited. They are models for a new way of writing that somehow just happens, always mutating works that are created in myriad ways that are beyond prediction. By looking at the practice of making them, they can serve as pedagogical models for our times, showing us how to make things in common that are astounding in their uncommonness.[44]

Audiences, critics and academics tend to privilege texts that are perceived to be produced in isolation by one artist, that exist in one form, that are not editable or available to change, or prone to decay and flux, and which are permanent rather than ephemeral. This privileging of the single-authored text leads to the screenplay being 'widely dismissed as a corporately authored and infinitely malleable commercial product',[45] whilst the privileging of literary works that are deemed to be singularly authored lead to an 'essentially Romantic perception of literature as the product of an individual, autonomous sensibility'.[46] This chapter has argued that the foregrounding of the adapted screenplay is a benefit to the teaching of screenplay studies and adaptation studies, and encourages its utilization so that, as Kevin Alexander Boon posits, 'critics and scholars might re-evaluate critical approaches that privilege an individual text, acknowledging and sometimes incorporating the multiplicity of texts into their analyses'.[47] Regardless of the authenticity of the screenplay, the steady increase in the publication and online outlets for film scripts looks set to challenge the adaptation scholar, forcing them to address the screenplay as literary artefact, paratext, intertext, hypertext, hypotext, and critical research tool – with arguably as much 'status' as its literary ancestor.

Notes

1. Dennis Cutchins, Laurence Raw, and James M. Welsh, 'Introduction', in *The Pedagogy of Adaptation*, eds. Dennis Cutchins, Laurence Raw, and James M. Welsh (Lanham, Toronto, Plymouth: The Scarecrow Press, 2010), p. xi.

2. *Ibid.*
3. Jack Boozer, 'Introduction: The Screenplay and Authorship in Adaptation', *Authorship in Film Adaptation*, ed. Jack Boozer (Austin: University of Texas Press, 2008), p. 24.
4. *Ibid.*, p. 2.
5. Robert Stam, 'Introduction: The Theory and Practice of Adaptation', in *Literature and Film: A Guide to the Theory and Practice of Film Adaptation*, eds. Robert Stam and Alessandra Raengo (Oxford: Blackwell, 2004), p. 45.
6. Thomas Leitch, 'Twelve Fallacies in Contemporary Adaptation Theory', *Criticism* 45.2, 2005, 150.
7. Boozer, 'Introduction', p. 1.
8. Leitch, 'Twelve Fallacies in Contemporary Adaptation Theory', p. 149.
9. *Ibid.*, p. 150.
10. Jennifer M. Jeffers, 'Life without a Primary Text: The Hydra in Adaptation Studies', in *The Pedagogy of Adaptation*, eds. Dennis Cutchins, Laurence Raw, and James M. Welsh (Lanham, Toronto, Plymouth: The Scarecrow Press, 2010), p. 123.
11. Steven Price, *Screenplay: Authorship, Theory and Criticism* (Hampshire: Palgrave Macmillan, 2010), p. 42.
12. Steven Maras, *Screenwriting: History, Theory and Practice* (London and New York: Wallflower Press, 2009), p. 7.
13. Price, *Screenplay*, p. 51.
14. Freddie Gaffney, *On Screenwriting* (Leighton Buzzard: Auteur, 2008), p. 7.
15. Kevin Alexander Boon, *Script Culture and the American Screenplay* (Detroit, MI: Wayne State University Press, 2008), p. 27.
16. Price, *Screenplay*, p. xi.
17. *Ibid.*
18. *Ibid.*, p. 27.
19. *Ibid.*
20. *Ibid.*
21. Kenneth Portnoy, *Screen Adaptation: A Scriptwriting Handbook* (Boston and Oxford: Focal Press, 1998), p. xii.
22. *Ibid.*, p. 5.
23. *Ibid.*
24. Robert McKee, *Story: Substance, Structure, Style and the Principles of Screenwriting* (London: Methuen, 1999), p. 368.
25. *Ibid.*
26. Steve May, 'Undergraduate Creative Writing Provision in the UK: Origins, Trends and Student Views', in *Teaching Creative Writing, Teaching the New English Series*, ed. Heather Beck (Hampshire: Palgrave Macmillan, 2012), p. 65.
27. Boozer, 'Introduction', p. 5.
28. Thomas Leitch, 'How to Teach Film Adaptations, and Why', in *The Pedagogy of Adaptation*, eds. Dennis Cutchins, Laurence Raw, and James M. Welsh (Lanham, Toronto, Plymouth: The Scarecrow Press, 2010), p. 5.
29. Cutchins, Raw, and Welsh, 'Introduction', p. xv.

30. Katy Macleod and Lin Holdridge, 'Introduction', in *Thinking Through Art: Reflections on Art as Research*, eds. Katy Macleod and Lin Holdridge (Oxon: Routledge, 2006), p. 4.
31. Charles Frayling, 'Research in Art and Design', in *RCA Research Papers*, 1.1 (London: Royal College of Art, 1993/4).
32. Macleod and Holdridge, 'Introduction', p. 5.
33. Patricia Leavy, *Method Meets Art: Arts-Based Research Practice* (New York & London: Guilford Press, 2009), p. 12.
34. *Ibid.*, pp. 228–229.
35. Hazel Smith and Roger T. Dean, *Practice-Led Research, Research-led Practice in the Creative Arts* (Edinburgh: Edinburgh University Press, 2009), p. 2.
36. *Ibid.*
37. Helen L. Yeates, 'Embedded Engagements: The Challenge of Creative Practice Research to the Humanities', in *The International Journal of the Humanities*, 7.1 (The Humanities Collection, 2009), pp. 142–143.
38. Marilyn Hoder-Salmon, *Kate Chopin's 'The Awakening': Screenplay as Interpretation* (Gainesville: University Press of Florida, 1992), p. ix.
39. *Ibid.*, p. 2.
40. *Ibid.*, p. x.
41. Mary H. Snyder, *Analyzing Literature-to-Film Adaptations: A Novelist's Exploration and Guide* (New York: Continuum, 2011), p. 225.
42. Ute Ritzenhofen, 'The English Patients: Teaching the Novel, the Screenplay, and the Movie', in *Adaptation and American Studies: Perspectives on Research and Training* (Heidelberg: Balestrini Universitatsverlag, 2011), pp. 141–142.
43. Maras, *Screenwriting*, p. 6.
44. Nathaniel Kohn, 'Disappearing Authors: A Postmodern Perspective on the Practice of Writing for the Screen', *Journal of Broadcasting & Electronic Media* 43.3, Summer 1999, 443.
45. Price, *Screenplay*, p. 12.
46. *Ibid.*, p. x.
47. Boon, *Script Culture and the American Screenplay*, p. 41.

8
Out of the Literary Comfort Zone: Adaptation, Embodiment, and Assimilation

Alessandra Raengo

'You'll hit with him! You'll run with him! You'll slide with him!'

The Jackie Robinson Story, poster tagline

'You know the flesh is hers; and given the way she inhabits it in the early scenes, you can't help wondering whether she also might own the glare, the scowl, the rolling gait and the purposeful mumble.'

Stuart Klawans, *The Nation*

This chapter pursues a deliberately unusual approach to teaching adaptation. It is motivated by an investment in understanding what is at stake when the very idea of adaptation comes under pressure, that is, when its very occurrence appears to be effaced. Focusing on these situations offers the possibility for adaptation studies to illuminate something that the very process of adaptation might be elaborating *vis-à-vis* its larger cultural and social context: for example, in the case studies under consideration here, the process of racial assimilation. I came to this conclusion studying the reception of two films centered on African-American characters: rather than referring back to the films' literary sources, film commentators discussed the actors' bodies as if they were both the source and the destination of the adaptation process, and the ultimate guarantee of its 'fidelity'. The first film is *The Jackie Robinson Story* (Alfred Green, 1950), an adaptation of the first Robinson biography in which the baseball player plays himself. The second is the

Oscar-nominated film *Precious: Based on the Novel 'Push' by Sapphire* (Lee Daniels, 2009).¹

The Jackie Robinson Story stands out not so much because it was based on a biographical text instead of a fictional source – think, for example, of Spike Lee's *Malcolm X* – but rather for the unprecedented fact that Robinson plays himself. An analysis of the discourses surrounding the film's production and reception reveals a sense of the necessity of this casting choice, both for the success of the project and for its concrete realization: nobody, the press argued, would have been able to reproduce Robinson's unique playing style; and no other African American personality was as beloved as he was at that time. In both cases Robinson's body held an authenticating role that was crucial in bringing the Integration Story to the big screen.

The protagonist's body performs an authenticating function in *Precious* as well, yet in this case as the by-product of consolidated practices (and politics) of reading authenticity *onto* the black body. The film adapts a highly lyrical and formally audacious novel by African-American poet Sapphire, where the character of Precious is very deliberately a textual figure that channels a number of students Sapphire encountered in her years working as a New York City schoolteacher.² Yet the connection between the excessive corporeality of the main character and her social circumstances has made it challenging for critics to respond to the film as a poetically driven work of fiction, even less as an example of art cinema, and to perceive the actress as clearly distinct from the role. Thus, regardless of how different actress Gabourey Sidibe is from the character she portrays, how spirited and vivacious rather than oppressed and stifled, how self-confident rather than hopeless, how much her diction sounds like that of a 'Valley girl'³ rather than the hardly comprehensible mumbling she skilfully conveys in the film, because of her sheer bodily constitution, her complexion, and her size, Sidibe is perceived as sharing the same predicament that afflicts her character.⁴

The pedagogical potential I want to discuss emerges precisely because the critical reception of both films collapses the distance between the actor and the role, the literary character and its cinematic counterpart. Consequently, in both cases the literary sources are effaced and the body itself appears to act as the source text as well as its ideal destination. Hence the challenge (and payoff) of teaching these two adaptations: how can we discuss the process of adaptation in its perceived absence?

To begin with, one would need to address the reasons for this effacement, which has to do with the overdetermination of the black body in the field of vision, the idea that subjects of colour are first and foremost captives of their visual appearance. One would turn to Frantz Fanon, as the main theorist of this process, and to visual scholars such as Nicole Fleetwood, who have explored the black body's ability to 'trouble' a visual field that already constructs it as 'troubling'.[5] Thus, in the context of the traditional iconophobic tendency of adaptation studies, racial overdetermination compounds matters even more.[6] Visual representation appears to outweigh and foreclose the capacity for expression, development, and realization of the body conjured up in the written page, beyond already familiar and predictable narrative and aesthetic possibilities. It is in this sense that both adaptations appear to deny their own process, because they are always already overdetermined by their visual outcome.

As I have argued elsewhere, a strategic analysis of the films' reception would quickly identify the understanding of the body as the adaptation's 'source' text.[7] Yet this very designation is still inadequate to the understanding of the role of the body *over* that of the literary source. More flexible tools are needed to address the different auspices under which different subjects might inhabit the field of vision, as well as the way some bodies more than others might be affected by the very process of adaptation. It was my initial work on *The Jackie Robinson Story* that brought me to this conclusion, as I realized that what was really being adapted through that film's casting was the process of *visual assimilation* of Robinson's body image in post-World War II American visual culture. Where, therefore, can we find a theoretical framework that can bring the role of the body into proper focus, both as an image and in its lived dimension?

I find a promising lead in the incipient 'biocultural' paradigm in adaptation studies,[8] whose seeds can be seen in the critical response to Spike Jonze's 2003 film *Adaptation*, which explicitly embraces the evolutionary sense of the term. In an early assessment of the film Robert Stam saw it as championing concepts of species hybridity and the idea of adaptation as a 'mutation'.[9] Similarly, for Linda Hutcheon the film develops an idea of adaptation as 'the biological process by which something is fitted to a given environment'.[10] The film we see is the script that the diegetic Charlie Kaufman (an alter ego of the real Charlie Kaufman who scripted the film) ends up writing partly about his failure to write the adaptation of the non-fiction book

The Orchid Thief by *New Yorker* writer Susan Orlean. Thus biological mutation and evolution are not only part of the content of the film, but inform both its structure and its understanding of the creative process, within a highly accomplished feedback loop that confounds the possibility to find a clear and unequivocal source text. Without a sense of a definitive ending point to the adaptation process, the film slowly fashions itself as an organism that, it is safe to assume, will continue to evolve beyond its arbitrary ending. Insofar as biological processes are employed as models for cultural processes, the film exemplifies a biocultural framework, as well as its payoff: to do away with the implicit unidirectionality of a more traditional ways of seeing the relationship between media as a relationship between (source and derivative) texts. Instead, the film's greater attention to transformations, evolution, and mutation aligns more closely with a growing 'vital' imagination in media theory that understands adaptive changes as occurring through feedback loops.[11]

I find this framework both helpful and necessary: not only does it champion mutation rather than fidelity, but, within it, adaptation appears more a matter of affect than text, more of an issue of modulation than intertextuality, and a question of life forms rather than authorship.[12] Or, as John Hodgkins proposes, it understands the adaptive process as a type of 'dissemination' of affective intensities 'from one medium to another where they take root and change from within'. This exchange between the texts' and the audiences' 'affective economies' is by definition bidirectional: '[a]ffect drifts both ways', he claims, thus somehow rendering the stability of the 'source' theoretically irrelevant.[13]

The idea of the bidirectionality of both affect and change is crucial to explain the reception of my two case studies not only because of how the protagonists' body image overdetermines the perception of the adaptive process, but also for how this very process might affect the living body that bears this image. Consider Robinson: as the man who broke the colour line in Major League Baseball, he enjoyed unprecedented media visibility and scrutiny, both on and off the field, functioning both as a symbol of the realization of America's democratic ideals and also, should the discrimination he suffered come to light, as a potential magnifying lens for America's profoundly rooted racial hatred and still unaccomplished social equality.[14] In casting Robinson as himself, *The Jackie Robinson Story* was able to defuse this possibility. Instead, in both the film and the book, the narration unfolds with a sense of predetermination, in which Robinson's fitness for the massive task of integration, as well as its successful outcome, are already guaranteed by his very presence on the silver screen. In both, people and places who vehemently resisted Robinson's entrance in organized baseball are omitted or fictionally renamed; episodes of systemic racism are virtually ignored or reframed for dramatic effect; and select individuals, who initially opposed the Integrationist Experiment, are shown developing admiration and affection for him, thus illustrating, as his wife Rachel eloquently put it, that 'Jack made it possible for America to love a black man'.[15]

Within this self-fulfilling structure, so tightly wrapped around Robinson's body, where would we find traces of the adaptation process we might effectively be able to teach? Again, I suggest that those traces are to be sought in the body itself. With this in mind, one would notice something theoretically important occurring in conjunction with Robinson's acting performance in the film: his coveted body is conspicuously heavier than at the time of the events portrayed, a fact that the press read as the condemnable by-product of his newly achieved celebrity status and an indication of the impending corruption of his moral integrity.[16] Yet we can regard this visual discrepancy instead as a signifier of dislocation and crisis of the tautological logic of the film: as much as Robinson's performance of the fictionalized version of himself constructs a highly sutured and suturing text that offered only one point of identification for the spectator ('You'll hit with him! You'll run with him! You'll slide with him!' claimed the poster tagline), his body in the film bears the signs of the very process of 'adaptation' that *he* was subjected to in order to fit within the terms of the post-World War II 'assimilationist imagination'. The carefully concealed process of assimilation he underwent – having to fit in, as well as hold back, deflect, and metabolize the racist abuse to which he was subjected – finally becomes visible *in* his body. More importantly, it is remarked upon and recorded in the reception of the film, despite the expectation of sameness, immutability, and fixity of Robinson's living body, supposed to always remain equal to the image of itself.

It is pedagogically important to realize that this very reading depends on the possibility of accounting for the organic and physiological life of the body that is both the trigger and the destination of the adaptation process. What is needed, then, is a way to push adaptation's biocultural metaphors to the edge of physiology, where we might think of the body as 'living' and not simply as textual, discursive, or even just visual. I find this move in filmmaker Claire Denis's idea of adaptations as *grafts*, which coalesced around Denis's reading of philosopher Jean-Luc Nancy's essay *L'Intrus*, an account of his heart transplant. Through the figure of the 'intruder', Nancy describes the transplant as both a crisis of representation ('Who is the "I" who speaks?' he asks) and the experience of a never fully resolved process of assimilation, always threatened by the possibility of organ rejection. Consistently, Denis conceives of her films – and particularly *The Intruder,* directly inspired by Nancy's essay – as both the graft and the host organism, both the 'outside' and the 'inside' of their 'sources', so that the relationship between the two is not one of derivation, but rather more akin to the negotiation between two competing immune systems.[17]

I am inclined to assess Robinson's casting as the perfect *graft* for the Integration Story in this sense, since he represented at all times its core, its outcome, its expression, and the evidence of its value. In teaching *The Jackie Robinson Story* from this perspective, therefore, one would encourage the identification of the 'immune systems' that have to be reconciled, at both a figurative and a literal level: on the one hand, one would seek evidence of how American visual culture had to accommodate for a black presence in otherwise lily-white media environments,[18] and, on the other hand, how Robinson's living body had to sustain and absorb the price of this assimilation. Thus, a bioculturally inflected attention toward mutation, bidirectionality, and the dissemination of affective intensities are crucial to understanding the two steps I have been outlining here: first, the possibility to see the body within a feedback loop between source and destination; and second, the opportunity to appreciate that, even though this loop is triggered by the specific way in which the black body inhabits the field of vision, the adaptation this same body is forced to undergo is not simply a visual process, but might take place at the level of the 'lived' body as well. I describe this as a *physiological* level, one that is always already implicated in the corporeal connotations of the concept of 'assimilation' itself.

In some respects, Gabourey Sidibe, the actress who plays Precious, finds herself in different circumstances. Her body never becomes the coveted object, a symbol of success and beloved mirror for everything that is supposedly great about American democracy. Hers is not the body that fits all frames, all genres, all social circumstances, in fact re-framing how public life is understood and experienced at a certain point in time. Sidibe's body is affected by the opposite problem: it indexes the difficulty to fit, both within the camera's frame, as well as within the generic and aesthetic understandings of the film. Sidibe's is a 'densely configured black female body', profoundly overdetermined by a condemning blackness compounded by a damning size.[19] The critical reception of the film does not fail to remark this point and, with constant slippages, repeatedly grafts the actress and the role onto one another: '[Precious's] head is a balloon on the body of a zeppelin', writes journalist David Edelstein, 'her cheeks so inflated they squash her eyes into slits. That's part of the movie's XXXtreme social realism, no doubt'.[20]

This 'pornotroping' of the black body – the idea that its very visual presence is intrinsically obscene or that the viewer needs to be *aroused* into empathy[21] – flattens and erases any discussion of form, style, art, and obviously, adaptation, as well as any possibility that Sidibe might ever be anything other than Precious. Rather, the body's obscenity is already *there*: implacable and undeniable. And in compounding one onto the other, the pornographic discourse of a social realism described with a triple X continues to graft an 'excess flesh' onto the character, the actress, and the film itself, a conflation that elsewhere I have rendered typographically as PRECIOUS.[22]

In previous discussions of the film I have argued that this 'excess flesh' is the result of a rhetorical and phenomenological act of catachresis, a way of grafting literal and figural elements as well as a specific cross-referencing of vision and touch triggered by the sight of blackness.[23] Racial catachresis is an affectively charged trope as well as a phenomenological structure that has the ability to trigger the impression of a corporeal growth, as if blackness had the capacity to fill, and overflow from, the very space between literality and figurality, vision and tactility. Racial catachresis is the outcome of an affect that is specific to the perception of the black body as excessive – an affect that from the body itself appears to extend to the terms of its representation.

This is the *graft* at work in *Precious*. We can see it in the flashback scene that reveals Precious's rape by her father. The flashback is triggered by a concussion caused by the remote control that Precious's mother throws at her head, whereby the girl's forward fall onto the kitchen floor is cut in mid-air to transition into a backward fall into the bed where the rape occurs. The father mounting her is seen across rapid cuts accompanied by sounds of bedsprings giving in under pressure, frying eggs, a cat meowing, and eventually the silhouette of the mother in the background – cuts that create a multisensorial experience where food/sex/semen/animality/complicity are all grafted together. Then, through a forward movement of the camera which breaks through the bedroom's ceiling, the same scene becomes also catachrestically grafted onto Precious's fantasy, where she appears as a movie star who is exiting the premiere of her latest film surrounded by a crowd of paparazzi and adoring fans.

A close textual analysis of the sequence shows this very clearly; yet for the pedagogical purposes I am pursuing here one would have to press this point even further, and ask: given this care to frame, re-frame, and emphasize the artistic act that grafts these *opposite* movements together (a forward fall which becomes a backward fall, a forward camera movement which transitions to Precious's body moving from the background to the foreground of the frame), given this complex editing structure that keeps the character's body at the centre of the 'figure–ground relation' between viewer and viewed; given all this, what really triggers the perception of the triple-X realism? What, other than the conviction that some raw quality of the character/actress's body is already the beginning and the end of anything that can be said about it?

Going back to the film's reception, one would notice how Daniels's aesthetic strategy of *mise-en-abyme* in reality backfired: the obscenity of her father's act was effectively grafted onto Precious's body itself, and yet seen as if spilling over to the victim's abject body, absorbed by it, or, even more troubling, stemming from it. Pressing this point further one could suggest that the visual presence of Precious overdetermines the process of adaptation because, unlike Robinson's, her body 'looks like pain' and therefore cannot index any form of adaptability. It cannot be absorbed or metabolized. Furthermore, it is a body silenced by its own size, a fact that explains the novel's focus on Precious's acquisition of literacy. This is a resistant move Margo Crawford describes more properly as *counterliteracy*, because it is developed, just like in the slave narratives, in reaction to expectations of muteness and inanimacy.[24] Yet, as she also argues, 'the novel does not (perhaps cannot) make the fact (the visual sign of traumatic excess) signify as much as it does in the film. The film does not (perhaps cannot) make Precious's writing practices matter as much as they do in the novel'.[25] Yet, what threatens the possibility to perceive the process of adaptation, the possibility to see a distinction between the black body and its representation, is the fact that if literacy is an over-determined question for the disenfranchised black subject, it is even more so for the hypervisible black body. If, as first illustrated by the slave narratives, disenfranchised black subjects can only prove their personhood through their literacy and eloquence, then what type of visual 'eloquence' can attest to an actor's distinct 'personhood' if he/she is already seen as the embodiment of his or her role?[26]

Ultimately Sidibe's/Precious's body does not offer the possibility to imagine its assimilation within the larger context of American visual culture. This is made clear from the film's opening, when we hear Precious's voice narrating over scenes of a typical morning at school. We see the inner city school environment and immediately hear her state her name and express her fantasies: 'My name is Claireece "Precious" Jones. I wish I had a light-skinned boyfriend with really nice hair. But first I want to be in one of those BET videos'. Immediately, however, this fantasy is shut down by Precious's recollection of her mother's comments: 'Mama says I can't dance. She says who would want to see your big ass dancing anyhow?' The issue to emphasize is this: given the number of fantasy sequences in the film that do show her dancing, while showered with attention and fame, who/what is this question really for? The question is rhetorical, within the film's diegetic world, but it does extend outside the text connecting to a larger issue of the possibility for, and the circumstances within which, Sidibe's body could be accommodated in mainstream American visual culture. Is that a body which can/could index success, freedom, joy ... pleasure?

Through this question, the film anticipates its strategic and relentless embracing of the excess of Sidibe's body-as-Precious to bust through the limits of the (generic, aesthetic, cultural, and so on) frame, to spill over onto the space of the viewer and generate an almost unbearable affect.[27] In fact, the camera movements that graft most fantasy sequences to Precious's reality leverage the phenomenological structure of catachresis, as the reversible relationship between the spectator's body and the film's body. Yet, by placing Precious's body at the site of the chiasm, between the viewer's sensorial movement toward the screen and the film's sensible movement toward the viewer, the film also reverses the direction and the investment in this reversible relationship with the screen, leading the viewer to retract from, rather than invest in, the film's sensible figuration.[28] Eventually, it places the viewer at the site of a more troubling chiasm, which connects, in a reversible relation, pleasure and abuse. It is this dynamic of investment and retraction that provides the tool to generate a process of visual counterliteracy in the viewer, a process that parallels the one Precious is undergoing as well. It is the viewer, the film argues, who needs to *adapt.*[29]

In other words, Daniels frames the elements that might lead to the perceived pornorealism of the film within the conventions of art cinema as a means to display Precious's complex affective and psychological world, and to introduce mechanisms of cinematic reflexivity that counteract the flattening of a subject that the XXXtreme realist reading insists on approaching as a specimen. These sequences, that is, function as alternative modes of visualization of what Sidibe's 'body can do',[30] for the benefit of the character, but more so for the audience. By visualizing Precious's fantasies the film allows her to graft herself within entirely new frames, situations, and genres, and therefore *test,* rather than *fall within,* the limitations of the audience's assimilationist imagination.[31]

To conclude, as an adaptation *Precious* is affected by multiple grafts: grafts related to the character's and actress's overembodiment, to the generic constraints of social realism, to the expectation that this subject matter can only be served by that genre, and to the fact that, even though the adaptation chronicles Precious's acquisition of independence from her abusive mother as well as literacy and subjective agency, she remains visually unchanged. Unlike Mariah Carey, who underwent a process of uglification to acquire a certain measure of 'invisibility' and 'plainliness' to play the part of the compassionate social worker in the film, Gabby, as Daniels pointed out, would not 'take off her [fat] suit' after the end of the shoot. Unlike Mariah Carey, who had to be de-glammed to 'belong' in the film's grim world, the sequences of Precious's glamorous fantasies continue to strike, disturb, and upset a viewing public that cannot *assimilate* what it perceives as incongruous: the sight of *that* liberated body.

By challenging some of the main tenets of an adaptation discourse that has already *evolved* toward a biocultural understanding of its own premises, these two case studies compel us to think about the moment, circumstances, and repercussions of embodiment not as an afterthought within a more serious and rigorous engagement with different textualities, but, especially for some subjects, as an element that overdetermines the adaptation process from the beginning. Seen within a biocultural framework, in the broad sense outlined here, and more specifically within the physiological connotations made available by the notion of the 'graft', they urge us to understand adaptation as a bidirectional relationship with the environment in which it occurs – an approach that, in the cases discussed, ultimately sheds light on the very limitations of the assimilationist imagination that coalesces around these bodies. More profoundly, within this framework 'adaptation' itself emerges as a profoundly melancholic process. It is melancholic in the Freudian sense that Anne Cheng has mobilized to think about the place of the Other's body in American literature and visual culture, as a body that is both expelled and desired, coveted and rejected, retained and lost, without possibility of substitution or resolution.[32] From this point of view the study of adaptation can really showcase its ability to reach beyond its own disciplinary boundaries and bring into focus important features of the circumstances in which it takes place: that is, the melancholic nature of American literature, cinema, and visual culture's relationship to race. And possibly, the melancholic nature of adaptation studies as well.

Acknowledgements

The author wishes to thank Charles Fox, whose insightful comments have greatly strengthened the pedagogical dimension of this chapter, as well as Drew Ayers for his kind reading of an early draft.

Notes

1. For the above-mentioned analysis of the film's reception see Alessandra Raengo, 'A Necessary Signifier: The Body as Author and Text in *The Jackie Robinson Story*', *Adaptation* 1 (2), 2008.
2. On the novel see at least Sika A. Dagbovie-Mullins, 'From Living to Eat to Writing to Live: Metaphors of Consumption and Production in Sapphire's *Push*', *African American Review* 44 (3), 2010 and Kathryn Bond Stockton,

'Somewhere a Child Is Desiring You: A Thought Experiment for Those Not in Need/Kid Orientalism: How a Global Future for Child Sexuality is Now Surfacing', Paper presented at the *Center for 20th Century Studies*, University of Wisconsin-Milwaukee, 2012.

3. Lee Daniels, 'A Precious Ensemble', in *Featurette* on the DVD for the film *Precious: Based on the Novel 'Push' by Sapphire* (US: Lionsgate, 2009).

4. For an analysis of the film's reception see Alessandra Raengo, 'Shadowboxing: Lee Daniels's Non-Representational Cinema', in *Contemporary Black American Cinema: Race, Gender, and Sexuality at the Movies*, ed. Mia Mask (New York: Routledge, 2012) and *On the Sleeve of the Visual: Race as Face Value* (Hannover: Dartmouth College Press, 2013), Chapter 2. See also the insightful special issue of *Black Camera*, 4 (1), 2012, devoted to the film, which has greatly consolidated my thoughts in relation to the pedagogical potential of this adaptation.

5. Frantz Fanon, *Black Skin, White Masks* (New York: Grove Press, 2008) and Nicole Fleetwood, *Troubling Vision: Performance, Visuality, and Blackness* (Chicago: University of Chicago Press, 2011).

6. Robert Stam describes iconophobia as the distrust towards embodiment, that is, toward the way a literary character is actualized in the concrete body, gesture, and voice of a film actor. See 'Introduction: The Theory and Practice of Adaptation', in *Literature and Film: A Guide to the Theory and Practice of Film Adaptation*, eds Robert Stam and Alessandra Raengo (Malden and Oxford: Blackwell, 2005).

7. See my essay 'A Necessary Signifier' mentioned above, as well as Chapter 2 in my *On the Sleeve of the Visual*.

8. See at least Kamilla Elliott, 'The Adaptation of Adaptation: A Dialogue between the Arts and Sciences', in *Adaptation and Cultural Appropriation*, eds Pascal Nicklas and Oliver Lindner (Berlin: De Gruyter, 2012), where she identifies a 'genetic turn' in adaptation studies already in Seymour Chatman, *Story and Discourse: Narrative Structure in Fiction and Film* (Ithaca, NY: Cornell University Press, 1978). She also cites the examples of Sarah Cardwell, *Adaptation Revisited: Television and the Classic Novel* (Manchester: Manchester University Press, 2002) and Julie Sanders, *Adaptation and Appropriation* (London: Routledge, 2006). I have derived the term 'biocultural' from Andrea S. Wiley, 'Adaptation and the Biocultural Paradigm in Medical Anthropology: A Critical Review', *Medical Anthropology Quarterly* 6 (3), 1992, 216–236.

9. Stam, 'The Theory and Practice of Adaptation', p. 3.

10. Linda Hutcheon and Siobhan O'Flynn, *A Theory of Adaptation*, 2nd ed. (London and New York: Routledge, 2013), p. 31.

11. See, at least, Eugene Thacker, *Biomedia* (Minneapolis: University of Minnesota Press, 2004) and the Deleuzian and biosemiotically inflected idea of the vitality of media in Jussi Parikka, *Insect Media: An Archaeology of Animals and Technology* (Minneapolis: University of Minnesota Press, 2010).

12. This is not to say that these issues no longer matter (see Jack Boozer, ed. *Authorship in Film Adaptation* (Austin: University of Texas Press, 2008)), but that they have to be placed alongside other considerations developed

under what I have described as a biocultural framework. I have found to be extremely helpful the chapter by Frank P. Tomasulo, 'From Susan Orlean's *The Orchid Thief* to Charlie (and "Donald") Kaufman's Screenplay to Spike Jonze's Film', in this same collection.

13. John Hodgkins, *The Drift: Affect, Adaptation, and New Perspectives on Fidelity* (New York: Bloomsbury, 2013), pp. 2 and 18.

14. Gerald Early, 'American Integration, Black Heroism, and the Meaning of Jackie Robinson', *The Chronicle of Higher Education* (1997).

15. Ken Burns, *Baseball*, DVD, directed by Ken Burns (1994): "6th Inning".

16. See at least 'Pauch May Take Punch out of Robby', *Chicago Defender* 25 February 1950.

17. The films are *Beau Travail* (1999), inspired by Herman Melville's novel *Billy Budd*, and *The Intruder* (2004), inspired by philosopher Jean-Luc Nancy's essay 'L'intrus', (Paris: Galilée, 2000). See Jean-Philippe Renouard and Lise Wajeman, 'The Weight of the Here and Now: Conversation with Claire Denis, 2001', and James S. Williams, 'O Heave! O Heave Away, Heave! O Heave!': Working through the Author in *Beau Travail*', both in *Journal of European Studies* 34 (1–2), 2004.

18. In my essay on the film I give several examples of this visual accommodation, the most glamorous being the harmonizing aesthetics used in the 1947 *Time* magazine cover, where Robinson's face is swallowed up by a sea of white baseballs.

19. Régine Michelle Jean Charles, '"I Think I Was Rape": Black Feminist Readings of Affect and Incest in Precious', *Black Camera* 4 (1), 2012, 143.

20. David Edelstein, 'When Push Comes to Shove', *New York*, 1 November 2009. Cited in Carol Henderson, 'The Abject and the Grotesque: Broken Bodies, Broken Dreams, and the Lost Promise of Harlem', *Black Camera* 4 (1), 2012, 210.

21. For the idea of 'pornotropes' see Hortense J. Spillers, 'Mama's Baby, Papa's Maybe. An American Grammar Book', *Diacritics* 17 (2), 1987, 65–81. For an account of the complicated relationship between empathy, victimization, and desire see also Saidiya V. Hartman, *Scenes of Subjection: Terror, Slavery, and Self-Making in Nineteenth-Century America* (New York: Oxford University Press, 1997).

22. For this argument and a close analysis of the film see Alessandra Raengo, 'Shadowboxing', and *On the Sleeve of the Visual*, pp. 60–8. Nicole Fleetwood employs the expression 'excess flesh' in her chapter on 'colorism' in *Troubling Vision*, pp. 71–104.

23. Catachresis is the trope we use to attribute a name to something that does not have one, by making metaphorical associations, and then forgetting that we did. For instance: the leg of the chair, or the feet of the mountain. Or, for example: black. Catachresis grafts literal and figural elements (it is figurative but it *performs* as if literal) in ways that have profound phenomenological implications because they create a cross-referencing between vision and touch. See at least Paul de Man, 'The Epistemology of Metaphor', *Critical Inquiry* 5 (1), 1978; Lee Edelman, *Transmemberment of Song: Hart Crane's Anatomies of Rhetoric and Desire*

(Stanford: Stanford University Press, 1987) and Vivian Sobchack, 'What My Fingers Knew: The Cinesthetic Subject, or Vision in the Flesh', in *Carnal Thoughts. Embodiment and Moving Image Culture* (Berkeley and Los Angeles: University of California Press, 2004).

24. Riché Richardson, '*Push, Precious*, and New Narratives of Slavery in Harlem', *Black Camera* 4 (1), 2012, argues that both novel and film share formal traits with slave narratives. On the connection between literacy and personhood see Henry Louis Gates, Jr., *The Signifying Monkey: A Theory of African-American Literary Criticism* (New York: Oxford University Press, 1988). On the intermingling of race and inanimacy see Mel Y. Chen, *Animacies: Biopolitics, Racial Mattering, and Queer Affect* (Durham, NC: Duke University Press, 2012).

25. Crawford, 'The Counterliteracy of Postmelancholy', p. 202.

26. This is in part a paraphrase of the question posed in Crawford, 'The Counterliteracy of Postmelancholy', p. 205.

27. Henderson reports Oprah's reaction after seeing the film, which she describes as ecstatic excess she registered in her own body. Carol E. Henderson, 'The Abject and the Grotesque: Broken Bodies, Broken Dreams, and the Lost Promise of Harlem', *Black Camera* 4 (1), 2012, 92.

28. As Sobchack explains, the term *cinesthetic* is meant to comprise the way in which the cinematic experience triggers and relies on both synaesthesia (or intersensoriality) and coenaesthesia (the perception of a person's whole sensorial being). At stake is the possibility to explain how meaning emerges from the conjunction of the spectators' bodies and cinematic representation; see 'What My Fingers Knew', p. 67.

29. In 'Somewhere a Child Is Desiring You' Bond Stockton emphasizes the stunning moment in *Push* in which Precious discovers how to orgasm during her father's abuse. The film has been criticized at times for seemingly shying away from the question of Precious's forms of pleasure, but I believe instead that it has made the provocative choice of leveraging the phenomenological structure of catachresis in order to make the viewer face the complexity of these feelings, between pornorealism and social protest.

30. This is the Deleuzian question that Michele Prettyman Beverly poses in her PhD dissertation 'Phenomenal Bodies: The Metaphysical Possibilities of Post-Black Film and Visual Culture' (Georgia State University, 2012): what can black bodies do in order to transcend, or live *through*, the visual constraints of blackness?

31. I feel compelled to mention that the film affords yet another reading of the physiological connotations of the idea of 'assimilation' in the way Daniels presents Precious's bodily functions – overeating, puking, giving birth, breastfeeding, and so on – as another complex terrain of struggle for both the character and the audience. Not only can Precious hardly be framed, the film appears to argue, but she can hardly be 'metabolized'.

32. Anne Anlin Cheng, *The Melancholy of Race: Psychoanalysis, Assimilation, and Hidden Grief* (New York: Oxford University Press, 2000), p. 10.

9
'Adapting' from School to University: Adaptations in the Transition

Natalie Hayton

The pedagogic value of using film adaptations in the English classroom in further and higher education has come under much debate and scrutiny, inevitably fuelled by attitudes regarding 'literary' and 'popular' culture.[1] The use of fine art to 'illustrate' texts, such as John William Waterhouse's 'The Lady of Shallot' (1888) in conjunction with Lord Alfred Tennyson's poem of the same name (1833 and 1842), or John Everett Millais's *Ophelia* (1852) to encourage a visualization of the action in *Hamlet* are regarded as 'worthy' adaptation comparisons, enabling students to pick out the symbolism used in the image to redirect them back to the text, such as the tapestry in the former, or the suggestion of a bridal gown in the latter. However, film is still seen as 'merely' pleasurable, and 'only' entertaining, and is still more likely to appear as an end of term 'treat' to consolidate knowledge in further education English classes, rather than offering new ways of viewing a text.[2] So, to the undergraduate in English engaging with university-level adaptation studies for the first time without a background in film, reading the image and developing theoretical knowledge in essentially three fields of literature, film, and adaptation, can, initially, be somewhat daunting. The examination of cinematic tropes and symbols is, of course, considered in film and adaptation circles as just as 'worthy' and compelling, but it is not my intention here to dwell on the literary versus popular debate. Rather, I raise this point in relation to the examples that will be deployed throughout this piece. This chapter concentrates on the transition from further education to higher education, and argues that the best way to smooth the transition is to include practical exercises that assist with the development of visual literacy and in acquiring the terminology and theoretical knowledge of a new discipline through an exploration of intertextual techniques, as well as involving students in the creative process via screenwriting and describing their own scenes. Taking examples from an undergraduate course on children's literature and their adaptations (a course designed by Deborah Cartmell), this chapter explores the ways in which students can learn to engage in reading at 'university level', learning sophisticated intertextual and contextual skills. The examples deployed, such as *A Midsummer Night's Dream*, *Alice's Adventures in Wonderland* (1865), *Charlie and the Chocolate Factory* (1964) and the *Harry Potter* series (1997–2007), provide a rich seam of adaptations from text to film, as well as sequels, retellings, and illustrations. My previous research into fairy tales informs the teaching of this course, where all of the texts discussed demonstrate an engagement and reliance on fairy tale tropes and their 'familiar narratives', providing an accessible route for students to engage with the complexity of intertextuality. This means that I adopt a research-led approach to teaching, integrating, and experimenting with my own theories in the field and demonstrating how research and teaching is a cyclical process.

To return to the question of 'worthy' texts, as Deborah Cartmell argues, children's literature, especially 'popular' texts, is often overlooked in adaptation and literary scholarship,[3] being regarded as 'simplistic' or 'heavy-handed' in their moral teaching. While scholarship into the representation of the child and children's literature is growing, with recent publications, such as Kimberley Reynolds's *Children's Literature: A Very Short Introduction* (2011) and Karen Lury's *The Child in Film: Tears, Fears and Fairy Tales* (2010) as well as the edited collections, *The Cambridge Companion to Children's Literature* (2009), *Children's Literature: Approaches and Territories* (2009), and *Children's Literature: Classic Texts and Contemporary Trends* (2009), there is still very little available on children's adaptations. This marginality is even more germane to a discussion of fairy/folk tales, as their origins in an oral culture means that their 'lack' of a definitive author and continual adaptation through retelling renders knowledge of an ur-text impossible. This means they too are frequently dismissed, because they cannot be neatly placed within a traditional literary value structure. To a certain extent fairy tales have also been overlooked in adaptation studies as they cannot be discussed in terms of fidelity, as 'homage to a source', or whether an adaptation has 'captured the essence of an author's work', as these theoretical approaches are simply not applicable. Scholarship has been slow to respond to the popularity of fairy tale adaptations on screen in the last decade (for adults and children), which includes Catherine Hardwicke's *Red Riding Hood* (2011), Julia Leigh's *Sleeping Beauty* (2011) and Tommy Wirkola's *Hansel and Gretel: Witch Hunters* (2013). These three films alone demonstrate the versatility of fairy tale adaptations in terms of genre, as the first film draws on the conventions of the dark romance, the second is a haunting portrait of the sex industry, and the third is an action-packed adventure/horror movie. Recent publications have attempted to recognize the significant and prominent position of fairy tales in cultural productions with Pauline Greenhill and Sidney Eve Matrix's edited collection *Fairy Tale Films: Visions of Ambiguity* (2010) and Jack Zipes's *The Enchanted Screen* (2011). Both of these works reference (but do not fully interrogate) the intertextual role that fairy tales also frequently play in productions. Elsewhere I have referred to the appearance of fairy tale characters and tropes within works telling another story as 'cameos', as they 'possess' the screen and the work briefly in a way that offers a multitude of palimpsestic readings, and, in some instances, they are arguably produced unconsciously.[4] These brief appearances can influence an audience's response to a character or scene through the use of semiotically charged props, such as a red cloak to invoke Red Riding Hood or a white rose to reference 'Beauty and the Beast', or by simply recalling the romance of the one-true-love paradigm associated with Cinderella's lost slipper. These intertextual moments are so familiar to audiences, partly due to the pervasive nature of fairy tales in contemporary advertising and film, but also because they have a long visual history associated with illustrated children's books; and they are for many of us our first experiences with narratives and literature. As Zipes explains, 'For each one of the classic fairy tales there are thousands of illustrated books. And yet, despite this enormous quantity, most are duplications or slightly varied images of standardized characters and scenes which have prevailed over the years'.[5] The reproduction of these images renders fairy tale appropriations, as Sarah Bonner claims, as 'ubiquitous' but also 'invisible', as their familiarity means that they are recognized but not always consciously acknowledged.[6] While there are many apocryphal folk tales that have fallen out of popularity, the unique position that a handful of fairy tales occupy in the cultural collective, such as 'Snow White', 'Sleeping Beauty', and 'Little Red Riding Hood' means that we do not even have to specifically recall our literary experience of reading these texts, as the knowledge of these stories permeates Western culture in multiple ways, making them ideal resources for teaching adaptation studies.[7]

In their first year of an undergraduate course, adaptation students are always keen to develop their visual literacy and acquire the terminology to describe their readings. In many ways this is a crucial part of getting to grips with adaptation studies, because, as we are all (students and scholars) aware, the field itself is replete with terms and taxonomies to describe adaptation processes.[8] As Cutchins says, 'We must teach students a usable taxonomy, a language that will allow them to recognize, abstract, and make sense of what they encounter within and between these texts.'[9] This can be difficult when simply identifying what type of adaptation one is engaging with can be confusing, selecting whether to use Geoffrey Wagner's model of transposition, commentary, analogy or David Bordwell's and Kristin Thompson's definitions of referential, explicit, implicit, and symptomatic; and there are many others to choose from.[10] Having said that, I would argue that the desire for a 'fixed' approach is questionable and that the plurality and fluidity of many adaptation taxonomies and theories is in fact their strength; the process of adaptation is one of exchange and often consists of the overlapping of narratives between media, and therefore there is no limit to how they may overlap and how one might wish to describe them. However, to the first-year undergraduate in search of a definitive answer, this approach, rather than exhibiting a diverse adaptation 'toolkit' may at first seem rather obscure and unhelpful. In this context, intertextuality as a conceptual framework through which to view adaptations is an ideal starting point for students making the transition from further education to university, because as well as there being numerous theoretical models for students to engage with and choose from, more importantly, the focus when exploring intertextual relationships is on the texts themselves: how they interact with each other, and what and how an idea is being conveyed through other works, thus providing students with the opportunity to develop their visual literacy and theoretical knowledge at the same time.

Identifying the intertextual appropriation of fairy tales in children's literature and their adaptations provides an enjoyable way for students to demonstrate their understanding of adaptation techniques as well as thinking about why we tell stories, and why we continue to tell the same stories. Intertextuality and self-reflexivity are not only the mainstays of contemporary works as a way of referencing influences and creating a layered textual experience, they have been a part of our enjoyment of stories for centuries. The ability to recognize familiar tropes and images is a fundamental part of storytelling and the longevity of fairy tales is perhaps a testament to this fact. As Hutcheon explains, the need for repetition is one of the ways in which we understand the process of adaptation itself:

> Like ritual ... repetition brings comfort, a fuller understanding, and the confidence that comes with the sense of knowing what is about to happen next ... the real comfort lies in the simple act of almost but not quite repeating, in the revisiting of a theme with variations.[11]

In terms of retelling fairy tales on screen, whether we are viewing for pleasure or engaging in critical appraisal, the same enjoyment in 'repetition' can be found, and this also translates into the classroom as students gain confidence by identifying a reference to a familiar fairy tale while considering the significance and effects of the 'variations' that an adaptation has employed. Once students have overcome their reservations to acknowledge that they are aware of fairy tale plots and characters ('I don't read fairy tales' can sometimes be heard at the beginning of this exercise) and engage in the identification process by coupling their existing cultural knowledge of fairy tales with different types of intertextuality (allusion, appropriation, un/conscious) the theory no longer seems so intimidating or potentially alienating, allowing for other connections to be made more freely as well as uniting the course material. An example of this can be seen in a work of children's literature that has been discussed in terms of intertextuality – even accused of being derivative because of its reliance on both literary and popular references. J. K. Rowling's *Harry Potter* series has been compared with myths of the chosen one, *Star Wars*, the Narnia books, and *The Wizard of Oz*, and its character Hagrid with Dr Doolittle, Mary Poppins, and Darth Vader,[12] to mention a few. But throughout, there are also some unmistakable fairy tale moments, with 'cameos' of Cinderella perhaps topping the intertextual billing. This is hardly surprising, as Cinderella is arguably the most adapted fairy tale of them all and works especially well with teen and high school films and television series, with its inevitable make-over sequence and ball/prom (*The Princess Diaries* (2001), *Sabrina* (1996–2003), and *A Cinderella Story* (2004) all engage with this format). In *Harry Potter and the Philosopher's Stone* (novel and film (1997 and 2001)) Harry clearly takes on a Cinderella role, and students enjoy the fact that here is a male Cinderella, as well as listing commonalities between them: Harry lives in the cupboard under the stairs, is dressed in his cousin Dudley's hand-me-down clothes, and is seen carrying out household chores at the beck-and-call of the Dursleys. By identifying this part of the book as engaging with a familiar fairy tale story, students are encouraged to consider the ideological implications of this and the acculturating messages associated with the literary fairy tale and Disney appropriation that typically promotes gender stereotypes and conformity.[13] Students' initial response is that Rowling is subverting or challenging gender stereotypes by creating a male Cinderella, but when asked to consider the portrayal of the characters throughout the books and the way they are all paired off at the end of the series, more traditional heterosexual dynamics are exposed.[14] This is then compounded by the interrogation of another 'Cinderella' moment in the fourth book, *Harry Potter and the Goblet of Fire* (2000), when the fairy tale is invoked again at the Yule Ball as Hermione undergoes the make-over treatment associated with the fairy tale heroine, including some magical orthodontics. The ball ends at midnight with Ron and Hermione quarrelling, as the latter points out that Ron should have asked her to the ball before someone else did rather than as a last resort, reinforcing the idea that the 'prince' must do the wooing. The film takes this further by depicting Hermione sitting on the hall staircase as she dejectedly removes and then throws her 'slipper' to the ground because her 'prince', Ron, has failed to declare his feelings. The visual signifiers of the make-over and the slipper reinforce the importance of feminine beauty and the concept of a one-true-love, which the adaptation represents by visually invoking the fairy tale through a familiar trope.

While the *Harry Potter* books and films contain some very important issues to discuss in the classroom, such as gender stereotypes and racial identity (muggles, wizards, and mudbloods) the veritable treasure hunt that the works offer in terms of identifying intertextual references makes for some useful readings and comparisons, and the mix of popular, literary, classical, and most importantly, the familiar, means that students do not feel overwhelmed by the idea of looking for mysteriously 'hidden' or 'high-brow' meanings. As Dennis Cutchins argues, intertextuality is perhaps one of the fundamental principles when teaching or studying adaptations, as 'adaptation studies seeks to understand not individual texts, but rather the relationships that exist between texts'.[15] Furthermore, Cartmell specifically examines this relationship between children's literature and their adaptations, asserting that it is built on reliance: 'The reflexivity apparent in both [children's] film and literature emphasizes both hostility and dependency, making the reading and spectating doubly complex and doubly pleasurable'.[16] She cites and examines Roald Dahl's *Charlie and the Chocolate Factory* and the 1971 adaptation, *Willy Wonka and the Chocolate Factory*, directed by Mel Stuart, as a prime example, explaining how the former denigrates screen entertainment, while the latter 'aspires' to 'literariness' through aural intertextual quotation (Shakespeare's *The Merchant of Venice* (ca. 1596), Oscar Wilde's *The Importance of Being Earnest* (1895)). While this analysis provides students with an insight into the hierarchical conflict between literature and film, as well the complexity of intertextual frameworks, *Charlie* is very useful when considering the development of visual literacy and how intertextuality functions beyond referencing other fictional works. As Cutchins argues, it is important not only to demonstrate to students how to interpret images and intertexts, but also to consider their role in ideological terms:

> Texts are always inter-texts, and borrow, rework, and adapt each other in complex ways, but at the same time, we can discern specific forces (social, economic, historical, and authorial) at work in particular texts and intertexts – that is to say, in specific 'adaptations'.[17]

Charlie and the Chocolate Factory can also be thought of in terms of a 'Cinderella' story as the protagonist follows the 'rags to riches' trajectory associated with the story, and many students are interested in approaching this text through a critique of capitalism. However, this often generates some interesting and contradictory feelings amongst the class as their memory of a text and its beloved author and characters suddenly transforms, and not always in a way they would like. Revisiting children's literature as an adult and applying a critical appraisal can often yield some surprising and upsetting results. While studying Roald Dahl's text the benevolence of Willy Wonka in his treatment of the Oompa-Loompas is typically not questioned by students until the class is confronted with a particular still from Tim Burton's 2005 adaptation. The image depicts the Oompa-Loompas sitting in Wonka's boat in rows like galley-slaves, oars in hand, with drummer behind them, waiting to row the visitors along the chocolate river. The Oompa-Loompas are also computer-generated, so that the image of Deep Roy (the single actor used to represent the whole race) is replicated to create a race of identical people all dressed in blue PVC factory uniforms. The familiar image of slavery provokes intense debate, with some students readily acknowledging the problematic relationship of the factory owner and his 'workers' originating in Dahl's text, while others feel automatically compelled to defend a beloved author and story associated with their childhood, asserting that Burton is to 'blame' for a racist portrayal. Although at first many read the chapter 'The Oompa-Loompas' as a 'rescue mission', when combined with Burton's image, the language Dahl uses, such as 'imported', 'shipped', and 'smuggled',[18] suddenly becomes much more significant, especially when considering contemporary debates regarding immigration and human trafficking. What is perhaps most significant here is the effective way that Burton draws on a familiar historical/colonial image to offer a commentary on Dahl's text in a way that does not condemn or condone, but merely asks the viewer to consider the imagery and issues (race and exploitation), raised in children's literature, regardless of whether it is produced wittingly or not, while contemplating its significance for each contemporaneous audience. This is made even more compelling when Burton's choice is combined with the knowledge that Dahl originally described the Oompa-Loompas in the 1977 text as 'black pygmies' with accompanying illustrations by Faith Jaques.[19] Using such overt images again allows students to develop their visual literacy by deconstructing the details: questioning the significance of the computer-generated figures of the Oompa-Loompas so that they are all identical, and considering the conflation of historical periods through the image of Roman galley slaves and drummer dressed in modern synthetic 'factory' uniforms. The issue of race is particularly significant when considering children's literature, as predominantly white characters populate these works, including the examples used here, and very few fairy tales have been adapted with multiculturalism in mind, opening up the intertextual debate to consider Genette's architextual structures. Drawing on Barthesian ideas of intertexuality, Brown argues that, 'When the literary text is situated in an intertextuality of interpretation and theory, it becomes more approachable by being more connected to the "real world" issues of today and yesterday.'[20] And this is precisely what the examples here have so far shown, whether in relation to ideological paradigms or historical events.

Cutchins also argues that adaptation studies should be pluralistic in its approach and that this in itself is a 'powerful pedagogical tool'. A focus on intertextuality that draws on fairy tales as the ultimate intertextual resources can be used for furthering this approach when teaching. Furthermore, studying children's productions can automatically generate a pluralistic approach, because as well as the fact that the children's literature and film market has produced tie-in merchandize for decades, including toys, clothing, video games (very few adult productions receive similar treatment), as I have already briefly discussed, children's literature is often accompanied, and in some ways bound, to illustrations. An obvious example here is Lewis Carroll's *Alice's Adventures in Wonderland* (1863), and many films, from Norman McLeod's 1933 live-action film, to Disney's animated feature in 1951, to Tim Burton's computer-animated and live-action movie in 2010, all strive to re-create on screen John Tenniel's illustrations of *Alice*. These films clearly demonstrate to students the pains that adaptors go to when creating anticipated scenes, such as falling down the rabbit hole or the meeting with the caterpillar, in an attempt to satisfy audience expectation. Burton again takes this further, as although he spends the first half of the film similarly re-creating those anticipated scenes he also chooses to make his production a sequel, with Alice returning to Wonder/Underland as a young adult, and interweaving a quest narrative for the heroine in which she must wield the vorpal sword to defeat the jabberwocky and rid Underland of the tyrannical Red Queen. As part of her transformative journey Alice must realize her own potency and agency, which her ally, Bayard, says is achieved by following a prescribed route, 'You must not diverge from the path'. Alice rejects this advice, saying 'I'll make the path from here'. So, not only do we have an implicit linguistic reference to 'Little Red Riding Hood' here, where straying from the path is rewarded rather than punished, but it is at this point in the film that the plot deviates from Carroll's texts, aligning the actions of the director with his protagonist.

The creativity involved in developing a visual and aural literacy, reading film and literature, and identifying intertextual frameworks and links, provides students with the confidence to explore their own ideas and theories. Furthermore, this course also offers the students the opportunity to produce their own adaptations, writing a screenplay and/or describing how they would adapt a particular scene. Perhaps because the *Alice* texts are so visual, and have been retold similarly many times, students are always keen to adapt this text when engaging in creative exercises and often pay no heed to fidelity concerns, instead concentrating on what they want their adaptations to convey:

> Adapting texts myself made me fully appreciate the fact that an adaptation does not have to be ... an exact replica of its source material. It showed me the possibilities of using a known story for a new message – and more importantly validated that choice.[21]

While for some the process of adapting scenes from the texts can seem a little challenging at first (as prior to university many have not had the chance to engage in creative practice), for many, this is the best way to engage with adaptation terminology and debates, as it encourages them to not only deconstruct an existing scene but to think about how they would put together their own in detail – considering all aspects of the *mise-en-scène*: costumes, lighting, composition, etc. as well as editing, casting, target market, and thinking about what their piece is conveying to an audience. One of the easiest ways of demonstrating how all these aspects of film construction are vitally important is to consider the conventions of genre by showing several clips of the same scene. For this, you obviously need an example that has undergone the adaptation process numerous times, and one that has been adapted very differently is especially useful. The opening sequences of films are also effective for this exercise, as cinematic works tend to establish genres and thus audience expectation within the first few moments. Three opening sequences from adaptations of *A Midsummer Night's Dream* are ideal for this exercise: Max Reinhardt and William Dieterle's 1933 version adopts the epic approach, beginning with Hippolyta's parade through Athens as the spoils of war; a BBC 1981 adaptation chooses to emphasize the political hostility between Hippolyta and Theseus by depicting them standing at opposite ends of the room on a black and white tile floor as if enacting a game of chess; and Michael Hoffman's adaptation chooses to view the couple alone on a balcony as they oversee their wedding preparations, and so creating a far more romantic scene. Again, the attention to visual and aural details allows the students to identify the signifiers of each genre, and by extension, think about how they would adapt the scene for other genres, as well as how genre frameworks can provide a useful starting point when exploring adaptation processes and creative motivations. This not only allows students to engage with the vocabulary and theory from *within* the process, but also makes them receptive to thinking about the subtleties of adaptation that as experienced film viewers we may forget to acknowledge. For example, when discussing the differences between literature and film in terms of plot, characters, and narrative voice, Albrecht-Crane and Cutchins argue that there is often no need to mention 'fundamental differences. As experienced film viewers we take them for granted. Like the background music in a department store, we have learned to internalize and thus ignore them'.[22] For the undergraduate student it is precisely through a detailed interrogation of film stills and soundtrack, identifying similarities and differences, that the relationship between texts is discovered, allowing them to hypothesize about media hierarchy and/or ideological paradigms. The idea of unconsciousness assumption is particularly germane here, as the same process of internalization is often associated with the unconscious recognition and assimilation of fairy tales. They populate our screen explicitly and implicitly and perhaps one of the most interesting examples (for myself at least) to be found in this course on 'children's' texts is in Michael Hoffman's 1999 adaptation of *A Midsummer Night's Dream*. As Hermia (Anna Friel) and Lysander (Dominic West) are shown entering the forest at night as the lovers elope from Monte Athena and the law that binds a daughter to her father's will, Friel is seen wearing a short red travelling cape that ties at the neck with an upright collar suggestive of a hood. The red cape can be read as an implicit, potentially unconscious, reference to the cautionary tale 'Little Red Riding Hood', emphasizing Hermia's sexual vulnerability, while Lysander's initial attempt at seduction and then desertion (albeit under the influence of Puck's love potion) casts him in a wolfish light. An analysis of 'Little Red Riding Hood' is also very useful here, as students are often unaware of the tale's themes on sexuality, again challenging their ideas on the role and function of children's literature and folklore and how it is appropriated. This then leads to a detailed examination of colour and costumes on screen, and how red specifically affects our perception of female characters, from its association with danger and vulnerability to passion and the *femme fatale*. This is a particularly effective example for this kind of approach, as here – unlike the *Alice, Charlie,* and *Harry Potter* books where there are very cinematic descriptions or illustrations – there is no textual counterpart from the source for adaptors to rely on: the visualization of Hermia's cape is purely a cinematic invention.

In terms of considering the representation of gender and sexuality in *A Midsummer Night's Dream,* I also ask the students to consider Demetrius's speech to Helena prior to this scene:

> You do impeach your modesty too much
> To leave the city and commit yourself
> Into the hands of one that loves you not,
> To trust the opportunity of night
> And the ill counsel of a desert place
> With the rich worth of your virginity.[23]

This dialogue not only reinforces the interpretation of Hermia as a Red Riding Hood figure in terms of the portrayal of sexual danger, it also allows students to think about the role of the forest itself, not only a site of magic and fairies, but, as in 'Little Red Riding Hood', a place of transformation and peril. From here students can interrogate and compare how the theme of sexuality and sexual danger that is a part of Shakespeare's text has been combined with a fairy tale trope for the purpose of film, as well as considering whether Shakespeare and Hoffman are offering commentaries on, or reinforcing, the patriarchal oppression of young women.

As this piece illustrates, an exploration of the way in which fairy tales intersect with children's literature potentially liberates undergraduate students from some of the misconceptions they may have about adaptation studies, as these works de-centre the notion that only canonical texts are worth examining in an adaptation context. Students consulting the library shelves for adaptation textbooks in search of clarifying terminology and theories can be forgiven for initially assuming that adaptation studies is primarily concerned with the transposition of canonical texts, as the number of books dedicated to Heritage, Shakespeare, Austen, and Dickens, for example, far outweighs discussion of the popular or marginal. These are, obviously, all worthy areas of examination, and as my final textual example demonstrates, even fairy tales can be used here to further understanding about intertextual systems, reminding us that adaptation is fundamentally a cyclical process, not only in terms of the way texts alter over time and across media, but in the way research informs teaching and vice versa. This approach supports James Naremore's proposal that adaptation studies should become more central in the Humanities:

> The study of adaptation needs to be joined with the study of recycling, remaking, and every other form of retelling in the age of mechanical reproduction and electronic communication. By this means, adaptation will become part of a general theory of repetition, and adaptation study will move from the margins to the center of contemporary media studies.[24]

Albrecht-Crane and Cutchins use this passage to introduce their edited collection, *Adaptation Studies: New Approaches*, but the proposal to move adaptation studies to the centre of contemporary media studies is also relevant to my own research-led teaching agenda in terms of promoting fairy tales as the ultimate intertexts in adult and children's cultural productions. Here, I hope I have demonstrated how utilizing fairy tales can enable an engagement with adaptation theories, so that through the familiar, what is new to the student (namely, adaptation terminology and debates) becomes more accessible, and in a way that counters conservative reactions to adaptations themselves. Fairy tales, perhaps more than any other texts, illustrate for students the narrative continuum of recycling and remaking without the reactionary trappings of fidelity and 'essence' debates, and with examples ranging far beyond children's literature, this knowledge makes them invaluable teaching resources.

Notes

1. For further reading on this debate, see John Broughton's 'How Youth and Popular Culture Meet Resistance in Education', in *Film, Politics, and Education: Cinematic Pedagogy Across the Disciplines*, ed. Kevin Shawn Sealey (New York: Peter Lang Publishing, 2008) and Thomas Leitch's 'How to Teach Film Adaptations, and Why', in *The Pedagogy of Adaptation*, eds Dennis Cutchins, Laurence Raw and James M. Welsh (Plymouth: Scarecrow Press, 2010).

2. Attitudes to cinema in the classroom in terms of 'reading reinforcement' and pleasure are discussed in detail by John Broughton in 'Inconvenient Feet: How Youth and Popular Culture Meet Resistance in Education', in *Film, Politics, and Education: Cinematic Pedagogy Across the Disciplines*, ed., Kevin Shawn Sealey (New York: Peter Lang Publishing, 2008), pp. 17–42 and by Kevin Shawn Sealey in his 'Introduction' to the edited collection, pp. 1–16.

3. For further reading see Deborah Cartmell's 'Adapting Children's Literature', in *The Cambridge Companion to Literature on Screen*, eds Deborah Cartmell and Imelda Whelehan (Cambridge: Cambridge University Press, 2007), pp. 167–180.

4. My doctoral thesis, *'Little Red Riding Hood' in the 21st Century: adaptation, archetypes, and the appropriation of a fairy tale* includes a chapter that explores the intertextual processes involved in the appropriation of fairy tales, called: 'Little Red Riding Hood as "Cameo" in Film and Television' and includes an examination of David Peace's Red Riding quartet (1999–2002) and its adaptations made for television (2009), Guillermo del Torro's *Pan's Labyrinth* (2006), and the BBC family show *Merlin* (2008–2012), and many more.

5. Jack Zipes, *The Trials and Tribulations of 'Little Red Riding Hood'* (London: Routledge, 1993), p. 335.

6. Sarah Bonner, 'Visualising Little Red Riding Hood', *Journal of the Graduate Society* 2, 2006.

7. As many critics have discussed, including, Jack Zipes in *Fairy Tales and the Art of Subversion* (New York: Routledge, 1983) and Elizabeth Bell in her 'Introduction' to *From Mouse to Mermaid: the politics of film, gender and culture*, eds Elizabeth Bell, Linda Haas, and Laura Sells (Indianapolis: Indiana University Press, 1995), the first point of contact with fairy tales for contemporary audiences is typically through Disney films and their accompanying productions and merchandize, and often in a way that usurps a literary text.

8. The many theories on intertextuality typically draw on Julia Kristeva's work in *Desire in Language: a Semiotic Approach to Literature and Art* (1980; rpt. Oxford: Blackwell, 1981), and Gérard Genette's *Palimpsests* (1982; rpt. Nebraska: University of Nebraska Press, 1997). Two contemporary approaches to a taxonomy of adaptation studies can be found in Kamilla Elliott's *Re/thinking the Novel/Film Debate* (Cambridge: Cambridge

University Press, 2003), and Thomas Leitch's *Adaptation and its Discontents* (Baltimore: The John Hopkins University Press, 2007).

 9. Dennis Cutchins, Laurence Raw, and James M. Welsh, 'Introduction', in *The Pedagogy of Adaptation*, p. xvi.

10. For further reading on these enduring approaches see Geoffrey Wagner's *The Novel and the Cinema* (New Jersey: Fairleigh Dickinson University Press, 1989), and David Bordwell's and Kristin Thompson's *Film Art: An Introduction* (New York: McGraw-Hill, 2007).

11. Linda Hutcheon, *A Theory of Adaptation* (New York: Routledge), 2006, p. 115.

12. I have taken this from Deborah Cartmell's notes for her first-year English course at De Montfort University (2012). For further reading on intertextuality in the *Harry Potter* series see Philip Nel's *J. K. Rowling's Harry Potter Novels: A Guide* (New York: Continuum, 2001), and Deborah Cartmell's and Imelda Whelehan's 'Harry Potter and the Fidelity Debate', in *Books in Motion: Adaptation, Intertextuality and Authorship*, ed. Mireia Aragay (Amsterdam: Rodopi, 2005).

13. For further reading see Jack Zipes's *Fairy Tales and the Art of Subversion* (New York: Routledge, 1983), and Marina Warner's *From the Beast to the Blonde* (London: Vintage, 1995).

14. For further reading on gender in the *Harry Potter* series see Ximena Gallardo-C's and C. Jason Smith's 'Cinderfella: J. K. Rowling's Wily Web of Gender', in *Reading Harry Potter: Critical Essays*, ed. Giselle Liza Anatol (Connecticut: Praeger, 2003).

15. Cutchins, Raw, and Welsh, 'Introduction', p. xii.

16. Deborah Cartmell, 'Adapting Children's Literature', p. 179.

17. Christa Albrecht-Crane and Dennis Cutchins, 'Introduction: New Beginnings for Adaptation Studies', in *Adaptation Studies: New Approaches*, eds Christa Albrecht-Crane and Dennis Cutchins (New Jersey: Rosemont, 2010), p. 19.

18. Roald Dahl, *Charlie and the Chocolate Factory* (London: Puffin Books, 1985), pp. 78–80.

19. For further reading on race in *Charlie and the Chocolate Factory* see Dominic Cheetham's '*Charlie and the Chocolate Factory*: Versions and Changes', *English Literature and Language* 42, 2006, 77–96.

20. Kathleen Brown, *Teaching Literary Theory Using Adaptations* (North Carolina: McFarland 2009), p. 13.

21. Student Testimonial: June 2013.

22. Albrecht-Crane and Cutchins, 'Introduction', p. 14.

23. William Shakespeare, *A Midsummer Night's Dream*, ed. Harold F. Brooks (London: Methuen, 1979) (II i 214–19).

24. James Naremore, *Film Adaptation* (New Jersey: Rutgers University Press, 2000), p. 15.

10
Coming Soon ... Teaching the Contemporaneous Adaptation

Rachel Carroll

A range of pedagogic, disciplinary, and institutional factors can inform the construction of a curriculum for a course on film and television adaptations; among these factors, the availability of published scholarship on the set texts (whether literary, film, or television) may be a key concern for tutors, students, and validating committees alike. These pressures might mean that in some circumstances those adaptations that have attracted significant academic interest are more likely to be adopted than those that have been overlooked, and in this way emerging canons can become self-perpetuating (see Cobb, this volume). Of course, the very notion of the canon has been critically contested and its potential complicity in hierarchies of cultural power and value interrogated, especially in relation to gender, class, and race. However, questions of canon persist, and perhaps especially so when a field of study is relatively new and where the existence of a demonstrable canon might be seen as a necessary condition for disciplinary credibility. In this context it may seem perverse to focus on adaptations which, by definition, offer no supporting critical apparatus. This chapter seeks to explore the value and benefits of teaching contemporaneous adaptations, by which I mean film or television adaptations whose release or broadcast is concurrent with the delivery of the teaching programme; it will do so through a focus on a specific case study in pedagogic practice – an active learning strategy presented under the title of 'Adaptation Watch'.[1]

Students participating in the Adaptation Watch exercise are asked to monitor the discourses of publicity and reception which precede and follow a film or television adaptation whose broadcast or release is concurrent with the course of the module. Working independently, both as individuals and in small groups, students gather and collate evidence from a range of sources – whether print, broadcast, or online – including previews, reviews, interviews, trailers, posters, prizes, awards, and merchandising; this material then forms the basis of group discussion. Significantly, for this task students are *not* required or expected to read the source text, as is standard pedagogic practice where adaptations are concerned; here the emphasis is placed on the televisual, cinematic, and critical contexts in which film and television adaptations are produced and consumed. This task has been employed in two contexts, both taking the form of final-year option modules offered within an English Honours programme at a UK university.[2] The first context is a module dedicated to the study of film and television adaptations that aims to explore the key critical, contextual, and historical contexts in which adaptation as a cultural practice can be understood. In this context the Adaptation Watch task is an integral part of a teaching programme that also incorporates the close comparative analysis of a selection of film and television adaptations and their source texts. The second context is a module on twenty-first century literary culture which aims to examine the changing conditions of literary production, consumption, and reception and their impact on books as a cultural form, authorship as a conceptual category, and reading as a collective experience; in this context film and television adaptations are studied alongside topics including literary prize culture, book clubs and reading groups, public reading events, celebrity authorship, and literary biopics.

The design and delivery of Adaptation Watch was informed by two pedagogic principles. Firstly, while close comparative analysis continues to be an invaluable methodology for adaptation studies, its propensity to privilege the literary source text over the adapted text – perhaps especially when taught in English Literature curricula contexts – can be problematic. Through a focus on discourses of publicity and reception this strategy seeks to promote an appreciation of televisual and cinematic contexts. Secondly, this exercise is designed to foster qualities of initiative, autonomy, and independence, and to do so in a context where the drama, suspense, and excitement of 'live' projects are positively mobilized in support of student engagement. Terry Smith suggests that the experience of the 'contemporaneous' is defined by the following qualities: 'its immediacy, its presentness, its instantaneity, its prioritising of the moment over the time, the instant over the epoch, of direct experience of multiplicitous complexity over the singular simplicity of distanced reflection'.[3] In this task, tutor and students alike occupy the identical moment of the contemporary; neither is privileged by the advantage that hindsight affords, and all experience – simultaneously – the same journey of enquiry and discovery. In this way, this exercise aims to dissolve the boundary between culture as an object of canonized study and culture as a lived experience to which we all contribute. Moreover, it seeks to enable students to recognize themselves as active producers – rather than passive consumers – of cultural meaning.

This chapter will offer three Adaptation Watch topics as case studies;[4] it will consider the intertextual relationship between source text, adaptation, and 'remake' in relation to *Brideshead Revisited* (UK, Dir. Julian Jarrold, 2008), the representation of black British history in the classic adaptation with reference to *Wuthering Heights* (UK, Dir. Andrea Arnold, 2011), and the relationship between literary prizes and adaptation, with a focus on postcolonial politics, in *Life of Pi* (US/Taiwan/UK, Dir. Ang Lee, 2012).

Revisiting *Brideshead Revisited*

British director Julian Jarrold's 2007 film *Becoming Jane* brought the aesthetics of the post-Andrew Davies literary adaptation to the task of imagining the life of a classic author. Making no special claim to historical authenticity – and taking some liberties with the known details of her life – this biopic of Jane Austen was nevertheless not denounced as a travesty by Austen enthusiasts. It is perhaps a testament to the new kinds of literary celebrity which have been cultivated by a culture of appropriation and adaptation that it takes its place in the ever-expanding canon of the Austen industry (from Karen Joy Fowler's 1994 novel *The Jane Austen Book Club* to Amy Heckerling's 1995 film *Clueless* to Hank Green and Bernie Su's 2013 web drama *The Lizzie Bennet Diaries*), increasingly taking its cue from the sensibilities of its consumers rather than from any deference to traditional notions of authorial control. The kind of cavalier fidelity evident in *Becoming Jane* seemed to signal an interesting shift in the expanded field of literary adaptation, with the signifiers of a particular kind of 'classic' adaptation being applied to the historic genre of the biopic, and Austen's life imagined as if she were a character in an adaptation of one of her own novels. However, any expectations that Jarrold might bring a similar ingenuity to his next project – the 2008 feature film *Brideshead Revisited* – seem to have been met with disappointment. Indeed, many reviewers compared Jarrold's film unfavourably with the 'original', whose memory loomed large over the marketing and reception of this film. However, the 'original' that most reviewers and audiences had in mind was not Evelyn Waugh's 1945 novel, but its celebrated 1981 television adaptation, directed by Charles Sturridge and Michael Lindsay-Hogg with a screenplay by John Mortimer. As Philip Kemp put it: 'For many [the 1981 adaptation] remains a towering achievement, no less bathed in an aura of romantic nostalgia than the Marchmain family and their great house of Brideshead, in Waugh's original novel'.[5]

In *Film Adaptation and its Discontents: From Gone With the Wind to The Passion of the Christ*, Thomas Leitch observes that the 1981 Granada Television production of *Brideshead Revisited* 'profited from an ... important lesson': 'a classic adaptation did not require a classic original'.[6] A film or television adaptation can acquire a 'classic' status within the canons of adaptation studies for a variety of reasons and this is exemplified in the 1981 *Brideshead Revisited*, which has become a key reference point in the field. Firstly, the broadcast of *Brideshead Revisited* attracted both critical acclaim, in the broadsheet press and beyond, and popular audiences. It was a significant cultural and industrial event, both in terms of popular television viewing memory and in setting new precedents for the commission and production of quality television drama. The 1981 *Brideshead Revisited* has attained a cultural prestige which continues to survive the passage of years; the release of the 2008 *Brideshead Revisited* seems to have acted as an occasion for the public renewal and reaffirmation of its value, now acquiring the additional credential of having withstood the test of time. Secondly, within the field of adaptation studies, *Brideshead Revisited* (1981) is widely recognized as having established key generic signifiers for the classic adaptation, especially in the context of television production and broadcast; as Sarah Cardwell puts it, it 'provided an instigation of various traits of content, style and mood which still define the genre today'.[7] Leitch writes that it was 'the first of the BBC miniseries to establish an aesthetic distinct from either the radio or the theatrical aesthetic of its television predecessors'.[8] In other words, it marks the emergence of the serialized television adaptation as a genre in its own right, rather than as a derivative of its precursors; moreover, this is achieved by the mobilization of specific production values and a particular period aesthetic. *Brideshead Revisited* was first broadcast in the UK not on the BBC, perceived as the traditional home of the classic adaptation, but on ITV, a commercial public service network, airing between October and December 1981 in 11 weekly episodes. Its capacity to attract and retain a mass audience was by no means a foregone conclusion, perhaps especially given its focus on the lives of an aristocratic elite. However, as Cardwell has written: 'The sedate pace of the narrative in *Brideshead*, though arising from fidelity to the source book, was subsequently adopted as a generic stylistic trait, along with other peculiarities of style, such as its particular use of framing and editing'.[9] Moreover, Leitch (and others) attribute its appeal to the seductive visual spectacle it presented: 'Locations from Oxford University to Castle Howard were chosen for maximum visual splendour and sumptuously photographed, and exterior shots carefully planned to include notable or recognizable architectural monuments'.[10] However, it is its charged mobilization of selected signifiers of national cultural heritage which have ensured that *Brideshead Revisited* (1981) has become central to a key set of debates in adaptations studies: those concerning the politics of the heritage film as it emerged in the context of the adversarial politics of Thatcherite Britain. The ideological meanings of nostalgia have been the particular focus of this debate and a yearning for the past is central to a narrative structure driven by the act of 'revisiting'. As Leitch puts it:

> *Brideshead Revisited* was canonized by a television adaptation that embalmed in exhaustive detail and epic length the narrator's achingly nostalgic attitude, at once disillusioned and enduringly romantic, toward a vanished idyllic past and the fugitive promise of social mobility in an England defined by class-consciousness.[11]

In this context, the decision to film the 2008 adaptation of Waugh's novel at the same location as the 1981 production – the historic house, estate, and gardens of Castle Howard in North Yorkshire – served to determine the terms of the film's reception in ways that proved unfavourable to the later film.[12]

In his article 'Refiguring National Character: The Remains of the British Estate Novel', John J. Su writes that: 'the country house represents a prominent object of nostalgia in [Waugh's *Brideshead Revisited* and Ishiguro's *The Remains of the Day*] and postwar British society more generally because of its long-standing association with continuity, tradition, and Englishness'.[13] In *Brideshead Revisited* (2008) the film location inadvertently activates nostalgia for a past adaptation; it serves as hallowed ground not so much in its role as Brideshead but as the site of the location of the 1981 production. The use of an identical – and unmistakable – location inevitably evokes the memory of the first adaptation and perhaps implicitly posits it as the source text, provoking comparisons in which the criteria of fidelity centre on the 1981 adaptation rather than Waugh's novel. While *Brideshead Revisited* (2008) announces itself as a classic adaptation, the very status of the source text as a 'classic' is in some way dependent on – and arguably an after-effect of – its adaptation in 1981. Moreover, its celebrated location takes on a celebrity aura analogous to a star persona, whose extra-textual identity is more insistent than the 'character' it is ostensibly enlisted to play. This raises the question of whether *Brideshead Revisited* (2008) should be considered an adaptation (of Waugh's novel) or a *remake* (of the 1981 television series) – a possibility which the title itself seems to ironically underline, given its potential to be misread as a cinematic sequel by the uninitiated. Constantine Verevis suggests that 'the concept of remaking is never simply a quality of texts, but is the secondary result of a broader discursive activity'.[14] Indeed, Catherine Grant writes that the status of a film as an adaptation is determined not only by its relation to a source text but by 'those discourses of publicity, promotion and reception which make known the generic framework within which to comprehend [it]'.[15] While discourses of publicity and promotion sought to identify this film as an adaptation of a classic novel, discourses of reception often figured it as an inferior remake.

As Grant's article demonstrates, the film remake can be a vehicle for an auteurist intervention as much as a commercial strategy designed to capitalize on a 'pre-sold' property. However, *Brideshead Revisited* (2008) was widely perceived as falling short of the interpretative originality expected of an auteur production. In a review for the *New York Times*, A. O. Scott described *Brideshead Revisited* (2008) as a 'strenuously picturesque adaptation', 'necessarily shorter [than the television series, broadcast on PBS in 1982]', 'less faithful to Waugh's book' and 'tedious, confused and banal'.[16] Scott concludes that it is a 'lazy, complacent film, which takes the novel's name in vain'.[17] Roger Ebert pronounces it 'a good sound example of the British period drama; mid-range Merchant Ivory, you could say', but judges that 'the movie is not the equal of the TV production, in part because so much material had to be compressed into such a short time'.[18] Writing in *The Observer*, Philip French expresses disappointment with this 'dull, perfunctory and moderately efficient'[19] film and in *The Guardian* Peter Bradshaw dismisses it as a 'handsome-looking, workmanlike but fundamentally uninspired and obtuse adaptation' which offers 'neither the time nor space to swoon'.[20] The language of automated labour which runs through these reviews – 'perfunctory', 'efficient', and 'workmanlike' – suggest that the seductive mechanisms of the classic adaptation are now not only familiar but visible to audiences once dazzled by the judicious placing of carefully costumed actors, with old school theatrical pedigrees, within the stately interiors of ancestral homes. Directors who merely set these signifiers in motion are now castigated as either working the machinery too hard to achieve the desired languorous tone ('strenuously picturesque') or as not working hard enough to bring something new and original to the proceedings ('lazy' and 'complacent'). Bradshaw, French, and Scott, make a point of referring to Waugh's book as a 'resplendent'[21] novel of 'rich fibre' and 'delight',[22] which 'live[s] and breathe[s]',[23] but the references to the length of this feature film – which could hardly match the 11 hours screening time of its television counterpart – suggest that it is the memory of the 1981 adaptation against which this film is being compared. 'Why revisit it?' asks Bradshaw and declares the outcome 'superfluous'.[24] A capacity to inspire and accommodate multiple interpretations, and to acquire new meanings for new audiences in successive historical and cultural contexts, is arguably a key characteristic of the classic text – such a text is not exhausted but renewed by 'revisiting'. The reception of Jarrold's *Brideshead Revisited* seems to instate the 1981 Granada Television production as simultaneously the original source and the definitive version, enlisting discourses of fidelity in defence of an adapted text elevated to the canons of quality television, while at the same time deploying the language of creative ennui to belittle the very act of adaptation as derivative.

Wuthering Heights and black British history

As the director of a literary biopic of a leading adaptation 'property' Jarrold's progression to the classic adaptation did not seem remarkable; by contrast, the news that an auteur director more often situated in a British social realist tradition was to direct a new film adaptation of Emily Brontë's 1847 novel *Wuthering Heights* was met with surprise and anticipation. As the director of the critically acclaimed *Red Road* (2006) and *Fish Tank* (2009) – both awarded the Jury Prize at the Cannes Film Festival – Andrea Arnold's cinematic signature has come to be associated with contemporary themes, poetic realism, psychological drama (including transgressive desire), and naturalistic performance. A period drama and literary adaptation marked a significant departure for Arnold and the critical reception of her film confirmed that her *Wuthering Heights* was very much an expression of a distinctive cinematic vision. Reviews were distinguished both by repeated references to Arnold's authorial signature (legitimized as an original creative intervention, rather than criticized as overwriting the 'original') and to the perceived conventions of the literary adaptation as a genre. In a feature article in *Sight & Sound*, Amy Raphael pronounces the film an 'anti-heritage take'[25] on Brontë's novel and one which 'tear[s] up the rule book for adapting period novels'.[26] Reviewing the film in the same publication, Kate Stables describes it as 'stripping away ... literary, romantic and supernatural trappings' and 'gutting the gothic framework of the novel'.[27] Writing in similar terms, Peter Bradshaw in *The Guardian* sees the film as 'strip[ping] the story ruthlessly down to its bare essentials'[28] and 'sweep[ing] away the period choreography of the conventional literary adaptation'.[29] Both Stables and Bradshaw celebrate the 'shock of the new'[30] delivered by this adaptation, with Bradshaw adding that such a sensation is 'something I never expect to get from any classic literary adaptation'.[31] Raphael even goes so far as to attribute a 'punk ethos'[32] to Arnold's film, in an essay whose title – 'Love Will Tear Us Apart' – evokes the post-punk music scene from the other side of the Pennines, conjuring a northern sensibility uniquely forged by industry and landscape. The language of 'stripping', 'sweeping', and 'gutting' is suggestive of an act of artistic renovation which is both iconoclastic (in terms of literary adaptation convention) and 'faithful' (in terms of its dedication to an idea of textual truth). The more conventional classic adaptation has often been castigated for its over-reliance on dialogue at the expense of the wider audio-visual qualities of the medium as a mode of storytelling; in this context Nicolas Becker's sound design is especially significant when interpreted as expressing a kind of sensual fidelity to the aural and material texture of the 'original'. In *The Independent*, Anthony Quinn notes that 'dialogue is pared to a minimum, while incidental music is banished almost entirely',[33] while in *The Observer* Philip French applauds the 'remarkable soundtrack … [which] incorporates wind, birdsong, barking dogs, rain, the flapping of shutters, the whispering of leaves, the chattering of insects and the creaking of trees into a great symphony of nature'.[34] Indeed, critics reached for new analogies to capture the novel kind of non-verbal fidelity manifested in this adaptation, with Bradshaw suggesting a radical reversal of the relationship between source and adapted text:

> In the most extraordinary way, Arnold achieves a kind of pre-literary reality effect. Her film is not presented as another layer of interpretation, superimposed on a classic's frills and those of all the other remembered versions, but an attempt to create something that might have existed before the book, something on which the book might have been based, a raw semi-articulate series of events, later polished and refined as a literary gemstone. That is an illusion, of course, but a convincing and thrilling one.[35]

However, it took the intervention of a commentator outside of the circle of established film reviewing to identify the importance of another departure from classic adaptation convention. In an article written in response to the release of Arnold's film adaptation of Brontë's *Wuthering Heights*, and published on *The Guardian's* website in October 2011, British actor Paterson Joseph wrote: 'Black actors belong in British costume drama. After all, we've been around for a lot longer than 1948'.[36] Joseph was responding to the casting of black British actors Solomon Glave and James Howson in the roles of the younger and older Heathcliff. This casting is significant in a number of ways; it can be understood as exposing and challenging the unacknowledged racial politics of the classic adaptation genre, but also as a gesture of fidelity to the source text which is an implicit critique of leading adaptations of the past.

In his essay, 'Secrets and lies: black British histories and British historical films', Stephen Bourne makes the following observation:

> Over more than a century of cinema, the black historical presence in Britain has been all but invisible in British popular films. In this entire period, black appearances in films with British historical settings have been limited to a few fleeting appearances by extras ...[37]

The literary adaptation is a key genre of the period drama and has played an important role in establishing its generic signifiers. However, as Sarita Malik has suggested in *Representing Black Britain: Black and Asian Images on Television,* non-white actors continue to be 'locked out'[38] of this branch of quality television drama and prestige film production. Two factors can be identified as conspiring to exclude black British actors – and black British histories – in this way. Firstly, the dominance of a particular set of source texts, located in the era of the British Empire and foregrounding the lives and experiences of subjects privileged by race, class, and colonialism. Secondly, the persistence of casting strategies which, on the one hand, have failed to represent the historical presence of non-white people in Britain and, on the other, have proved peculiarly resistant to integrated casting strategies (now commonplace in film and television adaptations of Shakespeare's plays). Indeed, Bourne suggests that 'there is ample ammunition for regarding "whiteness" as a specific generic trait of British period films, even if it is one that their audiences unthinkingly take for granted'.[39] Joseph is not the first British actor to speak out about this issue; in a interview conducted by Stephen Bourne in 1996, Carmen Munroe commented: 'I feel disheartened every time I look at the screen and see something like *Pride and Prejudice* [the 1995 BBC television production which attracted record audiences for British television drama] or *Sense and Sensibility* [Ang Lee, USA/ UK, 1996] that will exclude ... minority ethnic artists'.[40] The absence of non-white actors in classic adaptations perpetuates a misleading vision of Britain's history and cultural heritage and owes more to a fidelity to culturally constructed and ideologically problematic generic signifiers than it does to a presumed authenticity to period detail. The casting of black British actors in Arnold's film casts into relief the role of literary adaptation in erasing the visibility of black British identity and history from the collective cultural memory; however, this is not a rare example of integrated casting (in which the perceived race or ethnicity of the actor performing the role would have no significance in the narrative), but a motivated casting strategy which has its roots in the source text.

In Brontë's novel, the character of Heathcliff is repeatedly, if ambiguously, racially marked. Found destitute on the streets of Liverpool by Mr Earnshaw, the unnamed foundling is described by Nelly as 'a dirty, ragged, black-haired child; big enough both to walk and talk' and 'repeat[ing] over and over again some gibberish that nobody could understand'.[41] Mrs Linton later rebukes Cathy for 'scouring the country with a gipsy!',[42] a term which Susan Meyer describes as 'the generic designation for a dark-complexioned alien in England',[43] and Mr Linton refers to him as: 'that strange acquisition my late neighbour made in his journey to Liverpool – a little Lascar, or an American or Spanish Castaway'.[44] Mr Earnshaw describes the child he discovered as 'dark almost as if it came from the devil'[45] and he is dehumanized and objectified as an object of property in Nelly's account of the family legend: 'he picked it up and inquired for its owner – Not a soul knew to whom it belonged …'.[46] However, the casting of Heathcliff in television and film adaptations has followed persistent conventions which seem to defy these textual clues. Laurence Oliver's Heathcliff in William Wyler's 1939 *Wuthering Heights* has served as a template for later casting, with Heathcliff's 'otherness' being signified by dark, unkempt hair contrasted against a markedly pale complexion. This pattern is followed both in Peter Kosminsky's 1992 film adaptation and the Mammoth Screen/WGBH Boston co-production, directed by Coky Giedroyc and broadcast on ITV in the UK in 2009, where Ralph Fiennes and Tom Hardy mirror their co-stars (Juliette Binoche and Charlotte Riley) in the length of their dark hair and pallor. Even where cross gender casting is employed – as in *Sparkhouse* (BBC, Dir. Robin Shepperd, Screenplay by Sally Wainwright, 2002) – the 'Heathcliff' figure (played by Sarah Smart) is instantly identifiable by the contrast between her raven black hair and alabaster skin. This possibly Celtic fashioning of Heathcliff perhaps lends weight to interpretations of the novel which posit him as a child of the Irish diaspora; as Elsie Michie (and Winifred Gérin before her) has noted: 'Brontë's description of Heathcliff … links him to Victorian representations of the Irish children who were pouring into England in the late 1840s as a result of the potato famine'.[47] However, Arnold's adaptation explicitly evokes a different diaspora, not only in the casting but also in the script. In *Imperialism at Home: Race and Victorian Women's Fiction*, Susan Meyer identifies 1769 as the year in which Mr Earnshaw finds the child Heathcliff destitute on the streets of Liverpool:

> … the city was England's largest slave-trading port, conducting seventy to eighty-five percent of the English slave trade along the Liverpool Triangle … Thousands of black slaves were living in England itself in the late eighteenth century, concentrated particularly in the port cities of London, Liverpool and Bristol, to which they had been brought by captains of slaving vessels and planters, government officials, and military officers returning to the West Indies.[48]

Andrea Arnold's film adaptation makes this history visible not only by casting black British actors in the roles of the younger and older Heathcliff, but also by depicting Heathcliff as a child whose first language is not English and whose body is marked by scars and brands which seem to identify him as a child of the triangular trade. The abuse to which he is subjected – both verbal and physical – in the film adaptation then becomes an extension of a historically rooted racialized oppression; the violence of Empire is literally brought home to the English household and its displaced subjects made visible in such a way as to prompt the audience to question the ways in which prior adaptations may have marginalized a significant dimension of this radically troubling text.

'Prizing Otherness' and *Life of Pi*

Yann Martel's 2001 Man Booker Prize winning fabulist novel *Life of Pi* has been described more than once as 'unfilmable', an accolade in disguise which implicitly defines a book's literary value in direct proportion to its resistance to conversion to cinematic narrative. Its adaptation by an auteur director renowned for his 'genre versatility',[49] including critically acclaimed literary adaptations of Jane Austen's *Sense and Sensibility* (1995), Rick Moody's *The Ice Storm* (1997), and Annie Proulx's *Brokeback Mountain* (2005), ensured that its release would assume the status of a major cultural 'event' in both the film and literary worlds. When Ang Lee's film adaptation of Martel's shipwreck fantasy received 11 Academy Award nominations the conditions seemed to be set for a 'perfect storm' as far as the film and publishing industry's apparatus of cultural prestige are concerned. The release and reception of this film adaptation presented an opportunity to observe and analyze a specific form of cultural triangulation – namely, between contemporary literary fiction, literary prize culture, and the adaptation industry.

In *Marketing Literature: The Making of Contemporary Writing in Britain*, Claire Squires argues that literary prizes 'play a crucial role in the interaction between genre and the marketplace, and are one of the forces that come to influence notions of cultural value and literariness'.[50] Indeed, the production and circulation of cultural value through the mechanism of the literary prize is the key concern of James F. English's *The Economy of Prestige: Prizes, Awards and the Circulation of Cultural Value*. English suggests that the annual controversies which attend the award of leading prizes should not distract us from paying attention to their economic, cultural, and ideological power, arguing that: 'prizes are not a threat or contamination with respect to the field of properly cultural practice on which they have no legitimate place. The prize *is* cultural practice in its quintessential contemporary form [emphasis in original]'.[51] The close correspondence between the award of a prestigious literary prize to a contemporary novel and the likelihood of its being optioned for film or television adaptation is likewise a relationship which Simone Murray asks us to take seriously when she proposes that: 'literary prizes do not merely legitimate symbolic capital in a particular cultural segment, but moreover actively facilitate the conversion of that capital into other media sectors ...'.[52] Murray situates the literary prize within what she calls the 'adaptation network', an expanded field of contexts and conditions which shape the production, circulation and reception of adaptations:

> Literary prizes constitute a crucial but commonly overlooked node of the adaptation network. Chiefly, the literary prize's role

is to catalyse adaptation, by drawing attention to a particular text
... By broadening interest in the title beyond the reviews pages
of the literary community, typically increasing sales and public
recognition of the winning volume in the process and, through a
combination of all of these factors, markedly increasing the likelihood of the title's adaptation into other media formats.[53]

The literary adaptation has played a key role in the evolution of
the 'prestige' film production, and the award of an internationally
recognized literary prize often serves to provide advance cultural
legitimation through the perceived status of the literary 'property'.
Jim Collins has discerned the 'creation of [a] new terrain for quality
cinema, between blockbuster movies and the art house cinema'[54]
which he designates the 'cine-literary'; he offers the 'seamless, simultaneous, interconnection of novel, film, featurette, Web site, and
digital reading device' as the 'foundation of cine-literary culture'
within which 'reading the book has become only one of a host of
interlocking literary experiences'.[55] Collins posits Miramax, under
the creative co-direction of Harvey Weinstein, as playing a key role
in the creation of this new critically acclaimed and commercially
successful product and writes that: 'Weinstein's explanation of the
success of Miramax in a Hollywood dominated by high-concept
blockbusters – "our special effects are *words*" – suggest just how
important literary values were in that success story [emphasis in orig-
inal]'.[56] This turn of events is especially significant when considering
the critical history of literary adaptations, whose cinematic creden-
tials have often been perceived to be compromised by an emphasis
on the verbal at the expense of the visual. Ang Lee's *Life of Pi* presents
an interesting departure from the emerging conventions of the cine-
literary in that (to paraphrase Weinstein) this film's special effects
were its special effects, both in the judgement of its reviewers and of
the Academy of Motion Picture Arts and Sciences.

A recurring motif in the critical reception of Ang Lee's film, which
combined live action and computer generated imagery, was the discrepancy between the spectacular special effects and the quality of its
narrative content. In a review headed 'Great Tiger – a pity the narrative of *Life of Pi* is all at sea', Anthony Quinn's admiration for Lee's
'Wonder of the Universe movie, sumptuously shot, ravishingly col-
oured and absolutely up to the minute in its use of 3D technology'

was qualified by a disappointment with its dramatic lassitude: 'For long sections one forgets what the story is meant to be proposing at all, aside from the infinite possibilities of digital technology'.[57] Similarly, Peter Bradshaw in *The Guardian* applauds the 'technical brilliance' and 'stunning effects' of this 'awards-season movie' but is unimpressed by the 'shallow and self-important shaggy-dog story – or shaggy-tiger story'.[58] This judgment seemed to be confirmed at the 85th Academy Awards, at which *Life of Pi* received 4 awards from its 11 nominations. Literary adaptations have traditionally done well at the Academy Awards, to the point of attracting both criticism and anxiety about the future of original content; however, their success has tended to be confined to specific categories, including screenwriting and acting, with adaptations often serving as vehicles for star performers to demonstrate their credibility within a pseudo-classical repertoire. By contrast, *Life of Pi* received awards not only for direction but also for cinematography, music (original score), and special effects; in other words it was rewarded for its cinematic properties rather than its literary origins. Aside from the presence of respected Indian character actor, Irrfan Khan (alongside British film and television actor Rafe Spall) in the less admired framing narrative, screen time is mostly occupied by younger actors making their debut; indeed, a still image of Suraj Sharma, who plays the eponymous hero during his perilous sojourn of the lifeboat, provides the key iconography for the film marketing. This image offers a focal point for consideration of the novel's effective canonization by the combined forces of literary prize culture, adaptation, and film industry award: namely the relationship between literary prizes and postcolonial fiction, and between the film industry and the history of colonial representation.

In September 2013 the Man Booker Prize announced that eligibility for the annual award for best original novel would be extended to any novel in English and published by a UK publisher; media coverage of this significant change focussed on the Prize's global ambitions in an increasingly competitive – and crowded – literary prize marketplace, and on concerns about the potential dominance of the short-list by American authors. Less discussed was the future of the Prize's distinctive historic relationship with 'Commonwealth' fiction. Sponsored by an agribusiness multinational with historical links to the slave trade (famously denounced by John Berger in his 1972 acceptance speech) and designed to reward novels written by citizens of the UK or its former colonies (including the Commonwealth and Republic of Ireland), the relationship between the prize and postcolonial fiction has been complex. The Man Booker Prize has brought new readers and markets to non-UK authors, but on the condition that their fiction is written in English and published in the UK. It has championed new generations of postcolonial writing – as exemplified in the award of the 40th anniversary Best of Booker to Salman Rushdie's 1981 novel *Midnight's Children* – but it has been also been accused of privileging particular postcolonial voices and genres over others. In his essay 'Prizing Otherness: A Short History of the Booker', Graham Huggan proposes that there is a 'conflicted relationship between the oppositional politics of postcolonialism and the assimilative machinery of the "global" literary prize'.[59] Moreover, Rushdie's Booker success sets a problematic precedent for Huggan; he suggests that *Midnight's Children*, 'while critical of the commodification of an Orientalised India ... profited precisely by circulating such commercially viable Orientalist myths'.[60] The award of the 2002 Man Booker Prize to French Canadian author Yann Martel's novel *Life of Pi* would seem to support the thesis that the award privileges a certain brand of post-Rushdie 'magic realism'. Opening in the former French colonial possession of Pondicherry, written from the perspective of a boy who embraces Christian, Hindu, and Muslim beliefs (to the consternation of his secular parents) and centring on the shipwreck which tragically thwarts his family's migration from post-Partition India to Canada (on a Panamanian registered Japanese cargo ship with a Taiwanese crew), the novel is ripe with postcolonial significance. Moreover, the territorial politics of the family zoo are transposed to the lifeboat which Pi inhabits with the tiger, Richard Parker, and act as a fantastical metaphor for the challenges of peaceful co-existence. Such themes have a particular importance in the context of global post-9/11 politics. Indeed, Huggan has suggested that the novel 'might be said to be an antifundamentalist text that pronounces against dogma of all kinds while provisionally accepting the importance of religious belief as the basis for human interaction in the world'.[61] However, the critical reception of Lee's adaptation would seem to suggest that the film did not prompt the same kind of speculation about the possibility of a 'post-secular' world. Indeed, it might be argued that the film's spectacular imagery can more readily be situated in the complex history of cinema's fascination with the 'exotic'.

While the technically astounding CGI Richard Parker played a prominent role in the marketing of this film, those strategies which relied on still images made extensive use of a publicity shot of Suraj Sharma which evoked a older lexicon of unashamedly Orientalist imagery. The shot in question centres on Sharma standing on the canopy of the lifeboat in a posture of self-possession somewhat at odds with the desperate struggle for survival (in the face of starvation or predation) which dominates much of the film's action. Sharma stands squarely with feet planted astride and hands balled into fists at his side, the angles of his arm and legs accentuating the triangular outline of his torso; his upper body is exposed and he wears a head-dress resembling a turban. His posture and dress, combined with the fantastic exoticism of his location, recall the iconic image and star persona of the Indian-born child and adult actor Sabu Dastagir (1924–1963), more often credited simply as Sabu. Sabu appeared in a number of British and American adventure and fantasy films, including adaptations of fiction by Rudyard Kipling (*Elephant Boy*, directed by Robert Flaherty, 1937; *Jungle Book*, directed by Zoltán Korda, 1942) and versions of the tales from *One Thousand and One Nights* (*The Thief of Baghdad*, directed by Michael Powell, Ludwig Berger, and Tim Whelan, 1940; *Arabian Nights*, directed by John Rawlins, 1942). Indeed, Priya Jaikumar suggests that such was his screen presence and audience appeal that the 'Sabu film' attained the status of a film genre in itself 'with its animals, royalty, magic, superstition and battling beliefs in jungle or wilderness at a non-Western location'.[62] A charismatic and talented actor, Sabu's screen persona was a complex construction, capitalizing on his masculine beauty but containing his star power within strictly circumscribed racial and sexual boundaries. As Jaikumar argues:

> Sabu is rarely counted as a man in any of his films. His body is effeminised, made sexually ambiguous with its attributes of over- or under-dress, yielding his figure to a range of desires outside those ruled by conventions of heterosexuality, patriarchy and empire.[63]

One of the few South Asian actors to obtain star status within the Hollywood film industry, he seems at once the willing subject of the Orientalist gaze (which constructs him either as the 'natural' boy or an exoticized 'prince') and the inviting object of subversive desire (his body sexualized and objectified).[64] Moreover, Sabu's screen presence is closely associated with a series of films, produced or directed in the 1930s and 1940s by figures such as Robert and Zoltán Korda, Michael Powell, and Emeric Pressburger, which pioneered the use of the new technology of Technicolor. As Sarah Street writes in her essay '"Color consciousness": Natalie Kalmus and Technicolour in Britain', 'colour films that were successful ... were spectacular interventions in a conventional, economy-driven aesthetic system',[65] and more especially so in a national cinema in which social realism was the dominant mode and equated with the use of black and white. Sabu appears in two of the three films discussed as case studies in Street's essay (*The Thief of Baghdad* and *Black Narcissus*, directed by Powell and Pressburger, 1947). Indeed, Street argues that:

> early discourses on colour ... linked it with the 'exotic' and 'otherness'. Indeed all three films discussed in this essay are linked by their use of colour to highlight questions of racial difference and exoticism within generic contexts which favoured the foregrounding of colour: the outdoor melodrama and empire film.[66]

This history of technology and representation seems to be evoked in both the marketing and reception of Ang Lee's film adaptation which is able to mobilize a deeply rooted construction of the 'Orient' as a site of visual excess and splendour while at the same time dismissing the film as an empty spectacle.

In each of the case studies presented above, an aspect of the production, publicity, or reception of a contemporaneous adaptation – whether film location or casting strategy, marketing campaign, or industry award – provides a starting point for discussion; relevant critical frameworks are then mobilized to inform interpretations responsive to unfolding events. In this way fresh insights are offered into established critical debates and original readings and new questions for analysis are initiated.

However, I would like to conclude by anticipating a question which this strategy might potentially provoke: might not the insights gained through the contemporaneous study of any single film or television adaptation be identical to those achieved through more conventional means, after the passage of years and with the advantage of critical hindsight and the benefit of published scholarship? If the answer is 'yes', then we might reasonably question whether the benefits of this approach outweighs its challenges – including dealing with the contingencies of television broadcasting schedules (in 2007 the question of whether the new television *Frankenstein* would reach the screen before the end of the module kept us all in suspense) and the unevenness of film distribution (in 2008 the theatrical release of *Wuthering Heights* went ahead as scheduled, but was limited to art house film theatres). However, these very contingencies – if and when they occur – are instructive in revealing how specific televisual and cinematic contexts shape and even determine the reception and subsequent critical reputation of film and television adaptations. Moreover, the particular value of a focus on contemporaneous culture is the opportunity it presents to observe, evaluate, and contribute to the processes of opinion shaping and canon forming – and to recognize that these processes are by no means a transparent reflection of the 'value' or 'quality' of the adaptation itself. In this way, students are able to gain new insights into the construction of cultural value and the workings of the cultural industries which profit from it; moreover, they are able to recognize their capacity to act as active agents in the production of new meanings, both as students and as citizens.

Notes

1. The title was inspired by a popular live broadcast natural history programme, *Autumn Watch*, broadcast by the BBC at the time of first delivery.
2. I would like to thank students at Teesside University for the enthusiasm and insight they have brought to this task; their expertise and pleasure in navigating contemporary culture has been a source of real inspiration.
3. Terry Smith, 'Contemporary Art and Contemporaneity', *Critical Inquiry* 32 (4), Summer 2006, 703.
4. Other Adaptation Watch topics have included: *Frankenstein* (ITV/Impossible Pictures, 2007); *Atonement* (UK. Dir. Joe Wright, 2007); *Little Dorrit* (BBC, 2008); *Never Let Me Go* (UK. Dir. Mark Romanek, 2010); *The Crimson Petal and the White* (BBC, 2011).
5. Philip Kemp, 'Interview with Julian Jarrold', *Sight & Sound* 18 (10), October 2008, 37.
6. Thomas Leitch, *Film Adaptation and Its Discontents: From Gone With the Wind to The Passion of the Christ* (Baltimore: Johns Hopkins University Press, 2007), p. 174.
7. Sarah Cardwell, *Adaptation Revisited: Television and the Classic Novel* (Manchester and New York: Manchester University Press, 2002), p. 108.

8. Leitch, *Film Adaptation and Its Discontents,* p. 173.
9. Cardwell, *Adaptation Revisited,* p. 112.
10. Leitch, *Film Adaptation and Its Discontents,* p. 174.
11. *Ibid.,* p. 175.
12. In an interview with Philip Kemp, Jarrold explained: 'We went almost everywhere first but there was nowhere else that felt like a Catholic family had lived there', *Sight & Sound* 18 (10), October 2008, 38.
13. John J. Su, 'Refiguring National Character: The Remains of the British Estate Novel', *MFS: Modern Fiction Studies* 48 (3), Fall 2002, 554.
14. Constantine Verevis, *Film Remakes* (Edinburgh: Edinburgh University Press, 2006), p. 106.
15. Catherine Grant, 'Recognising Billy Budd in *Beau Travail*: Epistemology and Hermeneutics of an Autuerist 'Free' Adaptation', *Screen* 43 (1), 2002, 59.
16. A. O. Scott, 'Bright Young Things in Love and Pain', The New York Times, July 25 2008, http://www.nytimes.com/2008/07/25/movies/25brid. html?_r=0. Accessed 29 November 2013.
17. *Ibid.*
18. Roger Ebert, *'Brideshead Revisited* [2008]' [Review]. *Rogerebert.com*, http://www.rogerebert.com/reviews/brideshead-revisited-2008. Accessed 29 November 2013.
19. Philip French, *'Brideshead Revisited* [2008]' [Review]. *The Observer,* 5 October 2013, http://www.theguardian.com/film/2008/oct/05/period andhistorical.drama. Accessed 29 November 2013.
20. Peter Bradshaw, *'Brideshead Revisited* [2008]' [Review]. *The Guardian,* 3 October 2008, http://www.theguardian.com/film/2008/oct/03/drama. periodhistorical. Accessed 29 November 2013.
21. *Ibid.*
22. French, *'Brideshead Revisited* [2008]' [Review].
23. Scott, 'Bright Young Things in Love and Pain'.
24. Bradshaw, *'Brideshead Revisited* [2008]' [Review].
25. Amy Raphael, 'Love Will Tear Us Apart', *Sight & Sound* 21 (12), December 2011, 34.
26. *Ibid.,* p. 36.
27. Kate Stables, *'Wuthering Heights'* [Review], *Sight & Sound* 21 (12), December 2011, 82.
28. Peter Bradshaw, *'Wuthering Heights'* [Review], *The Guardian,* 10 November 2011, http://www.theguardian.com/film/2011/nov/10/wuthering-heights-film-review. Accessed 3 December 2011.
29. Bradshaw, *'Wuthering Heights'* [Review].
30. Stables, *'Wuthering Heights'* [Review].
31. Bradshaw, *'Wuthering Heights'* [Review].
32. Raphael, 'Love Will Tear Us Apart', p. 36.
33. Anthony Quinn, *'Wuthering Heights'* [Review], *The Independent,* 11 November 2011, http://www.independent.co.uk/arts-entertainment/films/reviews/wuthering-heights-15-6259989.html. Accessed 3 December 2013.
34. French, *'Wuthering Heights'* [Review].
35. Bradshaw, *'Wuthering Heights'* [Review].

36. Paterson Joseph, 'Why *Wuthering Heights* Gives Me Hope', *The Guardian*, 11 November 2011, http://www.theguardian.com/commentisfree/2011/nov/11/wuthering-heights-black-actors. Accessed 3 December 2013.
37. Stephen Bourne, 'Secrets and Lies: Black British Histories and British Historical Films', *British Historical Cinema: The Fistory, Feritage and Costume Film*, ed. Claire Monk and Amy Sergeant (London and New York: Routledge, 2002), p. 48.
38. Sarita Malik, *Representing Black Britain: Black and Asian Images on Television* (London: Sage, 2002), p. 142.
39. Bourne, 'Secrets and Lies: Black British Histories and British Historical Films', p. 49.
40. Munroe quoted in Bourne, 'Secrets and Lies: Black British Histories and British Historical Films', p. 49.
41. Emily Brontë, *Wuthering Heights* (Oxford: Oxford University Press, 1982), p. 35.
42. *Ibid.*, p. 48.
43. Susan Meyer, *Imperialism at Home: Race and Victorian Women's Fiction* (New York: Cornell University Press, 1996), p. 97.
44. Brontë, *Wuthering Heights*, p. 48.
45. *Ibid.*, p. 34.
46. *Ibid.*, p. 35.
47. Elsie Michie, 'From Siminized Irish to Oriental Despots: Heathcliff, Rochester and Racial Difference', *NOVEL: A Forum on Fiction* 25 (2), Winter 1992, 129.
48. Meyer, *Imperialism at Home*, p. 98.
49. Anthony Quinn, '*Life of Pi* [Review]', *The Independent*, 20 December 2012, http://www.independent.co.uk/arts-entertainment/films/reviews/film-review-great-tiger--a-pity-the-narrative-of-life-of-pi-is-all-at-sea-8427929.html#. Accessed 6 December 2012.
50. Claire Squires, *Marketing Literature: The Making of Contemporary Writing in Britain* (London: Palgrave Macmillan, 2009), p. 97.
51. James F. English, *The Economy of Prestige: Prizes, Awards and the Circulation of Cultural Value* (Cambridge, Massachusetts; London, England: Harvard University Press, 2005), p. 26.
52. Simone Murray, *The Adaptation Industry: The Cultural Economy of Contemporary Literary Adaptation* (New York and London: Routledge, 2012), p. 109.
53. *Ibid.*, p. 104.
54. Jim Collins, *Bring on the Books for Everybody: How Literary Culture Became Popular Culture* (Durham and London: Duke University Press, 2010), p. 145.
55. *Ibid.*, p. 119.
56. *Ibid.*, p. 117.
57. Anthony Quinn, '*Life of Pi* [Review]', *The Independent*, 20 December 2012, http://www.independent.co.uk/arts-entertainment/films/reviews/film-review-great-tiger--a-pity-the-narrative-of-life-of-pi-is-all-at-sea-8427929.html. Accessed 8 December 2013.

58. Peter Bradshaw, *'Life of Pi* [Review]', *The Guardian*, 20 December 2012, http://www.theguardian.com/film/2012/dec/20/life-of-pi-review. Accessed 9 December 2013.
59. Graham Huggan, 'Prizing Otherness: A Short History of the Booker', *The Post-Colonial Exotic: Marketing the Margins* (London and New York: Routledge, 2001), p. 118.
60. *Ibid.*, p. 115.
61. Graham Huggan, 'Is the 'Post' in 'Postsecular' the 'Post' in 'Postcolonial'?', *MFS: Modern Fiction Studies* 56 (4), 2010, 764–765.
62. Priya Jaikumar, 'Sabu's Skins: The Transnational Stardom of an Elephant Boy', *Wasafiri* 27 (2), 2012, 63.
63. *Ibid.*, 64.
64. See also Ian Iqbal Rashid, 'Song of Sabu: Hollywood Cinema and the Displacement of Desire', *Wasafiri* 23, 1996, 33–39.
65. Sarah Street, '"Color consciousness": Natalie Kalmus and Technicolour in Britain', *Screen* 50 (2), Summer 2009, 208.
66. *Ibid.*, 199–200.

11
Teaching Adaptations through Marketing: Adaptations and the Language of Advertising in the 1930s

Deborah Cartmell

F. R. Leavis identified advertising as the lowest and most insidious form of writing and in its blatant underhanded methods and shameless materialism, he put it to use to expose the tackiness of writers who aimed to be 'popular', or middle-brow as opposed to high-brow. In *Mass Civilisation and Minority Culture* (1930), he attacks writers like Hugh Walpole and Arnold Bennett for stooping to the tactics of advertisers by unapologetically appealing to the lowest possible denominator in order to attract the widest audiences. Leavis's unwitting legacy to adaptation studies can be traced to this volume and, with Denys Thompson, *Culture and Environment* (1933): both books teach (or warn against) the menace of popularization. I would like to consider the concerns expressed within these two books, among them anxieties regarding the decay of language, the standardization of literary texts and the distrust for new technologies, within the context of the rise of the talkie adaptation (1927–) and the marketing of film adaptations in the 1930s.

In *Mass Civilisation*, Leavis moves from discussing the defects of popular writing to the even worse example of film and then swoops down on advertising, to demonstrate the inferiority of these forms of entertainment that use cheap tricks to attract an audience. In 'reverse evolutionary' terms, the popular novel descends into the cheap thrills of cinema which in turn descends into advertising, which appeals to our appetite rather than to our rational faculties. English academics have been historically uncomfortable with literature that has a popular appeal and this is an integral part of Leavis's legacy to the teaching of literature and to the formation of the English canon for most of the twentieth century.

The belief that if a book is liked, then it must not be good has become unspoken but deep rooted in English literature departments and within the culture of English education in general, perhaps because of what Leavis would see as popular literature's unholy alliance with advertising. Significantly, these critics wilfully linked popular literature, cinema, and advertising in their writing. Q. D. Leavis, for instance, sees the commercial targeting of the audience rather than appealing to the author's own better inclinations as the root of the problem of inferior literature: she writes in *Fiction and the Reading Public* (1932) that 'fear of the herd, approval of the herd, the peace of mind that comes from conforming with the herd, are the strings they play upon and the ideals that inform [the popular author's] work'.[1] F. R. Leavis did not ignore advertising as something unworthy of mention. He tackled it head on. Although he saw literature as divorced from society (and therefore the public), for Leavis, teaching English was not a far cry, peculiarly, to teaching advertising, or to unpacking the strategically hidden messages embedded within writing specifically designed to promote a product. In *Culture and Environment*, the need to teach or expose what lies behind advertising is outlined. Leavis and Thompson make it their mission to teach the means employed to darken the minds of thousands at the expense of enlightenment in order to expose what they called 'substitute living' which was at the expense of the appreciation of literature.

Film is seen as an enemy to culture, like advertising, as a form of entertainment that appeals to the many rather than the few. Leavis and Thompson initiate their volume with the question about the value of English teaching: 'What effect can such training have against the multitudinous counter-influences – films, newspapers, advertising – indeed, the whole world outside the classroom?'.[2] The language used to sell these inferior products is unpacked in *Culture and Environment* by bringing it to the classroom and in providing 93 specimen exercises for 6th form classes at the end of the volume. The authors draw heavily on Jan and Cora Gordon's *Star-Dust in Hollywood*, an exposé of Hollywood in the late 1920s which ends with 'the madness of the movietone', which at the time of writing was shockingly going to cost 'as high as a dollar for every word spoken'.[3] The equation of words with money, writing, and commerce, was clearly the last straw in this book and one that would clearly strike a chord with the Leavis circle. That Leavis and Thompson were writing *Culture and Environment* with a copy of *Star-Dust in Hollywood* to hand is revealing of the motivations underlying their enterprise. Leavis and Thompson's topics for debate are aimed at teaching students how to recognize and evaluate texts through their links with the exploitive techniques of advertising. The questions reflect the ways in which they, sometimes implicitly, contrast literature with film. Some of their proposed topics, presented with some tongue in cheek due to the authors' assumption of their unequivocal outlandishness, are worth looking at here.

> 'Broadcasting, like the films, is in practice mainly a means of passive diversion, and it tends to make active recreation, especially active use of the mind more difficult'.
>
> How far in your observation is this so, and how far need it be so?[4]

This assumes that the reception or reading of film is passive, unlike the reading of 'good' literature that requires an exercised, or in today's terms 'fit', mind.

Another example is from *Star-Dust in Hollywood*:

> 'We lunched with a film director the other day and he told us that you were all making the folk-art of the future. Folk-art admits of any number of authors to any plot'.
>
> * * *
>
> 'Folk-author?' said Ornitz. 'Tell me. How does folk-art develop? Every story-teller borrows from his neighbor; that's all right. But he doesn't borrow his tales thinking of the box-office; he borrows them because he enjoys them himself'.
>
> (*Star-Dust in Hollywood*)
>
> Develop the distinction indicated here.[5]

Cinema, as the 'art form of democracy' (sneered at by Leavis's *Scrutiny* but praised as such by Raymond Williams)[6] is described here as motivated by commercialism rather than as emerging from a cultural heritage or individual tastes. Students are being asked to develop the distinction between two types of adaptation or so-called 'folk-art': one which borrows from the past in order to preserve and retell an important story, another that steals a text and exploits it for commercial purposes. Finally,

> 'One working woman welcomes the coming of the movies as an aid in child rearing, saying, "I send my daughter because a girl has to learn the ways of the world somehow and the movies are a good, safe way."' (*Middletown*, p. 267)

> 'The cinema is recognized for what it is, the main source of excitement and of moral education for city children. It is in the subtle way of picturing the standards of adult life, action and emotion, cheapening, debasing and distorting adults until they appear in the eyes of the young people perpetually bathed in a moral atmosphere of intrigue, jealousy, wild emotionalism and cheap sentimentality.' (*ibid.*, p. 268.)

> Develop the discussion of the educational value of the cinema suggested here.[7]

The passages are chosen for their shock value and, as Christopher Hilliard argues in his recent study of the *Scrutiny* Movement, Leavis's teaching was animated by a belief that 'a literary training armed to resist the intellectually deadening and emotionally limiting tendencies of mass culture' was indeed most necessary.[8] Analogous to the critique of the effects of the Industrial Revolution on the nineteenth century, advertising, journalism, film, and best-selling fiction were engines of modern civilization that were a threat to the appreciation of the 'higher' forms of culture. Film, and in particular the talkie, were catastrophic desecrators of language and, therefore, of culture itself. But Leavis in particular, like Machiavelli, was keen that we should know the enemy; and that good students should be taught to understand it so that they could join the cultural minority and abstain from it.

These writings of Leavis and his contemporary literary critics were produced in the early 1930s, in the new era of the talking film, which indirectly posed an even stronger threat to those teaching 'English literature' in so far as the films were now employing actual speaking words filleted from the classics and served up for popular consumption. Leavis has a lot to say about advertising, something to say about film, but hardly anything to say about film adaptation, and we can interpret this silence as reflecting an anxiety about the threat posed by film adaptation, which, as I have argued, was decidedly banished from *Scrutiny* from the first issue onwards.[9] E. S. Turner has demonstrated how the debunking of advertising was popular on both sides of the Atlantic in the early 1930s and the most exploitative advertising was the advertising of film: 'No industry did more to destroy the meaning of words'.[10] According to Turner, cinema managers were 'deluged' with

> 'campaign sheets' full of brash ideas for engineering local publicity and 'tie-ups'. Any manager who carried out one tenth of these suggestions was well on the way to becoming the most unpopular man in his community. He was urged to suborn local clergymen, Army officers and heads of stores to help publicize his attractions; he was told to invite senior pupils from schools to see films about adultery; he was prodded to promote kissing contests and leg competitions, to hire hunchbacks.[11]

From the advertiser's perspective, the talking picture placed the adaptation in a different light – it was now, as its promoters joyfully proclaimed, even closer to its literary source, so much so that advertisers were claiming these were the first adaptations of an author's work, in spite of numerous silent precursors, and that the adaptations could indeed better their literary predecessors.[12]

   The advertiser's assertion that a film can be better than the literary or dramatic work that it is based upon is explicit in the pressbook of *Taming of the Shrew* (1929), where the promoters, with the help of William Shakespeare, who is brought back from the dead, announce that the play is improved by bringing it to the screen. Undoubtedly, to the disgust of literary critics and 'high-brow' writers, advertisers of these first talkies boasted of these films' fidelity to their literary sources; so insistently and powerfully were these arguments made that they became the yardstick to measure an adaptation's merit, a measure that has prevailed to the resentment of both literary and film critics alike for most of the remaining twentieth century.

Promoters of these early talkie adaptations of texts, such as those by Shakespeare and Dickens, and other adaptations that market themselves as adaptations, produce an early version of adaptation studies, with suggestions as to how to consume the films as pedagogical tools, inviting exhibitors to offer them up to schoolchildren as entrances to the great works of literature. Marketing the films as a form of literary explication is most evident in the film adaptations of Shakespeare, from *The Taming of the Shrew* (1929) to *As You Like It* (1936). In fact, we can look at the pressbooks as providing the first forays into the field of adaptations, often positing the message that the film will help you to know the book.

The pressbook for *As You Like It*, for instance, regards the film as 'explaining' the play and issues a 'Study Guide' which as its publisher's name, 'Educational and Recreational Guides', states, mixes work with pleasure. Filmgoers can be reassured that 'Thousands of sample copies have been mailed to high schools, educators and clubs throughout the United States'.[13] This guide, in particular, combines an understanding of the film with an analysis of the play: 'Through information, photographs and questions, the student is enabled to analyse the entire production. Fascinating technical points in the production of the film are made and sections are devoted to the study of dramatic values, the characters and Shakespeare'.[14] The film is marketed for its educational value, for sweetening the bitterness of Shakespeare, for making Shakespeare fun: 'So you *think* you don't like Shakespeare? There's a surprise for all you folks!'.[15] Adaptation studies, although it did not exist as such in this early manifestation, took the form of serving to lighten the literary source in an ostensible effort to convert filmgoers to literature. The appeal was not to those who knew the hypotexts, but to those who did not. This approach would feed into the worst fears of those critics of adaptation who could not help but worry that the prevailing attitude would be: why read a book when you can see the film?

As we all know, judging a film solely in relation to its literary 'source' or hypotext is a dead end street, dooming the adaptation as necessarily inferior to the work it references. And the teaching of adaptations remained very much a minority vocation for those in film and literary studies, as it consisted almost exclusively of evaluating a film in relation to how the adaptation speaks to its literary hypotext, what Plato would have dismissed as studying a pale version of a pale reality, and what Robert Stam (in what must be the most cited text on adaptation)[16] calls 'iconophobia', drawing our attention to the uncanny resemblance between the effects of film adaptation and Plato's cave dwellers', mistaking 'flimsy simulations with ontological reality'.[17]

While Leavis and Thompson were keen to teach the evils of advertising, so as to alert students to the seductive powers that pull the audience down to the lowest possible denominator, perversely, as Christopher Hilliard argues, Leavis was in part responsible for the rise of Media Studies through his opening up of texts of advertising and popular fiction.[18] In fact, Leavis and Thompson's work on advertising and literature offers an (albeit) unwitting model for an approach to adaptations which to date has paid scant attention to the commercial paratexts which surround it. Adaptation studies, as Simone Murray has reminded us, should be concerned with the marketability of the entertainment that strategically positions the consumer as the primary target. Murray calls attention to a significant blind spot in the field that has, until recently, refused to take account of 'the stakeholders, institutions, commercial arrangements and legal frameworks which govern the flow of the content across media'.[19] Rather than conceal its industrial and commercial motivations, the field should seek to uncover and unpack these. Popular literature can be identified through the manifest nature of its generic conventions, and the revelation of adaptation itself as a genre (by the likes of Thomas Leitch and Christine Geraghty) has done much to further the field by alerting us to how an adaptation works as an adaptation, a form which makes explicit its reliance on or manipulation of a previous text and is identifiable through certain generic adaptation features that include a period setting, intertitles, period music, new media, and an obsession with authors, books, and words.[20] The last feature 'words' or 'author's words', I would argue is the most important of these commercial generic markers and was initiated in the new era of the talkies when words – spoken words – played a defining role in an adaptation's marketing.

Among the adaptations in this period in which Leavis was writing were 11 Dickens adaptations (most prominently, MGM's *David Copperfield* (1935), directed by George Cukor and *A Tale of Two Cities* (1935), directed by Jack Conway), four Shakespeare films (directed by Sam Taylor (1929), Max Reinhardt and William Dieterle

(1935), George Cukor (1936), and Paul Czinner (1936)), and some groundbreaking gothic/horror adaptations (including in 1931, Tod Browning's *Dracula* and James Whale's *Frankenstein* for Universal, and Rouben Mamoulian's *Dr Jekyll and Mr Hyde* for Paramount). There is a wealth of material in the paratextual materials of adaptations, material that has been largely overlooked in much of the literature to date. Pressbooks, trailers, and posters are an invaluable source for understanding adaptations in relation to both their hypotexts and their audiences.

Where Shakespeare movies failed in the early sound period, Dickens and other authors, most prominently Gothic writers, succeeded, perhaps partially due to an advertising strategy that was more closely linked to the product it was selling. Looking at promotional materials for Shakespeare adaptations, it is hard to match the advertising with the product, and the mismatch reflects the frantic attempts of those involved in the industry to popularize their product. An example of this is the promotion of an entirely forgettable and, in my view, the worst, Shakespeare adaptation of the early sound era, *As You Like It*, featuring Laurence Oliver, for the first time, in a Shakespeare film.

While the film was essentially filmed theatre, or arguably a film of an indifferent theatrical production, the advertising material attempted to convey the movie as topical and unequivocally accessible to all. The pressbook features cartoon characters either eagerly awaiting or reflecting on their experiences of *As You Like It*. One shows a burly, tattooed worker being asked if he's seen the film and he responds: 'Yeah! I think it's full of excruciatingly comic overtones'. The Pressbook reiterates that 'With an astonishing lack of reverential awe with which everyone ordinarily views Shakespeare, the producers of "As You Like It" have brought the play to the screen as Shakespeare intended it should have been produced in one of the screen's great achievements'.[21] These promoters were over-zealous in trying to convince their audiences that Shakespeare was easy and cinematic: they were wrong. Shakespeare on film was not a success in the early sound era.

Arguably, the Dickens adaptations of this period were more successful in their marketing tactics and did not need to conceal the difficulties of the author, as in the case with Shakespeare adaptations. If we look at the marketing of Dickens in this period, the posters establish expectations for their audiences through a winning blend of literary pedigree with Hollywood selling points. *Great Expectations* (1934) promises everything: from a cast of stars, including a star performance, adventure, romance, and a film which spills out from the book. MGM did Dickens like no other film company, with two major adaptations, *David Copperfield* and *A Tale of Two Cities*, both released in 1935. In the first film, *David Copperfield*, characters emerge from the book, with David himself the most diminutive and Micawber (W.C. Fields) the most prominent. Focussing on star power (65 in total), the film poster promises fidelity to the book by making it literally centre stage, with the addition of intrigue, tragedy, romance, and comedy. MGM's next Dickens film uses a similar colour scheme in its poster to recall the earlier film, and obliterates the novel's other romantic lead, Charles Darnay, in order to focus on Ronald Coleman as Sydney Carton and Elizabeth Allan as Lucie (who replace the book's love triangle with Sydney alone split between his love and his duty). The poster translates the book into romance and adventure, with the couple literally torn apart by the angry mob but with the individual triumphing above the crowd. Rather than Dickens's book we have Dickens's signature included on the poster, as a promise of the film's fidelity to the author.

So the posters advertise the prominence of the author, star cast, romance, adventure, period detail, and fidelity to the book. Rather than simply comparing the film to the book, it can be more revealing for students to read the paratexts as well, to compare the film to its promotional materials, how these exploit or undermine literary pedigree, how they translate the characters into 'stars', how they tease us with the promise of our favourite film genres, such as romance, comedy and adventure, how they speak to the tastes of a contemporary audience, and how they locate themselves within a particular consumer culture.

Gothic adaptations clearly thrived in the early sound period, and in contrast to the posters advertising Dickens or Shakespeare adaptations, these posters tend to obliterate the author and the author's words; the emphasis is on tormented individuals rather than groups of harmonious characters, and the colours (preponderance of black, yellow and sickly green) recall each other. The emphasis on perverse sexuality draws in a particular audience, decidedly not fans of Mary Shelley, Robert Louis Stevenson, or Bram Stoker, in spite of the fact that the films (at least *Dr Jekyll and Mr Hyde*, *Dracula*, and, to an extent, *Frankenstein*) acknowledge their literary 'source' in the opening credits. The promotional materials announce that these are very different types of adaptations, aimed at an audience oblivious or indifferent to their literary pedigrees, promising thrills, combining horror and sexuality, and proudly formulaic in their publicity images: prime examples of Leavis's concerns about advertising, the imposition of standardization, and the consequent decay of literature and language.

As Leavis and Thompson imply in *Culture and Environment*, students who study literature can also study advertising, using the same close textual analytical skills to uncover both what the advertisers are proclaiming and to whom they are saying it. While the posters and advertising are often very different from the films themselves, they give us an invaluable insight into the commercial world which the films inhabit, and for many, like Leavis and his circle, the advertising would be the only access these self-proclaimed film-haters would have to the films themselves.

For instance, we see in the posters advertising the 1934 French 4½ hour *Les Misérables* and in the 1935 English-speaking film, a number of similarities: most noticeably, the diagonally positioned title and the focus on the individuals over the historical content of the story. Both include the author's name and focus on heads rather than bodies – prioritizing the individual over the political. The film publicity is producing what Leavis would perhaps term, a 'standardization' of Victor Hugo's work. While the author is credited here, he is not in *Anna Karenina* (1935). Greta Garbo's star power usurped Tolstoy, the novel, and almost every aspect of the story in the poster, whilst other adaptation posters, such as *Alice in Wonderland* (1933), *A Midsummer Night's Dream* (1935), and *David Copperfield* (1935) capitalized on their star-studded cast and their literary origins in order to bring in the punters.

How does this analysis of the marketing of adaptations translate to teaching adaptations? In order to adapt a piece of literature, you have to understand how the adaptation will be sold, what will it bring that is different from what has gone before, how it will remind us of previous successful adaptations, and how it will appeal to a contemporary audience. Looking at adaptations through their promotional materials provides students with models of how and how not to promote or defend their own work and to appreciate the importance of the audience for whom the adaptation is aimed. The promotional materials frequently combine a heady mixture of claims to authenticity, pedagogical value (often with ideas for school trips), and accessibility: the old adage 'something for everyone' (F. R. Leavis's worst nightmare).

So how does this affect teaching? Rather than teach the dangers of advertising, we can employ the Leavisite methodology to a different end: in my experience, students take great pleasure (as Leavis's students almost certainly did) in unpacking an advertising image, finding in these images important information (rather than what Leavis and Thompson would identify as warnings) about the audience and the context in which the movie was made. Film posters in the first half of the 1930s were produced in the early period of sound, when the new technology was still a novelty to both filmmakers and audiences. And sound – or the spoken word – is made much of in these images, in particular in 'prestige films', or adaptations of canonical writers.

Little Women (1933) is one of the most successful adaptations of the early 1930s. The poster artfully articulates the unique selling points of the film, providing a template for those that follow. The size of the book and its centrality promise fidelity; Louisa May Alcott's name makes a seamless translation from author to film-writer and is juxtaposed with that of the star, Katharine Hepburn (who becomes the novel's author in this film adaptation, as the character of Jo does in all the subsequent adaptations of *Little Women*); the poster is painted rather than photographed, calling attention to its artistic quality (announcing that the film is based on art); and the prominence of words, books, and characters who flow out of the book screams out that this is every inch an adaptation. The poster's quality of painting resembles that of book covers appealing to young girls, such as those of the Nancy Drew mystery books, making their appearance from 1930 onwards. *Little Women* fed into future adaptations which begin to feature particular individuals associated with adaptations – Edna May Oliver, who goes on to perform in *Alice in Wonderland* (1933), *David Copperfield* (1935), *A Tale of Two Cities* (1935), *Romeo and Juliet* (1935), and *Pride and Prejudice* (1940); George Cukor, who becomes known as an adaptation director with films such as *David Copperfield* (1935), *Romeo and Juliet* (1936), *The Adventures of Tom Sawyer* (1938);

and David O. Selznick, whose productions include *David Copperfield* (1935), *Anna Karenina* (1935), *Gone with the Wind* (1939), and *Rebecca* (1940).

One way of teaching adaptations is by asking students to write their own adaptations, to take a scene or chapter from a text and adapt it, including a critical introduction that essentially 'sells' what they are doing. The worst adaptations produced by students that I have encountered are bad, not always because the author is unfamiliar with the text that they are adapting, but because the author is unable to persuade or, more precisely, *sell* what it is that they are doing, to explain why their film version would work, who it would appeal to, and how it provides a change from what has gone before: the very details we find in film posters of this period.

Leavis and Thompson (albeit unwittingly) teach us how to approach adaptations through advertising, and rather than teaching students to understand and therefore recoil from it, I would rather that we encourage students to understand and embrace it as a way of explaining adaptations, possibly to see the commerciality as artful in its own right.

I think I can understand Leavis's anxiety about popular culture, surrounded as he was by an overwhelming number of these advertising images, presenting films that he undoubtedly would never dream of seeing himself. Like many of his generation, his knowledge of these films would be through hearsay and advertisements. His instinct was not just to recoil from advertising but to teach people how to read the slogans as if they were in a practical criticism class, to consider their construction and to what and to whom they were appealing; in other words, how they were flattering their audiences with cultured and/or uncultured constructions of themselves.

Adaptation studies is in many ways about the relationship between what Leavis and Thompson identified as 'Mass Civilization' and 'Minority Culture' (what could be translated as 'film' and 'literature') and, perhaps due to a subliminal prejudice for anything popular, the field has been slow to realize the important part that advertising plays in adaptation studies. So, like F.R. Leavis and Denys Thompson in *Culture and Environment*, I would like to end by asking the sort of questions that our students could be addressing and to suggest some creative practices that the study of film adaptations in relation to their promotional materials can generate. In other words, we shouldn't conceal the film text as a commercial entity, but understand and celebrate it in our teaching. Among the questions that I find produce the most informative responses from students are those that ask for the advertising materials to be taken seriously:

1. What does a particular poster image tell us about how a film adapts a literary text?
2. Do the advertising paratexts reveal or conceal the central features of a film adaptation?
3. Make explicit the implicit messages contained in a poster advertising a film adaptation and use these in defending your own adaptation of the same 'source' text.
4. What is the relationship between a film adaptation and its pre-release publicity?

For those students engaged in creative responses to adaptations, producing their own adaptation of a literary work, I would propose that they put aside any instinctive distrust of salesmanship, and work as much on their pitch as on their product.

Notes

1. Q. D. Leavis, *Fiction and the Reading Public* (1932; rpt. London: Random House, 2000), p. 192.
2. F. R. Leavis and Denys Thompson, *Culture and Environment* (London: Chatto & Windus, 1933), p. 1.
3. Jan Gordon and Cora Josephine Turner Gordon, *Star-Dust in Hollywood* (London: George G. Harrap & Co., 1930), p. 281.
4. Leavis and Thompson, *Culture and Environment*, p. 115.
5. *Ibid.*, p. 143.
6. See William Hunter, '"The Art Form of Democracy"?', *Scrutiny* 1 (1), 1932, 61–65 and Raymond Williams, 'Cinema and Socialism', in *Raymond Williams: Politics of Modernism* (London: Verso, 1989), pp. 107–118.
7. *Ibid.*, p. 144.
8. Christopher Hilliard, *English as a Vocation: The Scrutiny Movement* (Oxford: Oxford University Press, 2012), p. 37.
9. See 'Adaptation and the Coming of Sound: Sam Taylor's *Taming of the Shrew*', in *A Companion to Literature, Film and Adaptation*, ed. Deborah Cartmell (Oxford: Blackwell, 2012), pp. 70–84.
10. E. S. Turner, *The Shocking History of Advertising* (London: Penguin, 1952), p. 209.
11. *Ibid.*, p. 210.

12. See the pressbook for *The Taming of the Shrew* as discussed in 'Adaptation and the Coming of Sound'.
13. *As You Like It*, Pressbook, 1936, n.p.
14. *Ibid.*
15. *Ibid.*
16. Robert Stam, 'Introduction', *Literature and Film: A Guide to the Theory and Practice of Film Adaptation*, ed. Robert Stam and Alessandra Raengo (Malden and Oxford: Blackwell, 2005), p. 5.
17. *Ibid.*, pp. 1–52, p. 47 (note 8).
18. 'The *Scrutiny* movement's work on the subject was the foundation of media studies in Britain and part of the patrimony of several generations of teachers and students, many of whom took positions on mass culture and modernity sharply different from those of Leavis and Thompson (p. 48).
19. See Simone Murray, 'Phantom Adaptations: *Eucalyptus*, the Adaptation Industry and the Film That Never Was', *Adaptation* 1 (1), 2008, 5–23, 6.
20. See Thomas Leitch, 'Adaptation, the Genre', *Adaptation* 1 (2), 2008, 106–120 and Christine Geraghty, 'Foregrounding the Media: *Atonement* as an Adaptation', *Adaptation* 2 (2), 2009, 91–109.
21. '*As You Like It* Grandest Fun Ever Brought to Screen', Pressbook, 1936.

Appendix A: Instructions for the Creative-Critical Project

ENGL208 Creative-Critical Project: a creative project accompanied by a 3,000-word critical essay

(1) The creative portion of the project should adapt one of the works we have studied on the course in a way that opens up the work interpretively and conceptually.

(2) The critical essay should interpret your work as you would creative work produced by someone else, analyzing it and articulating how it interprets the work it adapts. You may also, of course, describe your creative process and any challenges you faced in producing the creative work. The essay should, however, be sharply conceptual, engaging theory, criticism, or other secondary sources and setting your work in dialogue with their interpretations of the work you adapt.

We understand that not everyone is a skilled artist, musician, screenwriter, photographer, filmmaker, textile producer, chef, etc. Many students work innovatively with materials created by others, reworking them creatively: for example, adding various sound tracks to the same film scene and addressing how these (re)interpret the images.

Rules

- You may address only media on the course. You may not use texts or films already addressed in your earlier assessments.
- You must address theory, criticism, historical, or other secondary sources in your critical essay.
- The length of the creative portion of the project is up to you. Remember that this entire project is equivalent to a 5,000-word essay; we do not therefore expect entire screenplays, feature-length films. A film treatment plus a sample scene or two would be sufficient for a screenplay project; the best student films are

usually only a few minutes in length. The same guidelines apply to other modes of adaptation.

- Overlength critical essays will be penalized. Observe the 10 per cent rule. Underlength essays are self-penalizing. Put the word count at the end of the essay.

Submission instructions: Attach a cover sheet to your written analysis: be sure to include the title of your project there. On the cover sheet, write a description of any accompanying pieces (e.g. box containing board game; photo album; screenplay, etc. All pieces of your project must be clearly marked with your name and submitted together inside a single container (envelope, folder, bag, box, etc.). If you have an over-sized project that does not fit in a container, it must be labelled with your name and the essay must be securely attached to it. If you submit a file CD, DVD, or memory stick, be sure to indicate which program(s) can read your file.

We will deduct marks for improperly labelled or submitted projects.

Good luck! We look forward to seeing what you come up with.

Appendix B: Marking Descriptors for the Creative-Critical Project

Broad descriptor	Grade	Attainment	Creative skills	Analytical and conceptual skills	Professional and production qualities
Excellent	A+	Outstanding and exceptional work, demonstrating a significantly higher level of attainment than that expected at the stage of the programme being assessed. Publishable/exhibitable creative output.	An outstanding degree of creativity, originality, control, and rigour, sustained at an artistic level exceptional for the year of study.	Critiques will demonstrate outstanding conception and originality of thought, offering new insight into both work critiqued and the context from which the creative work emerges. They will show a mastery of the available critical and/or theoretical tools.	Showing outstanding skills of planning, preparation, and organization. Demonstrating exceptional levels of presentational skill and accuracy. Wide, adventurous critical reading will be in evidence.

(continued)

(Continued)

Broad descriptor	Grade	Attainment	Creative skills	Analytical and conceptual skills	Professional and production qualities
	A	Exemplary range and depth of attainment of intended learning outcomes. Work of this standard will be convincing and compelling and will surprise a reader, offering new insights and stimulation.	Work that demonstrates a high degree of originality, control, and rigour.	Critiques will demonstrate clarity and technical rigour, offering new insight into both work critiqued and the context from which the creative work emerges, demonstrating a thorough and impressive understanding and handling of the available critical and theoretical tools.	Showing excellence in skills of planning, preparation, and organization. Demonstrating very high levels of presentational skill and accuracy. Wide, adventurous critical reading will be in evidence.
	A–	Excellent range and depth of attainment of intended learning outcomes. Work in this category is excellent. It will stimulate and draw attention to one or more of a range of qualities it possesses.	The creative work will be distinctive.	Critiques will demonstrate clarity and technical rigour, offering new insight into both work critiqued and the context from which the creative work emerges, demonstrating a discriminating command of relevant materials and analyses.	Showing strength in skills of planning, preparation, and organization. Demonstrating high levels of presentational skill and accuracy. Wide, adventurous critical reading will be in evidence.

Good	B+	Very good attainment of virtually all intended learning outcomes. Work at this level will be competent and coherent throughout, occasionally, but not consistently rising to excellence. Some evidence of first-level work.	Very good work, with some signs of creative excellence, but not sustained as in first-class work.	Able to integrate or link textual, contextual, and theoretical knowledge and understanding. Convincing in its relation of the particular (textual detail) to the general (thematic concerns of the argument, or broader contexts of the question).	Showing very good skills of planning, preparation, and organization. Demonstrating good presentational skill and accuracy. Evidence of very sound researching and reading skills, with a depth and range of reference. Accurate referencing and scholarly apparatus in evidence.
	B	Conclusive attainment of virtually all intended learning outcomes. The work will demonstrate a relevant and perceptive engagement with the topic under consideration. Work at this level will be competent and coherent throughout, showing occasional signs of excellence.	Good creative work, with attention to detail, demonstrating a good depth of understanding.	Critiques will demonstrate an equivalent degree of stylistic and formal control to the creative work; characterized by clarity and technical rigour, they should offer a sustained analysis of the work critiqued, drawing on the context from which the creative work emerges.	Showing good skills of planning, preparation, and organization. Demonstrating good presentational skill and accuracy. Evidence of very sound researching and reading skills. Accurate referencing. There may be occasional, but not recurrent, presentational or spelling errors.

(continued)

(*Continued*)

Broad descriptor	Grade	Attainment	Creative skills	Analytical and conceptual skills	Professional and production qualities
	B–	Solid attainment of virtually all intended learning outcomes. Work at this level will be competent and coherent throughout.	Solid creative work, well thought out and executed, but lacking the scintillation of work in higher grade ranges.	Critiques should offer a sound analysis of the work critiqued, showing sound and thoughtful interpretation and a good level of analysis and evaluation, though they may not be as rigorous in argument or technical accomplishment as work earning higher grades. Some evidence of a grasp of textual, contextual, and theoretical knowledge.	Showing solid skills of planning, preparation, and organization. Demonstrating solid presentational skill and accuracy. Evidence of sound researching and reading skills. Accurate referencing. There may be occasional, perhaps recurrent, presentational or spelling errors.
Satisfactory	C+	Work at this level will be satisfactory throughout and sometimes engaging, but will not consistently achieve the control and competence characteristic of higher work, though some signs of B grade work are in evidence.	Creative work will be solid rather than original, adequate rather than strong.	Critiques are competent, but may have some missing or descriptive elements rather than analytical parts; they offer some insight into the work critiqued, but draw only slightly on a wider critical context.	Showing sound skills of planning, preparation, and organization. Demonstrating satisfactory presentational skill and accuracy. There may be some presentational or spelling errors. Evidence of competent researching and reading skills. Mainly accurate referencing.

C	Work at this level will be satisfactory throughout, but will not achieve the control and competence characteristic of higher work.	Either conventional approaches predominate the creative portion, and only slightly manifest creativity or too little work has been put into realizing promising creative ideas.	Critiques are mostly satisfactory, but are either too elliptic or lacking in analytical elements.	Showing reasonable planning, preparation, and organization. Demonstrating basic presentational accuracy. Some evidence of researching and reading skills. Recurrent spelling or presentational errors. Inconsistent or erroneous referencing may be in evidence.
C–	Work at this level will be mostly satisfactory, with some lapses.	The work struggles to achieve an integrated form; authorial control will be inconsistent. Weak style, unclear expression.	Critiques struggle to substantiate analysis by detail. Approach to the work may be more descriptive than analytical. Conventional or derivative approaches predominate, and draw only slightly on a wider context.	Showing some deficiencies in planning, preparation, and organization. Demonstrating a basic presentational accuracy but with recurrent evidence of spelling errors, lack of proofing, erroneous referencing. Range of reference is limited.

(continued)

(Continued)

Broad descriptor	Grade	Attainment	Creative skills	Analytical and conceptual skills	Professional and production qualities
Weak	D+	Acceptable attainment of intended learning outcomes. Work shows some attempt to meet and achieve the creative project requirements.	An attempt to grasp analytical issues and concepts, but often understanding incomplete or erroneous. Creative work lacks originality and inventiveness; little time and effort have been given to the creative portion.	A willingness to attempt the analysis of creative work, albeit of a weak or elliptic or conventional nature. Tendency towards the subjective and impressionistic and reference to a wider literary context is either arbitrary or absent.	Some signs of planning, preparation, and organization. Some presentational accuracy. Evidence of limited researching and reading skills. Very narrow range of reference. Multiple and recurrent spelling and presentational errors.
	D	Acceptable attainment of intended learning outcomes. Less successful in fulfilling the project requirements than higher marked work.	Creative work is rarely original or inventive; subject matter will tend towards the predictable and formulaic, with little evidence of original thinking; little creative momentum or structural control.	A high degree of generalization and insufficient evidence. Description predominates. Tendency towards the subjective and impressionistic and reference to a wider literary context is either arbitrary or absent.	Some signs of planning, preparation, and organization. Limited presentational accuracy. Evidence of very limited researching and reading skills. Little or no secondary reading in evidence. Little, partial or no scholarly apparatus (referencing, bibliography) in evidence. Multiple and recurrent spelling and presentational errors.

| D– | Barely acceptable attainment of intended learning outcomes. Evidence of limited familiarity with the relevant primary material. Work will show some familiarity with the requirements of writing in the chosen form. | Creative work will be basic, predictable, and generic, with little evidence of original thinking. Critiques are superficial and brief, demonstrating little or very partial grasp of the contents of the course. | The level of analysis is basic and may be partly erroneous or absent. Rudimentary grasp of relevant issues. | Scant sign of planning, preparation, and organization. Very limited presentational accuracy. Evidence of very limited researching and reading skills. Little or no secondary reading in evidence. Little, partial, or no scholarly apparatus (referencing, bibliography) in evidence. Multiple and recurrent spelling and presentational errors. |
| Fail | F1 | Attainment deficient in respect of specific intended learning outcomes. | Creative work will be basic and unoriginal, predictable and unengaging. | Critiques will be superficial and slight. Poor interpretation. Little evidence of analysis and evaluation. Possibly incoherent and arbitrary. | Very limited signs of planning, preparation, and organization. Little presentational accuracy. Evidence of very limited researching and reading skills. Multiple and recurrent spelling and presentational errors. |

(continued)

(Continued)

Broad descriptor	Grade	Attainment	Creative skills	Analytical and conceptual skills	Professional and production qualities
	F2	Attainment of intended learning outcomes appreciably deficient in critical respects.	There is barely any evidence of genuine engagement with the course and the different currents necessary to create a successful piece of work.	Lacking secure basis in relevant factual and analytical dimensions.	Very limited signs of planning, preparation, and organization. Little presentational accuracy. Evidence of very limited researching and reading skills. Multiple and recurrent spelling and presentational errors.
	F3	Attainment of intended learning outcomes appreciably deficient in respect of nearly all intended learning outcomes. Showing no grasp of the subject. The work is simplistic and clichéd and usually under-length.	There is no evidence of engagement with the course or with the different currents necessary to create a successful piece of work.	Irrelevant use of materials and incomplete and flawed explanation. Regularly inaccurate in matters of fact and description. Completely incompetent interpretation.	No convincing signs of planning, preparation, and organization. Mainly inaccurate presentation. No obvious researching or reading skills.
	F4	No convincing evidence of attainment of any intended learning outcomes. The work is short, banal, and clichéd.	There is no evidence of engagement with the course or with the different currents necessary to create a successful piece of work.	Treatment of the subject directionless and fragmentary. No grasp of the requirements of undergraduate study.	No convincing signs of planning, preparation, and organization. Mainly inaccurate presentation. No obvious researching or reading skills.

Chronology of Key Publications and Events

1915, rev. 1922: Vachel Lindsay, *The Art of the Moving Picture* (New York: Liveright, 1970).

1936: Allardyce Nicoll, *Film and Theatre* (London: Harrap).

1944: Sergei Eisenstein, 'Dickens, Griffith, and the Film Today', *Film Form*, trans. Jay Leyda (New York: Harcourt Brace, 1947), pp. 195–255.

1948: André Bazin, 'Adaptation, or the Cinema as Digest', *Esprit*, 16(146), 32–40.

1951: André Bazin, 'Theatre and Cinema', in *What is Cinema?*, trans. Hugh Gray (Berkeley: University of California Press, 1971).

1957: George Bluestone, *Novels into Film* (Berkeley: University of California Press).

1969: Robert D. Richardson, *Literature and Film* (Bloomington and London: Indiana University Press).

1973: *Literature/Film Quarterly*, founded by Jim Welsh and Tom Erskine and published at Salisbury University, Maryland.

1975: Geoffrey Wagner, *The Novel and the Cinema* (Michigan: University of Michigan Press).

1978: Seymour Chatham. *Story and Discourse: Narrative Structure in Fiction and Film* (Ithaca, NY: Cornell University Press).

1984: Dudley Andrew, *Concepts in Film Theory* (Oxford: Oxford University Press).

1985: Joy Gould Boyum, *Novels into Film* (Berkeley: University of California Press).

1987: Neil Sinyard, *Filming Literature: the Art of Screen Adaptation* (London: Croom Helm).

1989: Literature/Film Association begins in the US, hosted by Dickinson College (Philadelphia: Carlisle).

1990: Seymour Chatham, *Coming to Terms: The Rhetoric of Narrative in Fiction and Film* (Ithaca, New York, and London: Cornell University Press).

1990: Robert Giddings, Robert K Selby, and C. Wensley, *Screening the Novel: The Theory and Practice of Literary Dramatization* (London: Macmillan).

1992: Henry Jenkins, *Textual Poachers: Television, Fans and Participatory Culture* (London: Routledge).

1992: Linda Seger *The Art of Adaptation* (London: Routledge).

1993: Peter Reynolds, ed. *Novel Images: Literature in Performance* (London: Routledge).

1996: The Film/Fiction series begins (until 2001). Edited by Deborah Cartmell, I. Q. Hunter, Heidi Kaye, and Imelda Whelehan and published by Pluto Press.

1996: Brian McFarlane, *Novel to Film: An Introduction to the Theory of Adaptation* (Oxford: Oxford University Press).

1999: Deborah Cartmell and Imelda Whelehan, eds, *Adaptations: from Text to Screen, Screen to Text* (London: Routledge).

1999: Timothy Corrigan, *Film and Literature: An Introduction and Reader* (New Jersey: Prentice Hall).

2000: Robert Giddings and Erica Sheen, *Screening the Novel: The Theory and Practice of Literary Dramatization* (London: Macmillan).

2000: James Naremore, *Film Adaptation* (London: The Athlone Press).

2001: Ginette Vincendeau, ed. *Film/Heritage/Literature: A Sight and Sound Reader* (London: BFI Publishing).

2002: Sarah Cardwell, *Adaptation Revisited: Television and the Classic Novel* (Manchester: Manchester University Press).

2002: Jim Collins, *High-Pop: Making Culture into Popular Entertainment* (Oxford: Blackwell).

2003: Kamilla Elliott, *Rethinking the Novel/Film Debate* (Cambridge: Cambridge University Press).

2003: Andrew Higson, *English Heritage, English Cinema: Costume Drama since 1980* (Oxford: Oxford University Press).

2003: Thomas M. Leitch, 'Twelve Fallacies in Contemporary Adaptation Theory', *Criticism*, 45(2), 149–171.

2004: Robert Stam and Alessandra Raengo, eds *A Companion to Literature and Film* (Malden and Oxford: Blackwell).

2005: Robert Stam: *Literature through Film: Realism, Magic, and the Art of Adaptation* (Malden and Oxford: Blackwell).

2005: Robert Stam and Alexandra Raengo, eds: *Literature and Film: A Guide to the Theory and Practice of Film Adaptation* (Malden and Oxford: Blackwell).

2006: John M. Desmond and Peter Hawkes, *Adaptation: Studying Film and Literature* (Boston MA and London: McGraw-Hill).

2006: Henry Jenkins, *Convergence Culture: Where Old and New Media Collide* (New York: New York University Press).

2006: Linda Hutcheon, *A Theory of Adaptation* (London: Routledge).

2006: Julie Sanders, *Adaptation and Appropriation* (London: Routledge).

2006: Launch of the Association of Adaptation Studies.

2007: Christine Geraghty, *Now a Major Motion Picture: Film Adaptations of Literature and Drama* (Lanham, Maryland: Rowman and Littlefield).

2007: Thomas Leitch, *Film Adaptation and its Discontents* (Baltimore: Johns Hopkins Press).

2008: *Adaptation in Literature, Film and Performance* (Intellect) begins.

2008: *Adaptation* begins (Oxford: Oxford University Press).

2008: Jack Boozer, ed. *Authorship in Film Adaptation* (Austin: University of Texas Press).

2010: Deborah Cartmell and Imelda Whelehan, *Screen Adaptation: Impure Cinema* (Basingstoke: Palgrave).